D0063971

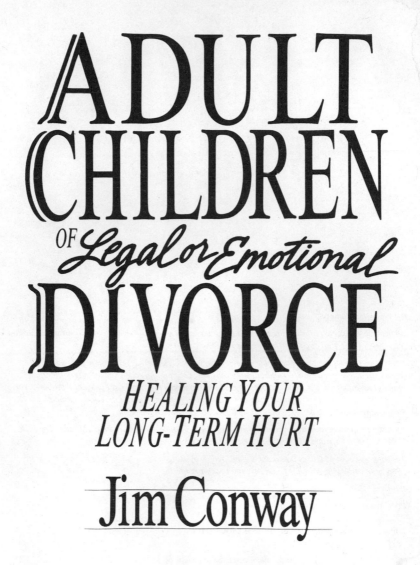

ADULT CHILDREN

OF *Legal or Emotional*

DIVORCE

HEALING YOUR LONG-TERM HURT

Jim Conway

INTERVARSITY PRESS
DOWNERS GROVE, ILLINOIS 60515

InterVarsity Press is the book-publishing division of InterVarsity Christian Fellowship, a student movement active on campus at hundreds of universities, colleges and schools of nursing in the United States of America, and a member movement of the International Fellowship of Evangelical Students. For information about local and regional activities, write Public Relations Dept., InterVarsity Christian Fellowship, 6400 Schroeder Rd., P.O. Box 7895, Madison, WI 53707-7895.

All Scripture quotations in this publication are from the Holy Bible, New International Version. Copyright © 1973, 1978, International Bible Society. Used by permission of Zondervan Bible Publishers.

The song on pages 196-97 is "Break the Chain." Words by Morgan Cryar. Music by Ty Tabor. © Copyright 1986 by Ariose Music. All rights reserved. Used by permission.

ISBN 0-8308-1381-0 (pbk.)

Printed in the United States of America ∞

Library of Congress Cataloging-in-Publication Data

Conway, Jim.
    Adult children of legal or emotional divorce/by Jim Conway.
        p.   cm.
    "Saltshaker books"
    Includes bibliographical references.
    ISBN 0-8308-1738-7 (hdbk.)
        1. Adult children of divorced parents—Pastoral counseling of.
    2. Adult children of divorced parents—Religious life.   3. Christian
    life—1960-   I. Title.   II. Title: Saltshaker books.
    BC4463.65.C65   1990
    248.8'4—dc20
                                                        90-43614
                                                            CIP

13   12   11   10   9   8   7   6   5   4   3   2   1
02   01   00   99   98   97   96   95   94   93   92

To my grandchildren:

Nathan James Christon Russell
Samuel Marc Jonathan Russell
Hayden Anne Sanders
Davidson Thaddeus Jacob Russell
Julian Schneider (who died before birth)
Emily Ives Sanders
Carlene Joelle Schneider

Who have drawn the best grandfathering
traits out of me.
Who give me unimagined pleasure and joy.
Who—I anticipate—will be a continued link for
emotional wholeness and spiritual righteousness
for future generations.

Acknowledgments

No book is ever produced by one person working in a vacuum. Although the ideas were mine, many people helped form the final manuscript. To them I owe a great debt of gratitude.

Sally, my wife, shared equally in the early research and the formation of the project. She encouraged me to keep writing even when I was in deep emotional pain from remembering my past. She also served as first editor of the entire book.

Barbara, Brenda and Becki, my daughters, each interacted with the manuscript and cheered me on to completion.

John and Dennis, my small group; Earl, my counselor; and Chuck, my pastor, read early drafts and challenged me to keep writing as they assured me the book would be helpful to many hurting people.

Susan, Marilyn, Vicki, "Alison" and Diane, secretaries and administrative assistants, entered and re-entered the manuscript into the computer dozens of times.

Linda, Don and Andy, my three InterVarsity Press editors, gave suggestions which vastly improved the readability and focus of the book.

Finally, thanks to the people who filled out surveys, who gave personal interviews and whom I have counseled in my thirty years of ministry. Thank you all for your invaluable insights and encouragement. I planted, these friends watered, but only God can cause the growth.

Preface

Scott, a college student, told me he planned to get married and have a family. He explained, "I'll be a good dad to my kids. My dad divorced my mom when I was five, and it has really bothered me all my life that I grew up without a father. I know how to be a good dad because I never had one."

Scott's desires are great, but unless he gets help he probably will not be a good father. He will instinctively follow his parents' patterns and escape when things get bad—even if that means abandoning his own children.

Scott can learn to be a good dad. But to do that, he must work through his childhood issues of abandonment, mistrust, anger and denial.

This book is intended to help people of all ages heal from childhood hurts caused by their parents' legal divorce or by parents who were emotionally divorced even though they "stayed together." In fact, the trauma from an emotional divorce can be just as painful as from a legal divorce for children because the marriage was torn by constant conflict, denial and escapism.

This book is not an attack on my parents. They did the best they could. They came into marriage and parenting with the background of some painful childhood experiences of their own. The illustrations about my family are included only to help people understand the full devastation of unresolved childhood problems. I have no intention to embarrass my family; in fact, the latter part of the book tells of the resolution of some of my own difficulties.

I have come to thank God for my problems because they have given me insights into life and the ability to empathize with people. I might never have gained these if I had not come from an emotionally divorced family.

And this book is more than my story. It is based on a national survey of over two hundred adult children of divorce, plus research conducted with university students whose parents had divorced, extensive personal interviews with other adults of divorced parents, and case histories from my years of pastoral counseling.

Part One

Facts about
Adult Children
from Legal or
Emotional Divorce

1
Who Are These Adult Children from Legally or Emotionally Divorced Families?

Many adults walk around, looking like a great success in life and yet feeling *very empty inside.* They are fooling most of the people around them and often are even fooling themselves. The realities are mind-boggling! Think of the number of people from every walk and status of life—mothers and fathers, teachers, clergy, police officers, truck drivers, politicians, doctors—who are running our country from their hollowness.

Several years ago I began to share with audiences that I felt my life did not begin until I was almost nineteen. For most of my life I thought that everyone grew up with a dull pain inside, everyone felt alone, and everyone felt estranged from their parents and—like me—just pretended to be part of a family.

My wife, Sally, thought I was referring to my new and exciting relationship with God, which had begun when I was an eighteen-year-old high-school senior. To some degree that was true.

As the years went by, however, I began to talk more about my terribly low self-image when I shared some of my story. I told about my fear of people and my feelings of not belonging in the world. Slowly I began to identify some of my problems as coming from my parents.

My mother was raised by a stepmother in a very difficult home environment. Her father was cruel and authoritarian. Even before she was a teenager, my mother was forced to go to work as a maid and bring all her income home to her father. He believed that children were to produce income for the family. Only recently I discovered that my mother was repeatedly sexually abused by her father.

Therefore, when I came into the world, I had a mother who wanted to love me but who hadn't had the nurturing home life she needed to instinctively care for children. Unfortunately, some of the traits she most abhorred in her parents were the very parenting methods she used in raising me.

My parents probably never should have married each other. Many years ago my father told me that while getting dressed the very next morning after they were married, he said to himself, "I have married the wrong woman." As a result of feeling he had mismarried, he followed a pattern of avoidance. He stayed away from my mother as much as possible and became totally preoccupied with work.

I think they were attracted because of unmet childhood needs—my mother to escape her home and my father to feel successful. Their choice in marriage was really a reaction to their homes and environments rather than a conscious, rational choice.

Because the marriage was rocky from the beginning, some people suggested that having a child might strengthen the relationship. I was the child who was to improve and stabilize the marriage. What an awesome task to place on a newborn baby! From early childhood I felt responsible for my parents.

So I grew up with a mother who did not have the native capacities to love me and a father who was essentially absent my entire life. My parents were legally married, but they were emotionally divorced.

As I look back and tearfully begin to put the pieces together, I see my mother as a woman, blighted by her childhood, who entered marriage hoping to find love and a sense of "home." Tragically, however, she was forced to get her emotional nourishing from her children and friends—not her husband. As a way of coping, she denied she had any needs. Or if she had needs, they were unimportant and didn't deserve to be fulfilled.

As my parents felt more and more estranged from each other, my mother turned increasingly inward with her feelings, and my father turned more to his work and to other people.

My Family Secrets

Many years later my mother told me that my father got his emotional fulfillment through the attentions of other women. A number of times, though, she stood up for my father and denied that he would be involved with anyone else.

On one occasion a policeman came to the door, asking for my father. My mother said he wasn't at home, but she offered to help. The policeman said that a woman had accused my father of making sexual advances to her while he was working at her house.

My mother declared, "You're mistaken. You have the wrong man. My husband would never do a thing like that! We have a good marriage, and we go to church every Sunday and Wednesday. The woman must be imagining things, or she has confused my husband with somebody else."

The officer complimented my mother for defending her husband, and the matter was dropped. But the incident was indicative of my parents' dysfunction.

All through my life I had a deep sense that things were bad between my parents, but I figured that was normal—all homes were like that. I also began to "keep the family secrets," much the way my mother did. I consciously and unconsciously protected my father. After all, how could I admit that *my* father was involved with other women? How could I admit *my* parents were emotionally divorced? How could I admit *my* home and *my* parents were dysfunctional?

I May Look Successful, But I Feel Empty

By the time I was in my fifties, I became increasingly aware of a deep-seated anger inside myself. I felt a terrible sense of emptiness. By outward standards I was a success—an author, speaker, seminary professor, pastor and counselor. Our three daughters had married successfully, and Sally and I were involved in many joint efforts of writing and speaking. Yet I felt a horrible void and a gnawing sense of unfulfillment within.

I remember my feelings when my book *Friendship* was released in the spring of 1989. I opened the package, saw the first copy off the press, and felt, "It's not good enough. It's a disgustingly thin book. I've got to work harder." I felt no sense of accomplishment, and wouldn't allow myself to enjoy the fruits of my labors.[1]

Even though people began telling me that the *Friendship* book was helping them, my response to myself was, "How can that be, since I am such an empty person? How could I say or do anything that would be of encouragement or help to someone else?" I pushed the book out of my mind, refused to allow it to nourish me, and pressed myself on to other projects.

It's Not "Them"—It's Me!

Earlier I had been senior pastor of a large student church on the edge of the University of Illinois campus. I had noticed that students who came from divorced families had trouble studying, relating to people and feeling confident about themselves.

They were also afraid of marriage. I saw them as "clingers." They were desperately looking for love. Sometimes they got into unhealthy dating relationships and sexual commitments because of this desperation. These people who seemed to be searching for "home" were perfectionistic, had difficulty trusting and were marked by a deep-seated anger.

Sally and I conducted a study of these students to determine their needs and what could be done to help them. At that time it seemed to me they were just a small segment of kids from the many divorced families who somehow had not worked through their problems. Later I would realize these emotionally troubled kids were the majority.

Some years after we left Illinois, an editor friend asked Sally and me to submit proposals for future books. One of the proposals we suggested came from our earlier observations of university students from divorced families. That proposal drew immediate attention.

As a result, we expanded our research to people across the country who came from divorced families. I also began reading everything I could about adult children from alcoholic, abusive or other dysfunctional homes.

After I had gathered the national data, read dozens of books and carefully searched the journals, I was prepared to write. But each time I attempted to start, I found myself wrestling with an internal resistance. I knew all the information, I had the data before me, but I couldn't write. What was wrong? Deadline after deadline that I had set in my personal calendar went unmet. As I kept delaying, I excused myself by saying that I was doing more research. The truth of the matter, however, was that I finally was beginning to realize I was not just writing about "them" but about *me.*

I experienced exactly the same feelings adult children of divorce from all over the country had shared with me. I kept saying to myself, "But my parents aren't divorced. Why should I be feeling and reacting the same way adult children of divorced parents do?" Finally a flash like a giant strobe light: "I *did* come from a divorced family! My parents were *emotionally* divorced from the day they were married."

That emotional divorce was as crippling to me as if they had gotten a legal divorce—maybe more crippling. If they had been legally divorced, at least I might have had the chance to experience a somewhat stable home.

All my research and reading now began to make sense. Yes, I wanted to help those adult children of divorce, but I also realized I was starting a new journey toward my own personal healing from my parents' emotional divorce.

Please Be Impressed—Please Love Me

About that time I also had a growing awareness that I always have wanted people to know me because of what I do, not because of who I am. I have tried to impress people by letting them know about my two master's degrees and two doctorates, my magazine articles, books, radio and TV appearances, ministry trips around the world, my pastoring a large church and teaching at a seminary. Sounds like I'm still struggling, doesn't it?

At age fifty-seven, reality crashed home—I had never liked me, no matter how much or what I did. I had wished that other people would like me because of what I was doing. I had even hoped if I did more or better, I would like myself.

A number of books helped to open my eyes even wider to the dysfunctional family from which I had come. One of those important books was *Healing the Shame That Binds You* by John Bradshaw. In one section of the book he discusses a book written by Alice Miller, entitled *Drama of the Gifted Child.*

He comments on Miller's book: "More often than not, these narcissistically deprived people are talented, gifted, highly successful, superachievers who have been praised and admired for their talents and achievements. Anyone looking at them from the outside would believe that these people have it made. They are strong, stable and full of self-assurance. The exact opposite is the case."

Then Bradshaw goes on to quote Alice Miller: "Behind all this, there lurks depression, the feeling of emptiness and self-alienation, and a sense that life has no meaning."

Bradshaw continues, "Once the drug of grandiosity is taken away, as soon as they are no longer the stars and superachievers, they are plagued by deep feelings of shame and guilt." This deprived person "becomes a 'human doing' without any real sense of his authentic self. Such a person feels emptiness, homelessness, and futility."[2]

Wow, suddenly I realized they were speaking about *me*—and somehow I had known it all along!

Divorce or Dysfunction—Both Tragic

A journal article entitled "Long-Term Effects of Divorce on Children: A Developmental Vulnerability Model" really hit me. The author, Neil Kalter, points out that not only do children of legally divorced parents experience psychological problems, but children with both parents present will feel the same as divorced children if one or both parents or the marriage is dysfunctional. "It is important to note that youngsters who grow up in two-parent households are not immune to these difficulties in achieving a valued sense of gender identity. Fathers who hold themselves aloof from their sons and are only minimally involved in their emotional growth and development, who are subtly or directly rejecting of daughters and their femininity, who are peripheral figures in day-to-day family life, and who [belittle] their wives can be found in all too many two-parent homes. Children in such families are vulnerable to problems similar to those of their counterparts from divorced, single-parent households."[3]

These authors were driving the point home to me:

It is possible for an emotionally divorced home to produce the same negative psychological development in the children as if the parents were legally divorced.

That environment ultimately produces an adult who is physically grown but who carries the damning dysfunctional baggage of a wounded child.

Stop the Hurt of Divorce—Emotional or Legal

The long tentacles of pain from a dysfunctional family reach deep into the adult years and beyond, into the next generation and the next—until finally someone decides to take the ax and chop off the tentacle. Only then will the suffocating influence of divorce—emotional or legal—finally stop distorting, crippling and sucking life's joy out of everyone it touches.

The key is that someone must make the decision to become healthy, to have healthy relationships, to pass on health to the children and grandchildren. The issue is choice—a decision to be healed.

A Blighted Ph.D.

Phil was an exceptionally bright young man working on his Ph.D. He was good-looking, seemed to relate well to people, and took an active part in the singles group at church. But I noticed he always felt uncomfortable around women. As I observed him more carefully, I discovered he was uncomfortable around people in general.

When I had an opportunity to talk with him in depth about his background, he told me that his parents were divorced. Before the divorce his father would take him along to visit the "other woman." The young boy stayed in another room reading or watching television while his father had sex with the girlfriend.

Phil was forced to "keep the secrets"—to pretend that wrong was right—to not question his father. He learned to deny all of his natural feelings about the immoral situation.

The boy's logical mind thought, "I must be wrong and my father must be right. What he is doing by hurting my mother and seeing several girl-friends seems very wrong to me, but he is an adult, so certainly he's doing what is right."

Childhood thinking is very black-and-white. It is also deeply committed to a belief that parents are the perfect embodiment of truth and rightness. Therefore, if there is a conflict between what the child feels or thinks and what he observes his parents saying or doing, the child decides he is wrong. A child does not have the capacity to challenge the caretakers.

Phil repeatedly suppressed his feelings that his parents were wrong. As a result, he started questioning all of his own feelings and observations. At the same time, his nagging feelings that his parents were wrong caused him to mistrust his parents. This was the beginning of his lifelong trap: I can't trust myself and I can't trust anyone else.

Not Really on His Own
Phil smiles and talks pleasantly to people. He is a leader in the singles group. He appears to be very successful. He is on his way to completing his Ph.D. Yet inside he carries a pathetic amount of negative baggage because of his parents' dysfunction.

He has been unable to develop intimacy with people because he has come to believe that people are not to be trusted. Neither can he have confidence in his own feelings. He has dated many girls one or two times but never has been able to go deeper in a relationship. He does not trust them or his own emotions. "So," he said sadly, "I figure it's best to stay away from people."

As I talked to him, Phil's eyes darted around the room like a trapped animal, betraying the typical insecurity and low self-esteem that is so common with adult children of divorce. Finally he looked at me and said, "I don't think I'll ever marry, because my marriage would certainly end in divorce."

How sadly accurate is his statement. If Phil does get married, even to a very stable woman, their marriage will probably fall apart. He probably will be unable to become emotionally married unless he works through his childhood issues of mistrust and fear of intimacy.

A Mid-Life Pattern

The stories are endless because millions of us have come from emotionally or legally divorced families.

Donna, a woman in her late thirties, sat in my office sobbing. She asked if I could help her with her marriage problems. She was desperately afraid she was going to lose her husband who was beginning to go through a mid-life crisis.

She knew he was strongly attracted to other women, and she felt she was losing the battle. She thought of herself as on the end of a rope in a game of tug-of-war. Her husband was in front of her. They were both being pulled toward a deep, black chasm. At the other end of the rope were several sexually seductive women who seemed to be pulling them into the pit of marital collapse.

Donna was terrified as she told me the story, because her husband seemed to be losing heart—giving up. As she cried convulsively, Donna's body looked to me as if it were about to fall into several pieces like an old doll whose arms, head and legs are held together inside by one decayed rubber band.

In the midst of her emotional and almost physical disintegration, she sobbed out to me, "I know it isn't his fault or the fault of those other women. I'm frigid! I have been unable to have sex with my husband other than when he forced me when our two children were conceived."

The pattern was frighteningly similar to Phil's story in reverse. Donna continued, "How could I ever trust a man after what my father did to my mother? How could I ever believe that I could keep my husband, when my mother was unable to keep her husband? It's hopeless! It's hopeless! It's hopeless!"

I'm Suffocating

Archibald Hart, professor at Fuller Theological Seminary in Southern California, has written a book entitled *Children and Divorce*. He talks about his own parents' divorce and his hope for their reconciliation.

"But the worst was yet to come," he said. "Shortly after the divorce was finalized, my mother announced that she was getting married. I felt that my destruction was now complete. The fantasies of reconciliation were shattered. My conscious wish and prayer that somehow God was going to pull off a miracle and unite us all again vanished into thin air. nce again, feelings of despair and hopelessness set in. I had known nothing of my mother's courting. (She had started seeing another man shortly after the separation.) But it was clear to me that this new relationship was driving the final nails into the divorce coffin. I felt like I was the one inside!"[4]

Repeatedly, these adult children of divorce speak of being caught in the middle of confusion, hostility, pain, frustration, hurt, resentment, fear, rejection and discouragement. All of the time they believe it's their fault. Something is inherently wrong with them, they think. They refuse to believe that their parents, their caretakers, are dysfunctional.

I'm with You in Your Pain

Maybe you're beginning to see yourself in this chapter. I want to encourage you not to be afraid to feel the painful events of your childhood. You've made a good start. Keep reading and let that little child inside of you speak to you. Comfort that little kid. It's okay! We'll get healed together.

I want you to know, as we begin this book, that I'm not writing to you just as an author or researcher—I am writing to you out of my own pain. I'll talk to you about what works and what doesn't.

This book is not a "parent bashing" book. My intent is only for healing. I hope the stories about my family and other families will help you feel the pain of your past and work toward your own healing.

We'll spend the first part of the book understanding who we are and how we got this way. *Don't skip over this part!* It's important that you thoroughly understand and feel who you are. To heal you must confront and feel what really went on in your childhood.

In the last half of the book we'll talk about the healing process itself and the practical steps you can take from where you are today toward becoming that healthy, whole person you want to be. So be brave! It may be very painful in spots, but let's keep working together.

Let's *make the decision* to be healed. Let's cut off the tentacles from the past that are squeezing the life out of us. Let's *expect wholeness* for ourselves and all the people important to us.

We are on our way toward healing!

2
A Growing National Awareness

M ANY PEOPLE ARE AFRAID OF THE CHOICE TO be healed because it hurts too much. When we choose to be healed, we are choosing to look through adult eyes at our childhood, our parents, their dysfunction and their divorce, whether legal or emotional.

A Grown Woman with a Crying Child Inside

Two days ago I talked to Marie, a woman age fifty-three, whose last child had recently moved out of the home. Shortly after that, Marie went to her doctor for a physical check-up because she felt "run down."

The doctor said, "Everything seems okay, but how are you feeling inside?" The doctor's kind words opened the floodgates, and Marie sobbed and sobbed uncontrollably. Then she confessed that she had cried constantly for the last several days. Her life was totally out of control. She didn't know what was happening to her. Wherever she went and whatever she did, she experienced a deep sadness. Her grief poured out in what seemed like an endless flow. After they talked for forty-five minutes, the doctor encouraged her to seek counseling help, which she did.

The counselor gently helped Marie walk back into some frightening and shameful childhood experiences. They were terrifying! She loved her mother and father, yet she had to face the reality that they had been emotionally divorced from each other most of their lives. How could she accept the fact that her mother really loved another man?

Her hatred for her mother's lover produced intense violent feelings. Even as we spoke on the phone, Marie was seething with rage as she remembered coming home from school and finding the other man in her mother's arms. Marie hated that man! Her parents' marital problems and her personal problems as an adult were all *his* fault.

Marie had kept a picture of that horrible man on the back of her bedroom door when she was a girl. Each day after school when she was confronted with the sickening sight of him with her mother, she would go to her room, lock the door and throw darts at his face. She thought, "If only he would die, then my mother would be free."

Now, as a grown woman, Marie was beginning to face several frightening realities. Perhaps her mother had been *equally* at fault in the affair with the other man. Maybe the emotional divorce between her parents was not totally the man's fault. And perhaps Marie's own failed first marriage and poor choice of a second husband were directly tied to her dysfunctional childhood.

"No, my parents would never get legally divorced—because they were Christians," Marie said. "What a joke!" The shattering effect on all of the children in Marie's family was the same as if their parents had gone to court and split up.

It has long been accepted that young children are negatively affected by parental divorce. Recently, however, we have learned that the long-term effects continue even after those little children become adults.

An Endless Parade of Tragedy

The most comprehensive long-term study to date on the effects of divorce on children has been done by Judith Wallerstein. David Van Biema, writing about the Wallerstein study, says, "Millions of Americans whose parents were divorced struggle to escape a lingering shadow that darkens their own search for love. A generation unlike any other has come of age, one in which millions have been marked by a profound and early sorrow. They are the children of divorce. They are just the front rank of a seemingly endless phalanx."[1]

In the 1950s, divorce was relatively uncommon and still not socially acceptable. That changed drastically in the next decades. By the mid-sixties one out of every three marriages ended in divorce. By 1980 the rate was one out of two.

Twenty years ago—even though the rate of divorce was starting to explode—most psychologists told us that kids would bounce back quickly after a family break-up. We were told that after two or three years of grieving, children of divorce would be almost as good as new. Millions of people have since learned, through sad experience, that those untested psychological ideas were false.

During the sixties and seventies I personally became increasingly troubled by the skyrocketing divorce rate. Would it ever level off? What could I do to help?

In 1980 Sally and I were invited to address the National Association of Deans of Men and Women for Christian Colleges. In order to prepare for one of our presentations, we did in-depth interviews with about two dozen undergraduate and graduate students at the University of Illinois. We selected only students whose parents had been divorced within the last five years. We were astounded at the impact that parental divorce was causing in these students' lives. These next few vignettes will give an overview of what we found.

Devastated Students

One university woman reported that she was traveling overseas when her parents announced they were getting divorced. She immediately cut short her educational tour and rushed home to try to save her parents' marriage. When she got home, she was shocked to discover that her forty-year-old mother was running around, dating wildly as if she were sixteen.

Mark, an undergraduate student in engineering, told us that his parents divorced when he was in high school. A friend of his saw the legal notice of the divorce in the paper and teased him. Mark lied and said, "That's not true, my parents aren't getting divorced!" The friend continued to make fun of him. Mark became so angry that he jumped on the other boy and smashed him in the face. Mark felt an inexpressible shame over his parents' divorce and tried to cover up.

Tim told us matter-of-factly, "While I was home one weekend, I heard my mother cry out from the bathroom. I ran in to find her lying crumpled on the floor. She had slit her wrists and blood was spurting all over the sink, the floor and her clothes. I guess she was really taking the divorce badly." Wow, what an understatement!

One result of our in-depth interviews was a multi-media presentation, using the exact quotes of students as they shared their agonies. As we showed it at the meeting of the college deans, a new awareness emerged. They began to more fully understand the unique problems of students from divorced families who were attending their schools.

Now It's Safe to Get Our Divorce

For many years we have known that very young children and teen-agers experience emotional disturbance, destructive behavior patterns, plus social and educational dysfunction when their parents are having deep conflict before divorce and when the family finally breaks with a legal divorce.[2]

Children of divorce can become emotionally withdrawn; they may start trying to be perfect and make everything around them perfect; or they may exhibit behavioral problems as they try to get anyone's attention. Often they begin failing in school, have trouble relating to people, and show insecurity in the way they talk and act.

Children whose parents divorce are more likely to commit suicide, become homosexuals, get into trouble with the law, use drugs and become sexually promiscuous.

But even though we knew all about these bad effects on children, as a nation we didn't believe there would be any long-term effect when these children of divorce became adults.[3]

New Revelations

A news note from *InterVarsity* entitled "Divorce and Students" points out this false belief:

It's not uncommon for parents to wait until their children leave for college before they divorce. The rationale has been that the divorce is less painful for college kids than it is for small children. But new studies are coming up with different findings.

According to a study being conducted by Katherine Stone Kaufmann, a clinical social worker at Harvard, 80 percent of the students described their parents' divorce as one of the most significant events in their lives. Many reported feelings of guilt, believing that their parents would have stayed together if they hadn't left for college. As many as 60 percent believed that their departure for college played a part in the parents' decision to divorce.

There was one other significant finding. Seventy-three percent said they doubted their own abilities to form and maintain intimate relationships. . . .

According to Kaufmann, "everyone has totally underestimated how devastating divorce is to students. It's really a tough time, and they're going to need help getting through it."[4]

College students have enough problems finding out who they are and what they should do in life without having to also handle their parents' problems. One student from the University of Illinois said, "I'm torn between them. If I visit my father he continually runs down my mother. When I visit my mother, she verbally attacks my father. They each want me to be on their side and attack the other parent. They seem to forget that I love both of them. I'm not getting divorced—*they* are!"

By the mid to late eighties, studies which followed divorced children for many years began to paint a grim picture, showing that the devastation created by divorce followed these children into their adult years. Paul Amato, from the University of Nebraska, in a journal article entitled "Long-Term Implications of Parental Divorce for Adult Self-Concept," says the children of divorce have a "lowered sense of power in their later life." He continues, "As children of divorce grow into adulthood, they carry with them at least one source of vulnerability . . . feelings of powerlessness and helplessness."[5]

Surprisingly, these feelings did not appear until these children of divorce became adults—some not even until they were into their mid-life years.

Documented Long-Term Effects

Judith Wallerstein, whom I mentioned earlier, followed sixty divorced California families to see the long-term effects in the adult lives of the children raised in these broken families. At the end of five years she published a book entitled *Surviving the Breakup: How Children and Parents Cope with Divorce.* The news was not good. She found over one-third of the children to be intensely unhappy and dissatisfied with their life in the post-divorce family. The unhappiness of the children tended to follow a strange pattern of high unhappiness at the time of the parental separation, declining after about eighteen months, only to rise again about five years after the divorce.

Her report at the end of five years was very unsettling. She said, "Thirty-nine percent felt rejected and unloved by the father. We found 37 percent of all the children and adolescents to be moderately to severely depressed. As at the 18-month check point, depression was the most common psychopathological finding and was manifested in a wide variety of feelings and behavior, including chronic and intense unhappiness (at least one child with suicidal preoccupation), sexual promiscuity, delinquency (drug abuse, petty stealing, some alcoholism, breaking and entering), poor learning, intense anger, apathy, restlessness, and a sense of intense, unremitting emotional deprivation."[6]

In 1989 Wallerstein published another book about her long-term study of children from divorced families. Entitled *Second Chances: Men, Women and Children a Decade after Divorce,*[7] this book told what was happening at the ten-year mark in her study. Things were not getting better. *Time* magazine, reporting on the Wallerstein studies, said, "Of the 131 children who belonged to the 60 families studied, three out of five youngsters felt rejected by at least one parent. Half grew up in settings in which the parents were warring with each other even after the divorce. Two-thirds of the girls, many of whom had seemingly sailed through the crisis, suddenly became deeply anxious as young adults, unable to make lasting commitments and fearful of betrayal in intimate relationships.

"Many boys who were more overtly troubled in the post-divorce years, failed to develop a sense of independence, confidence or purpose. They drifted in and out of college and from job to job."[8] These children of divorce were not outgrowing their problems. Rather, their problems were becoming permanently limiting factors which were dominating their whole lives.

Exploding Support Group Network

Alcoholics Anonymous has had support groups for decades. Finally in 1983 the National Association for Children of Alcoholics was formed with approximately 20 members. By 1987 the group had over 7,000 members, and new groups were springing up all over the country. Books poured off the presses during the last half of the eighties, specifically targeting these adult children of alcoholics.

It's interesting to note that two of the major writers for children of alcoholics say the problem is really much greater: "Children of alcoholics are but the visible tip of a much larger social iceberg which casts an invisible shadow over as much as 96 percent of the population in this country. These are the other 'children of trauma.' " (They are referring to all children from emotionally or legally divorced homes or dysfunctional families.)

"Surviving their childhoods rather than experiencing them, these children of trauma have also had to surrender a part of themselves very early in life. Not knowing what hit them, and suffering a sourceless sense of pain in adulthood, they perpetuate the denial and minimization which encased them in dysfunctional roles, rules, and behaviors."

These writers go on to point out that the "children of trauma" generally come from "perfectionistic, judgmental, critical, or non-loving families who appear normal and functioning well on the surface. In all of these families rigidity prevents normal childhood development. In the name of love, children are ignored, isolated, abandoned, and abused."[9]

What Is an Adult Child?

So why do these writers speak of these people as adult children? It's because they are "all grown on the outside, but feel little and bad on the inside."[10] John Bradshaw, in *Healing the Shame That Binds You*, says, "Being abandoned through the neglect of our developmental dependency needs is the major factor in becoming an adult child. We grow up; we look like adults. We walk and talk like adults, but underneath the surface is a little child who feels empty and needy, a child whose needs are insatiable because he has a child's needs in an adult body. This insatiable child is the core of all compulsive/addictive behavior."[11]

In this book when I speak of "adult children," I am referring to adults whose lives are continuing to be damaged because of their parents' emotional or legal divorce and the dysfunctional marriage before the divorce.

Our Second Study

In 1988 Sally and I carried out national research among these "adult children" whose parents had been divorced. The people who responded were generally mid-life, although ages ranged from sixteen to seventy-two. The results of the survey verified what we had seen in 1980 and in our counseling for more than thirty years.

Rich, a man in our study who was in his mid-40s sadly wrote, "Divorce not only damages the couple involved, but even more the children. In my opinion, it is almost *worse than murder* itself. At least with murder you kill the victim quickly. With divorce, all parties involved suffer lifelong damaging effects to the emotions and self-esteem at the deepest level. This is like a slow death from which recovery—if it happens at all—is slow and painful.

"Only God can undo the damage to my self-image, my feelings of incompetence, my limited social skills, and my inability to trust others."[12] In the next chapters we'll look at some of these tragic losses experienced by adult children of divorce. In a few more chapters we'll start to look at how you can get help and healing from all your painful past.

3
What Has the Adult Child Lost?

T HE LOSSES FOR CHILDREN OF DIVORCE ARE immense. As I sifted through 102 questionnaires from people all over the country, I repeatedly was brought to the point of tears. "How could these people have endured all this pain and still go on?" I asked myself. "Why did they keep on going? Why didn't they take their lives?"

At least one child of divorce did. Our local newspaper headline blazed, **"Boy who killed himself was focus of custody fight."** The tragic story was told of a ten-year-old boy who hanged himself behind his father's barn. Just hours before, the boy had been the focus of a heated courtroom custody battle.

The boy had threatened to kill himself a year earlier. Tragically, even though the boy had written in his journal that he was considering suicide, a psychiatrist had found him not to be suicidal—no one really believed his pain.

About thirty minutes after he told his father that he was going to the barn to feed the rabbits, the fifth grader was found hanged. The boy had been caught in the middle—he wanted to stay with his mother, but he also loved his father.[1]

"Why didn't more of us take our lives like that ten-year-old boy?" I wondered. As I read the comments from survey people expressing loneliness, sadness, rage and the inability to function, I kept asking myself, "What enabled so many of us to survive?"

Susan, a California woman, wrote to us, "I keep friends at a distance." The full pain of her statement is apparent as later she wrote, "My mother tried to kill me as a two-month-old baby and my father put me in a foster home."

Susan spent two-and-a-half years in orphanages and time in thirty different foster homes between the ages of two months and ten years.

Susan's pain is still very evident as she writes, "My father never came around to see me in those foster homes. Sometimes I'd wait for hours to go to a movie with him—but he never showed." Her pain isn't just something that happened in the past; she is now deprived in her everyday relationships. She is still "waiting" for someone to really want her—to love her.

As the statistics from the people we surveyed were compiled, I began to feel the full impact of their losses in numerical form. I was astonished to see how deep the pain, how intense the anger, and how long-lasting the hurt were in these adults whose parents had divorced.

Loss Assessment

Looking through the list that follows, you begin to grasp some of the scope of the losses these people have lived with. We had asked people a series of questions, such as "Did you feel cheated out of part of your life because of your parents' conflict and divorce?" They were then asked to respond on a scale from ten, meaning "very much," to zero, meaning "not at all." Later we took these statistics and collapsed them into yes and no answers. Look at these surprisingly high statistics of loss. These are not just numbers—they are human pain!

Did you feel cheated out of part of your life?	70% yes
Did you feel extra responsibilities were forced on you?	63% yes
Did you feel torn in your allegiance between your mother and father?	58% yes
Were you emotionally abused?	57% yes
Did you suffer financial hardship?	57% yes
Did you feel dysfunctional at school?	53% yes
Did you become a parent or a counselor to either of your parents?	51% yes
Were you afraid to date or marry?	37% yes
Did you withdraw from your family?	36% yes
Did you become a parent or a counselor to any of your siblings?	35% yes

In addition, we asked people to rank some of the emotional losses they felt at the time of their parents' conflict or divorce:

72%	Were Unhappy
65%	Felt Powerless
61%	Felt Lonely
52%	Were Afraid
50%	Were Angry
48%	Felt Abandoned
40%	Felt Personally Rejected
30%	Were Hostile
30%	Felt Worthless

These were the emotions being experienced by people *at the time* of their parents' conflict and divorce. Later in the survey we asked them if they were still struggling with various issues. Following are the percentages of people *still struggling* with old issues:

58%	Constantly seek approval
54%	Block out some of their past
53%	Judge themselves too strictly
51%	Feel they are different from other people because of their parents' conflict and divorce
50%	Feel stunted in their personal growth
47%	Take themselves too seriously
45%	Still guessing at what is a normal family
42%	Overreact to situations over which they have no control
40%	Still having trouble with relationships
35%	Trouble relaxing or having fun
21%	Trouble following through on projects

These are real people! Many of the people in the survey were over forty, some even over seventy. The best way to give reality to these shocking numbers is to think of a friend or coworker from a legally or emotionally divorced family and put his or her face and name with these sad feelings.

The losses are staggering and immense. As I think about the collective human losses of these lives, I feel as if I'm skiing as an avalanche breaks loose above me. I turn downslope, desperately trying to escape. But I'm swallowed up by the terrifying, suffocating wall of snow and rocks.

Depressing Data

In a study entitled "Adult Children of Divorce: Curative Factors of Support Group Therapy," done in 1987, Kent McGuire summarizes the information available to that date about the terrible losses of adult children of divorce.

"Researchers have found that, as compared to children from intact homes, adult children of divorce tend to experience an increased level of the emotions of depression, anger, hostility, sadness, sorrow, anxiety regarding future relationships, difficulty in dealing with memories, increased vulnerability to stress, feelings of emptiness, uncontrollable rage, worry, isolation, bitterness, a sense that in many areas they may never be better off than those from intact families, a sense of being overwhelmed, and a reduced level of self-esteem."

McGuire's study showed that adult children of divorce have "more behavioral problems, less work effort, less empathy, pathological lying, frequent truancy and delinquency, and less appropriate social behavior."

McGuire also discovered that adult children of divorce have many problems relating to people, such as "lower satisfaction of courtship, short-lived sexual relationship, higher divorce rates, and difficulty in expressing and controlling emotions."[2]

The losses for these adult children of divorce undermine the very foundations of their lives. In the following condensed list, I've itemized the losses that I commonly see being sadly lived out by people from legally or emotionally divorced homes. They have:

☐ lost their parental models
☐ lost their stable and secure environment from
which to be launched into adult life
☐ lost their parental counselors and confidants
☐ lost the full realization of their future
☐ lost some of their childhood history

☐ lost the ability to love, appreciate, and be at peace
with themselves

☐ lost the ability to be intimate and close or to trust other people

☐ lost the ability to contribute through work without compulsion

The Losses Affect Future Generations

Marvin is fifty-two years old and lives on the East Coast. His whole life has been affected by his parents' divorce. He feels like part of a row of tumbling dominoes. Pathetically, he wrote to me, "I have now given, like a chain reaction, the same problem to my two children—a broken family. I am insecure. Before I felt I was just shy, now I feel broken."

Sadly, he speaks of his parents as not being real and his dad as some distant, untouchable, uncaring person.

"I do not remember Mom and Dad as married. I can only see them together when I see their old photographs. I still reach out to Dad as if my arm were extended, but he is always distant."

Each time I have felt Marvin's feelings about his dad, I picture a little boy who has fallen over the edge of a cliff and is clinging to a branch as he calls for help. I see the dad look over the edge. The boy pleads, "Dad, please help me." But the father turns away, afraid to risk.

Marvin is fifty-two, but he is still very angry at his parents for their divorce. He says pathetically, *"It hurts because my mom insists that divorce doesn't hurt the children.* It hurts that she speaks in nasty ways against my dad. True, he never was warm, but he still is my dad—a part of me."

The tragedy is that Marvin was six years old when his parents divorced. His life has been like a series of earthquakes, with loss after loss after loss, or, to use his words, "a chain reaction."

How Will I Explain It to My Children?

Debra, a thirty-three-year-old woman, told me what happened to her adult brothers and sisters when her parents divorced. Her parents were separated when she was twenty-three years of age and divorced when she was twenty-eight. Listen to her story:

"My parents' divorce seemed to create and enhance bad patterns among all of my family members. My youngest brother began using alcohol heavily.

"Then my sister ended up being wooed by the husband of a co- worker of mine who was my father's age. She had two illegitimate children by him and I had to deal with the ongoing trauma of my co-worker friend as well as my sister.

"At the same time my oldest brother became very withdrawn, very much of a loner."

Debra's family shows the sad effects of a divorce which takes place when the children are teens or young adults. Debra's life continues to bear the scars, which are clearly seen in her work and relationships:

"Sometimes work for me was a welcome break. Other times I felt distracted so that I was not able to perform at my best. I had room in my life only for friends who were willing to share my 'problems,' because that's what my life was mostly about." Sadly Debra's spiritual life has become a numb, hollow experience:

"Initially, my prayer life increased, but as the years and the consequences kept coming, I came to the point where I believed only that 'God is.' I didn't see him as answering prayer, only as allowing more and more problems."

When I asked Debra about what future problems she might experience, she said, "How am I going to explain to my children why Grandma and Grandpa don't live together and why we have to go to separate places to celebrate special occasions? How will I explain why Grandpa is married to someone younger than Mommy?"

The losses to Debra personally, in her marriage, and for her own children are immense and never-ending.

Success Yet Pain
The lives of adult children of emotionally or legally divorced families frequently are composed of two very distinct layers. The external layer, for many, is one of personal success and achievement. We know how to take responsibility. We know how to control. We know how to put up a good front and do whatever is needed in any situation. We have learned how to "read" people. Many of us have used these skills, produced by our dysfunctional homes, to make ourselves look very successful.

However, the second layer, that inside layer—that wounded little child—is a very uncomfortable and unhappy core of anger, perfectionism, depression, lust, cynicism and excessive control. Within us is a deep-seated mistrust of other people and ourselves. Because of this large core of insecurity and mistrust, we adult children of divorce have learned to follow the three crucial rules for survival: "Don't talk, Don't trust, Don't feel."[3]

Protect Yourself—Push People Away

Adult children from emotionally or legally divorced families have a deep need to protect themselves—to be safe from any more pain. We say to ourselves, "If I don't talk to anyone about what's going on, if I don't raise any questions, then I won't get into trouble or experience further hurt."

JoAnn is fifty-three years old and holds a master's degree in education. She told me that her three biggest problems are:

☐ Fear of rejection

☐ Fear of being vulnerable

☐ Difficulty in asking for help

JoAnn is a sharp contrast to the ten-year-old boy who hanged himself. JoAnn decided to take care of herself since no one else was doing it. JoAnn made an insightful, yet so tragic, comment:

"Because I was abandoned, I made the decision at age five to be strong—to take care of myself. I decided not to ask for help because no one would help me—I'll do it myself."

When I later asked, "What helped you to survive at the time of your parents' conflict and divorce?" JoAnn said, "My decision to *be strong.*" This decision may well have kept her alive. To me it seems that her decision set her overall life direction which continues to enable her to be successful.

JoAnn comments on her success, but also reveals her tragic losses, when she says, "This led to my development as a very strong, capable person. But I also became a person who could not be real and vulnerable or ask for help. I find it tough to become intimate with others.

"I learned the unrealistic expectation that marriage should always be happy. As a result, I tried hard never to allow conflict in my marriage."

JoAnn paid the price that many adult children from divorced homes have paid: they become people-pleasers. "Keep everybody happy" is their motto.

That's the way to reduce the conflict and tension around you.

To the people around her, JoAnn is a successful school administrator. They think her self-confidence is one of her greatest strengths but silently wonder why she is so aloof. They don't understand that JoAnn has a little five-year-old girl inside, gritting her teeth against the world and wishing someone would love her.

Inability to Handle Conflict

Adults who have been raised like this are afraid of conflict because, unconsciously, it brings back all the conflict they felt in their childhood. Not only are they dealing with current problems in life and relationships, but each problem triggers those awful, overwhelming childhood feelings.

Lois is a forty-four-year-old single woman whose parents divorced when she was seven. She told me how she developed a "secure zone" around herself. She used her mind to turn off her pain, to deny reality, to block out what was going on around her. "When the screaming got loud, I mentally turned off the sound."

As a seven-year-old child she found another way to protect herself. She said, "In those days I felt I had a guardian angel who protected me." She hung onto the guardian angel and felt safe. Without that, she might not have been able to handle her life as a child.

It is easy to understand why she developed those coping techniques. "I felt different from my friends and had a terrible self-image. I always felt if I could have had a brother or sister to share my problems, it would have helped immensely. But I was all alone. So I built a wall and blocked out much of the unhappiness I felt."

Lois didn't have anyone to talk to as a kid growing up in an emotionally divorced family. Then her parents divorced and her mother quickly remarried. The second marriage didn't make things any better for Lois.

"I hated my stepfather. I had a real father, whom I dearly loved and who loved me. I resented being forced to call this second man 'daddy' without my own feelings being taken into consideration. My mother's second marriage was also very unhappy, so my own thoughts about ever getting married were very negative."

Lois survived by living in a pretend world—but that unreal pretend world is still the place where she hides when conflict builds around her.

The Problem Is Not the Divorce Papers

It's shocking, but absolutely true! Much of the negative effect in the lives of adult children is not because a divorce paper was filed, but because of the conflict before and after the divorce.

Some couples, especially those from very strict religious backgrounds, believe that if they stay married—even though they have continuous conflict—they are not sinning and not harming their children. However, it is the dysfunction of their relationship which causes the tremendous negative impact, not the actual divorce.

One report is very direct, saying, "A conflict-ridden intact family is more [damaging] to family members than a stable home situation in which parents were divorced."[4]

An important study entitled "Young Adult Children of Divorced Parents: Depression and the Perception of Loss" showed that the depression children felt was not related to the act of the divorce itself. When a child or young adult was not able to have contact with a parent because of court rulings or lack of parental interest, they were more depressed.[5]

Millions of Damaged Adults

Studies such as these remind us that not only children and adults coming out of divorced families are damaged, but damage is also caused by dysfunction within a family.

Even if the parents had stayed married, the child would have been damaged.

Wow! As I read these studies I realized what had happened to me. I understood why I felt insecure, abandoned, as if I didn't belong in the world. I could understand why I always thought I had to "try harder" so people would like me. The pieces of the puzzle were starting to come together. Finally, there were reasons for my feelings. And I was not the only one— millions felt what I felt.

We are dealing with many more "adult children" than we thought— people whose parents were not divorced but whose homes were very dysfunctional. These children from non-divorced yet dysfunctional families will exhibit all the same losses and long-term personal trauma that we have been looking at in adult children of actual divorce.

Before we move to the next chapter, let me clarify one point. I'm not at all endorsing divorce. But we must clearly understand that emotionally divorced parents also damage children. The solution is not divorce. The solution is working on the bad marriage and the bad parent-child relationships so that positive patterns will replace negative ones—then family members will not experience long-term damage.

Now let's move to the next part of this book where we'll look in more detail at the common problems experienced by adult children of divorce—tons of people like you and me.

Part Two

Major Problems for Adult Children of Legal or Emotional Divorce

4

Cheated
out of
Life

---

*Y*OU MAY FIND IT PAINFUL TO READ ABOUT THE *troubling experiences adult children of divorce have gone through. In fact, you may be tempted to jump over these chapters and start reading again at part three, which talks about how to heal.*

Please resist the temptation to skip! Reading these stories will become part of the therapy for your own healing. The primary reason that adult children of divorce don't get healed earlier in life is that they have not wanted to look at their past or to feel their pain again. Healing comes as you face your past with adult abilities to handle your past. So keep reading and feeling—you are moving toward health.

As you read chapters four through ten, you will find it helpful to fill out the survey in appendix D, near the end of the book. The survey will help turn on the light in those dark rooms of your past.

Rage in Older Age

Charlotte, a single woman in her sixties, came to Sally and me after a conference. Her face was lined with the marks of anger rather than the soft lines of aging. I felt as if I were standing at the slope of the Kilauea volcano in Hawaii. I could feel the heat from her rage and almost felt the ground shaking under our feet. I was afraid at any moment the gory insides of hatred and wrath would erupt from Charlotte.

What had happened to produce such intense anger in her? With as much control as she could muster, Charlotte told us her story. As it spilled out, I could imagine myself standing on a tube of day-old lava whose crust was cool enough to walk on, but underneath the red hot lava flowed at 2,000 degrees Fahrenheit.

She explained that her parents had always had a rocky marriage. Increasingly, through her childhood, her mother had turned to Charlotte for the normal emotional nourishment that her husband should have given. Charlotte became an adult before her time, not knowing it was abnormal to care for her mother in this way.

Her mother thought it was wonderful that they had such a close relationship. But Charlotte, the child, the teen, was being sucked dry by her mother.

As a young woman Charlotte went off to college and finished one year. This was a signal to the parents that it was safe for them to get a divorce. The breakup was terrible, with deep bitterness on both sides. Her mother was unskilled and in many ways did not know how to take care of herself. She truly had been exploited by her husband, but she used the exploitation to manipulate Charlotte into caring for her.

The result was that Charlotte dropped out of college and went to work full-time while her mother set up housekeeping for the two of them. Her mother carried on as the homemaker while the daughter filled the role of breadwinner. The emotionally sick relationship continued, with the mother drawing nurturance and support from the daughter by reciting the old exploitations of the father. She controlled Charlotte by guilt and hatred.

Chains of the Past Bound Her

Even though Charlotte clearly sided with her mother against her father, she had an insistent feeling that something was wrong. Why should she take care of her mother? Hadn't the roles really been reversed for many years? Was it right that she should give up college and her future to protect her mother?

Remember, Charlotte had come to believe as a child that parental actions and thoughts are always 100 per cent accurate. Children think, "If I think or feel differently from my parents, I must be wrong." So as a child, Charlotte continually repressed those nagging feelings of truth coming from her own personality. Thus, she was set up to distrust men, distrust herself and feel insecure about her own decisions and judgments. On top of all that, she resented her mother for whom she was caring.

Finally, after years and years of denial and exploitation, her mother died. By now Charlotte had passed through mid-life and was nearing retirement. She was finally free of the depressing obligation. But at the same time, she became painfully aware that she had lived her entire life in response to the childhood baggage from her parents' emotional divorce and then their real divorce.

She had given up college. She had given up her career dreams. She had even given up marriage. It finally dawned on her—with crushing devastation—she had given up her whole life. Her life had been a continual response to the damning patterns of her dysfunctional parents.

As I felt the intensity of the rage within Charlotte, part of me wanted to cheer her on. "Finally, finally, finally, you've been willing to confront your past," I thought. There was hope for her now. Life could be different. Life *would* be different!

But another part of me was desperately sad for Charlotte. Much of her life could not be made over. She could not go back and live through her twenties and thirties, raise children, and enjoy her young husband and family. She could not enjoy the forties and fifties with children moving off into stable homes and careers. She could not enjoy grandchildren and the process of growing old with her husband.

Neither could she go back and live her life as a single person with a fulfilling career and rich friendships.

No—she was a lonely, unhappy woman, about to retire. She was an "adult child of divorce."

Wounded Deeply Within

Usually men are the least expressive about their problems, but sometimes their statements are the most poignant.

Mike, a twenty-seven-year-old guy from the South, perceptively said, "In a broken nest there are no whole eggs."

He had five brothers and sisters. It has taken years for some of the major cracks in their eggs to appear. His mom and dad were divorced twenty-three years ago, but it hasn't been until the past several years that Mike and his brothers and sisters began to deal with the emotional baggage they had been carrying around with them.

This young man described himself as having a poor self-image. Then he quickly rattled off a list describing this low self-image: "I am insecure, afraid of relationships, afraid of the unknown; I don't know how to be a father because I've not had a father model; I am a perfectionist; I always look for the approval of older males."

With great insight Mike projected his personal problems from his parents' divorce into our national future:

"I fear for the *next* generation—the product of the disintegrating marriages of the baby boom generation. We won't see the worst of it for twenty years, until the people who are now twenty-five to thirty-five begin dealing with what happened to them when their parents divorced."

This young man's graphic picture of feeling cheated continues to haunt me as I think of all the future potential emotional damage: "In a broken nest, there are no whole eggs."

The Unremovable Bullet

Bill was a thirty-two-year-old minister whose parents had divorced five years earlier. He was a very bright, confident, optimistic person, with a deep desire to help people. He was also a good communicator and liked to work with people. I thought of him as the ideal pastor type.

A year and a half after he graduated from seminary, his bubble burst. His parents, who had been married almost thirty-six years, got divorced. He was absolutely stunned. Everything in his life had seemed to be going so well. Now all of a sudden the foundational support fell apart, and his whole life came crashing down. In a matter of minutes, his concept of marriage and long-term relationships became suspect.

There were drastic changes in Bill. He was unable to continue his post-graduate studies because he couldn't concentrate, so he dropped the program. Suddenly, this confident leader-type man became plagued with self-doubt and insecurities. He wondered how he could ever lead anyone else when he felt so shattered himself.

His relationship with God, which was very close, became distant because he wondered if God really could be trusted. He didn't believe that God caused his parents' marriage to fall apart, but he wondered why God wasn't answering any of his intense prayers for healing in his parents' marriage.

He described himself as "sexually conservative," yet sex suddenly became a great problem for him. Because he was seeking love and affection, he started sleeping around with several women, even though his actions violated his morals.

It has been five years since Bill's parents divorced, yet his life is not yet together. He is a minister, yet he serves with uncertainty, and the leadership potential that was so obvious in seminary is greatly diminished. He is afraid even to face what he feels about his parents. But on rare occasions, he is willing to admit that he feels cheated. Even as he says that, it's obvious that he is trying to hold down the intense anger he feels. He graphically described the situation: "It's hard for a wound to heal when the bullet is still in the body."

His parents' divorce was like a gun that fired a bullet, and that bullet is still deeply lodged within his personhood.

Our world is beginning to realize that divorce affects more than just the two people getting divorced, and the effect is not short-lived. Lifelong consequences haunt the parents getting divorced, the children, and the extended family—for generations to come.

I Feel Cheated

A massive feeling among many adult children of divorce is that they feel "cheated out of life." They feel they were deprived by not having a normal home, having no models and living in a dysfunctional environment with parents in constant conflict.

They feel cheated because their self-images, schoolwork and careers were all negatively affected. Their marriages and children also have been adversely influenced. Plus, they fear that their grandchildren will be damaged.

In some senses they are very clear about what they lack, but in other instances they are unsure of what they missed. There's a common feeling among these adult children of divorce that they are "aliens" in the world—everyone else is normal and they are the odd people. Perhaps the most painful problems they experience are with themselves. One young woman told me, "I feel like I don't belong in my body." Her whole self-concept was blurred; she saw her physical self in the mirror and yet the person inside didn't identify with that body—the person inside didn't know who she herself really was.

People who say they feel cheated out of life may react in several very negative ways:

☐ *Anger.* Many harbor a deep sense of anger because they feel cheated. Sometimes the anger is very specific. One thirty-eight-year-old woman, writing to me about her parents' divorce which had happened ten years earlier, said with seething anger, *"Having a bad father has got to be much worse than having no father at all!!!!!"*

It's interesting that she underlined the phrase "having no father at all" three times and then added five exclamation marks as if to drive home the point and express anger that she still felt—ten years later.

☐ *Distrust.* Because these adult children of divorce feel cheated, many are living with a troubling feeling that "the world is out to get them." When anything goes wrong in their lives, they say to themselves, "You can't trust the world—you can't trust people. They're always going to exploit you. They'll always disappoint you or take advantage of you."

Pam's parents divorced when she was twenty-one. Now, six years later, she is afraid of being hurt as her mother was when her father abandoned her for a younger woman. As a result, Pam has only surface relationships. Unless she works through her distrust of men, Pam will never marry. Or if she does, her marriage will probably fail, because she will not be able to fully trust her husband.

Pam is also highly critical of herself and other people. Because she assumes other people will let her down, she places unrealistic expectations on them. Consequently, she often is disappointed by other people, so she withdraws quickly for fear of more disappointment.

Pam is not only unsure of other people, but she is unsure of herself. Maybe she will disappoint other people, or maybe she will repeat the same bad relationship that her parents had.

Pam needs assurance that she is a normal person, but she can't trust other people to tell her the truth, so she is left with only her own limited and uncertain perception of life.

Pam has gotten involved in drugs and alcohol and is sexually active. But she turns to these things only because of her desperate need to quiet the throbbing pain of loneliness and insecurity in her heart.

Unfortunately, Pam is the child in the family who kept the family secrets: her father was involved in an affair before the divorce and her mother is a frigid, unfeeling woman. The outside world is just supposed to think that Pam had two very normal parents who "just couldn't get along."

I wonder how far Pam will go along through life simply marking time, hoping that somehow she will grow out of this problem and become a "normal" person again.

☐ *Fear of the Past.* "I ought to look at my past—but I'm afraid," adult children of divorce say. Claudia is one of those fearful people. We first met her when she was a sophomore in college, helping Sally and me with a project. Very shortly, the conversation centered on her divorced family. She smiled and cheerily told us about how good things were between her mother and herself. But she was uneasy talking about the divorce, her father or her childhood when her parents were together.

Over the next couple of years, Sally and I had many contacts with Claudia and each time we parted, she seemed to be reaching out for a hug. She had a big smile on her face, but she also carried a big hurt in her heart. Somehow she hoped that the hurt would go away if she never looked at her past.

During the time we were asking people from many parts of the country to fill out the same survey found in appendix D, Claudia said she'd like to do it too.

When she brought her survey back she said, "This was hard for me to do. Yet because I committed myself to fill it out, I went through it, and a wonderful thing happened. I feel as if something has opened up inside of me. I now realize that much of my past, which I had stuffed away, had to get out in the open for me to be healed—so that someday I'll be ready for my own marriage."

☐ *Living Two Lives.* Adult children of divorce have been blighted within themselves because unresolved problems from their dysfunctional family have been blocked out. Most fail to integrate their past into their current lives. This separation leaves them with a sense of "unfinished business." Frequently they feel as if they are two different people. They are uncertain about how bad their home really was—or whether they themselves are good or bad people now.

Keith is a successful businessman. He is surrounded by all of the symbols of success—his nice office, respect from other people in the company, a new luxury sports car, and a magnificent home in the most prestigious development in his city.

Yet Keith lives a double life: his present one and the one from his childhood. He has tried to bury his hurt and pain that come from his parents' divorcing when he was a child. In fact, he has so effectively denied his past that he can live months without ever thinking about his divorced parents.

Even though Keith has pushed his parents to the edge of his consciousness as he lives his daily life, his other life continues to haunt him. He is looking forward to the day when they are both dead. He said, "When my parents die, I'll be very sad because of their choices, but at least I'll know they will not be here to hurt and disappoint our family any more."

No one in Keith's successful life knows about how really bad it was in his childhood and youth, but he cannot successfully hide the facts from himself.

I mentioned to you that in the early stages of preparing to write this book, I thought I was studying about other people. But my feeling of being cheated out of life was something I always felt very deeply.

I envied my friend Ross because his dad and mom really liked each other. His dad was involved with Ross's life in small things such as calling him in for supper and larger things like helping Ross get elected president of our junior-high class.

My dad was too busy working to support our family or involved with his own life. I made my own fun. I felt like a kid growing up on my own. Most of my fun was when I was away from home, being a "boy commando," building forts in the landfill, stealing fruit from neighbors' trees at the peak of each season, or playing street games of baseball, football, basketball or hockey. Home was a place of correction and a place to sleep.

I've always had problems at adult parties when I'm asked to talk about the warmest room in my house—there weren't any. So I'd make up one. "After all, it's only a game and probably everyone else lies about their homes too."

The easiest way to handle my homelife, as a child and as an adult, was just to forget it—ignore it—block it out.

□ **Denial.** To function normally, the human personality must resolve hurt. A very common defense is to repress any thoughts and feelings related to a specific hurtful event. In the case of divorce, many adult children block out an entire section of their lives.

We can understand why adult children of divorce would bury some of their past. I've asked hundreds of people, "Now that you are years away from your parents' dysfunction and divorce, what are your feelings?" Over 50 per cent have said they were still blocking some of their past. Some people more than thirty years beyond their parents' divorce were still dis missing and covering up part of their past, along with their feelings associated with that era.

The Denial Power of the Mind

Some people have trouble believing that the human mind actually can block out memories and feelings, but this blocking is very common in many areas of our lives. For example, when I was a pastor I visited widows in retirement homes. Their stories about their relationship with their husband were not always accurate.

When Mary was a young mother, her husband, Ralph, had deserted her to run off with another woman. Ralph hadn't provided any child support and essentially had no contact with the children during their growing-up years.

After the children were gone and Ralph's second wife had died, he contacted Mary. He visited her or called only occasionally, but Mary had rewritten her history with this man. She had selectively picked out the good stuff and conveniently forgotten her pain. She ignored the loneliness, the lack of child support, and his absence year after year at every holiday, birthday and anniversary. She told me only the *good* things about Ralph!

For our own survival, our personality chooses to keep the memories that are tolerable and to block out the memories that are too overwhelming.

Blinded by Pain

The shocking headline read, **"Cambodian Women Believed Blinded by Horror of Slayings They Witnessed."** The article revealed an unusual phenomenon called "functional blindness." Gretchen Van Boemel, an electrophysiologist, reported that in over fifty years of research only thirty cases of this type of blindness have been documented in the USA. Yet she had identified at least 150 Cambodian women living in Southern California with "functional blindness." She said, "They had witnessed things so horrible that they had willed their eyes not to see."

The horror they saw was something like their husbands being murdered in front of them. These women then cried and cried. When they stopped crying, they couldn't see.

One Cambodian woman saw the Khmer Rouge soldiers tie up her parents, cut their throats, and throw them into a river. Another woman saw her child bashed to death against a tree.

Sophisticated brain-wave tests have shown that these women should have normal eyesight. Doctors say there is no physical explanation for the blindness. They suffer from a vision loss caused by psychological factors.

"They just don't want to see anymore."[1]

We're Not Fighting

The same type of blocking happens emotionally in troubled homes. Some children are taught by their parents at a very early age not to believe what they hear or see. For example, parents may be fighting in their bedroom behind the closed door. The child hears the angry words, things being thrown around and mother crying. The child may even overhear the parents saying they ought to get divorced or that one of them is going to leave.

However, in a few minutes the parents come out and seem relatively well composed. The child asks, "What happened?" The parents assure the child, "Nothing happened—everything is okay." The child says, "I thought I heard you fighting." The parents respond, "No! We had a little disagreement, but we were not fighting!"

So now the child has to redefine these events. He thinks back to his sweaty palms, the tight muscles in his stomach, his pounding heart. He remembers feeling afraid that he might be abandoned and feeling angry toward his father as he heard him hitting his mother. He also remembers the disappointment that he felt toward his mother as she cursed at his father. But his parents told him, "Nothing is wrong." So he must have imagined all of this.

The child may block this incident out of his mind as never having happened. It's simply thrown into his subconscious, along with the other blocked incidents that never happened.

Even though they've been blocked out of consciousness, *these "feeling pictures" don't go away.* They'll live on, festering in the unconscious until there is some resolution. That explains why adult children of divorce have unexplained feelings of sadness, loneliness, depression, anger, and a deep mistrust of people. These negative feeling pictures are the roots of the damaged self-image and blurred boundaries which we will examine in the next chapter.

5
Damaged Self-Image and Blurred Boundaries

WHEN I WAS BROUGHT INTO THE WORLD AS a newborn infant, I was absolutely dependent on my parents for all my physical needs such as food, shelter and care. An unwritten agreement between my parents and me said my parents were responsible to introduce me to the world, to help me make sense of how I fit into history, and to help me discover my unique God-given gifts and abilities.

My parents also were the ones charged with the emotional and spiritual development of "little Jimmy." My ability to value and appreciate myself primarily would be in direct ratio to my parents' affirmation of me.

This is true of every person. If the people who are supposed to love, care for and encourage the child *hurt* him or her instead, through negative statements, neglect, or physical or emotional abuse, the child will then believe he or she is worthless. That child will feel like some sort of "alien" or blight on society.

My parents were preoccupied with their own personal and marital problems, so they didn't keep the unwritten contract. As a result, I felt very inadequate. I knew I would fail at anything I tried. So I didn't risk anything unless I knew success was sure.

Kent, a young man from Colorado, recently verbalized the feelings I've so often felt. "If I had a son like me, I'd be proud of him. I must have told myself that a thousand times. I think I say that in order to convince and comfort myself." Then he turned his face away and asked in anger— "Where was *my* dad? When are my accomplishments going to be outstanding enough to get *his* attention?"

You're Not Wanted

The world is filled with people like Kent and me whose parents didn't keep the unwritten contract of parenting. Cheryl is one of those millions. She is a bright, attractive college student, but she repeatedly was told by her mother, "I wish you'd never been born." She was told that her birth caused a heavy financial burden. Cheryl's father blamed her mother for getting pregnant, so there was constant dissension between her parents.

Imagine that you are Cheryl. How would you feel if you had been rejected since birth? Is it any wonder that you would have a low self-image? In fact, it is astounding that Cheryl had enough initiative to stay alive, to go through school and to actually finish college. She did it even though she felt terrible about herself.

As I've counseled people from divorced homes, I've heard them use these phrases indicating their low self-image:

"My opinion doesn't count."

"I try never to make waves."

"Whatever I do, it will never be enough."

"I can't do it."

"I keep trying to make everything perfect."

"I don't trust people."

"I'm afraid to get married."

"I'm afraid my children will become like me."

Does Anyone Love Me?

It is commonly expected that by the time people get to be forty, they ought to "have it all together." That is not the case with Marjorie. She has never felt as good as other people. She's always felt like an outsider. The burning question that sums up her life is, "Does anyone love me?"

Marjorie remembers always fishing for compliments as a little girl. If she helped her mom set the table, she would follow it up with questions such as, "Did I do a good job?" There was no internal sense of security.

Little Marjorie and my little granddaughter Hayden are very different. When Hayden helps with a task around the house or yard, she stands back, smiles at her work and gleefully yells, "I did it!"

But Marjorie constantly needed other people to say to her, "You did it." Marjorie started doing helpful things in order to get affirmation. Increasingly, she would even do things she hated to do, just to hear someone tell her that it was good.

If Only I Could Be Perfect

By the time she got into grade school, kids almost instinctively spotted her as a person who could be manipulated by a little bit of praise. So Marjorie would be anything they wanted her to be and do almost anything they wanted her to do. She literally became the servant girl and the "goat" for the other kids in grade school.

The reason Marjorie got very few voluntary compliments at home and repeatedly had to pull them out of people was that her parents were emotionally divorced. They were preoccupied with their marital struggles and didn't have time to notice that Marjorie was becoming a very confused child.

During Marjorie's teen years, her family continued to disintegrate, each person going separate ways. Marjorie was still trying to get approval from them or anyone. She desperately tried to be perfect, yet people kept brushing her aside. Her life seemed unimportant and a waste of time.

During these teen years she became suicidal. "Why go on living?" she thought. "The harder I work, the less I get. People only love me for what I do for them, not for what I am." So at one point she took a whole bottle of sleeping pills, hoping to end it all.

Marjorie's brother and younger sister believed that her attempt was real. But her parents never believed it. "I was serious, but I was also naive about how many pills it would take to kill me. I think my parents thought I was just trying to get attention. They didn't realize how desperately I was starved for love, for someone's approval.

"They never talked to me about it—I simply had a long sleep. It was almost worse to go on after that, because now I felt that my parents didn't care whether I lived or died."

This amazing woman did go on with life, got married and raised several children. But she still describes herself by saying, "Even though I am now a wife and a mother, in many ways I feel I'm still only a child."

DAMAGED SELF-IMAGE

People with low self-images have a driving urgency to do better, try harder and please more. All of us who feel inadequate ultimately want to be perfect and have everything around us perfect so that people will love and respect us. Of course, we fail, because no one is perfect and every situation has flaws. We understand that intellectually, but we keep trying to do the impossible. As a result, we struggle with many of the following issues as we try to be better—to be perfect.

☐ *Insecurity.* The recurring theme for us perfectionists is insecurity. "Who am I? Am I worthy of being loved? If I try a little harder, or if I am a little more perfect, will I finally be accepted?" Insecurity plagues us, nagging us to work harder.

☐ *Control.* Perfectionism also drives the person to try to control all of life. Unconsciously I say, "If I can perfectly control my environment, my relationships, my responsibilities—then I can be in the power position and I'll feel more secure."

On the surface this desire to be perfect seems like a wonderful idea, but it has a definite downside. A mid-life woman put her finger on it very precisely when she said, "I don't try anything unless I can get an A."

☐ *Fear of Risk.* The perfectionist or the insecure person is not willing to risk. Everything has to be guaranteed ahead of time. The perfectionist chooses to stay out of new relationships because they might eventually fall apart. So that person decides to be alone rather than risk failure.

Frequently perfectionists stay in careers where they are safe, rather than to risk new opportunities. One man told me, "I am highly critical of both myself and others. Consequently, I'm often disappointed by the actions of others and I withdraw quickly for fear of repeated disappointment. My fear which keeps me at a distance from people damages my relationships with peers, colleagues and friends."

☐ *Never Enough.* Another problem of the perfectionist is that enough is never enough. The perfectionist can never be satisfied to be the first or the best. No matter what his accomplishments have been, he still feels empty inside. He thinks, "Maybe if I try a little more, I'll feel good about myself." But "more" is never enough.

Let's suppose for a moment that you are this terrific, world-class pole-vaulter, but you're also a compulsive perfectionist. Let's also suppose that the world record is about 25 feet, and you have just set it.

The normal pole-vaulter who has just set the record would experience a great deal of elation, but that person would also pick up the pole to see if it's possible to set an even higher record. If he failed on each of the next three attempts, he would feel he had done his very best and would be satisfied with his record.

But you are the one who has just set the 25-foot record. Instead of asking the officials to set the pole at 25 feet 1-inch, you ask them to set it at 26 feet, a whole foot higher than anyone else in the world has ever approached. You take your pole back to the beginning of the runway. Your eyes have the glint of fierce determination. Your jaw is set. You lift the pole and your feet pound down the runway. You jam the pole into the socket and soar into the air. Your upper body and arms thrust your body over the 26-foot marker. You have now set a world's record a full foot higher than anyone else in the world has ever achieved!

The perfectionist in you says more would be better. So you ask them to set the cross-pole at 30 feet, 5 feet higher than anyone else. Now you pick up a special longer pole that you've been practicing with. Again your feet pound down the runway. You soar into the air. The stadium is hushed in silence as your feet turn upward and you are pulled as if by magic over the 30-foot horizontal bar. There's a stunned silence for a moment, and then a deafening cheer. You have now passed the world's record by 5 feet!

The fans express a mixture of disbelief and amazement in the midst of their wild crescendo of cheering.

But, you are a perfectionist. Enough is never enough. So you ask for the bar to be set at 50 feet—double the height of the world's record. After you clear that unbelievable goal, the perfectionist in you will always ask for the bar to be higher. Let's set it at 75 feet. Let's set it at 100 feet, 500, 1000. Suppose you clear the bar at 1500 feet, will enough ever be enough for you?

The answer is no. Because you think if you cross the bar just a little higher, maybe people will love you. Maybe you will feel secure. Maybe you will feel worthwhile. The truth is, until the security comes from inside you, you can cross the bar at 1500 feet and still feel worthless and unloved—a failure.

True security comes as we have deep, trusting relationships with other people who love and affirm us whether we succeed or fail. This is why knowing God personally (knowing that, amazingly, he *treasures* us and considers us to have *value*) can be such a powerful, life-changing force in our lives.

☐ *Fear of Intimacy.* Another problem for perfectionists is the difficulty in being intimate and vulnerable. We are afraid we won't be liked if someone knows very much about us.

I tend to be a perfectionist, but I have learned that other people don't like perfectionists. I've found it's easier for people to relate to me when I talk about my weaknesses than when I talk about my successes. They see me as more human.

Sometimes I tell a group to whom I am speaking, "I'm going to introduce myself to you by first telling you about my degrees, my books and articles, my travels around the world and other achievements." Then I go on to tell them about how inadequate and insecure I feel because of my dysfunctional childhood.

Finally I ask, "With which person would it be easier for you to share a problem—the successful one or the one who feels weak?" People have always felt closer to the weak Jim.

Adult children of divorce usually won't speak of weakness for fear they will lose the power position or lose control. True intimacy, however, is achieved by vulnerability rather than by power.

☐ *Anger.* Another trait of people with a low self-image is anger. The anger is linked to inadequacy ("Why should I be so inferior and unable to be what I want to be?") and to the inability to control ("Why can't I make life and people be the way they *should* be?"). The angry person will always have endless reasons to be angry because someone else will always have or be more. Life can never be made perfect.

☐ *Guilt.* In addition, people with a low self-image frequently feel guilty for not being perfect and for not being able to control events so life turns out right. On top of the guilt they feel for being imperfect, they feel guilty for getting angry at themselves, at other people and at God.

Another adult child of divorce said, "Since I was three years old I've believed that I caused my parents' divorce." His parents and older brothers and sisters reinforced his guilty feelings by their sarcastic remarks to him. He always felt that if he had been a better child his parents wouldn't have divorced. He has borne the shame all his life.

After he described how that faulty belief caused him to feel guilty all through his life, he said, "My greatest problem now is really loving myself and feeling I am worthwhile. I need help!"

He is angry that his family made him feel responsible for the divorce. Then he added, "Both of my parents are dead and I feel guilty just thinking bad things about the dead." Mentally he knows that the three-year-old boy didn't cause the divorce, but at age forty-three he still feels the childhood blame.

☐ *Immobilized.* Many adult children of divorce are trapped by their low self-esteem—it immobilizes them in their relationships and in their work.

Phyllis is an example of a person who was told all through her childhood that she was a worthless person. When her parents started to fight, even as a very young child, she would get between them and demand that they stop fighting. They would push her out of the way, telling her it was none of her business or that she was just making things worse.

She repeatedly tried to get her parents to love each other or hug each other, but she was told, "You're stupid, you don't understand, get out of my way."

Phyllis's parents did divorce, and the result of her being an unsuccessful peacemaker was that she felt very inadequate. She also always tried to keep things peaceful by being a compromiser and a people-pleaser. Then she felt guilty for never having her own opinions.

It was a dead-end street for this woman. If she didn't please people, she felt bad. If she did please them, she felt guilty.

Phyllis had a lot of negative self-talk going on inside her, which kept on immobilizing her so that she just couldn't do anything. For example, as she would start to work around the house or prepare a meal, she would talk to herself, using the negative input she had learned as a child: "You've never really been a very good housekeeper, and your meals aren't too hot either. Even though you keep trying to please people, you don't seem to be able to accomplish that either. You try to do special things for your husband, but he doesn't appreciate it, just like your parents didn't appreciate your trying to help."

Then she would attack herself for not being more of a person. "You really are a worthless person, and you ought to feel guilty for not being yourself. You spend all of your time compromising, trying to please other people instead of becoming your own person."

This self-talk kept her going in circles so much that she did, in fact, do a poor job of taking care of the house and preparing meals. Then when she didn't get things accomplished, her husband was angry. Their marriage relationship was continually threatened.

Sometimes the person who feels inadequate blames God. "If God really loved me, he would help me to feel secure and to be a productive person," Phyllis would say to herself. Then she would feel guilty and her self-talk would make her fear God, "You'd better be careful what you think about God. He might stop loving you if you keep talking that way."

So again, Phyllis would be paralyzed, embarrassed to tell God what she really felt, feeling guilty for everybody and everything around her. Sadly, the cycle in Phyllis was a downward one of being paralyzed by her low self-esteem, which caused her to fail even more, which in turn increased her guilt, spiraling her into depression.

☐ *Depression.* Another dimension of a low self-image—depression—involves a group of feelings that follow the familiar downward spiral through several layers:

Loss
Frustration because of the loss
Denial (an attempt to block out the loss)
Anger
Guilt because of getting angry
Bitterness
Hopelessness
Depression
Withdrawal, isolation, or the ultimate act of suicide

How Destructive Patterns Lead to Depression

When parents divorce, their children lose "home," security, past history and the hope of a positive future. Children feel abandoned as the home disintegrates.

Children or young adults of divorce often react by trying to get the parents back together. If they are unable to get their parents to reconcile, they may move into denial, blocking out the hurts they feel. The children then try to reorient their lives in a new direction, forgetting this sad chapter of parental dysfunction.

Whether or not they are successful in blocking out their feeling of loss because of their parents' divorce, they will still feel anger. "This is unfair! Why did it happen to me and to our family?" They feel that life is out of control—their control.

Guilt follows anger. The child feels responsible in some way for the parental dysfunction or feels guilty for being angry. Unless the child or young adult gets help, bitterness may follow guilt and then comes a rapid slide toward hopelessness, a sense of giving up on the situation or on life. "It will never change. I will never change. They are forever divorced. Our family is forever ruined."

Depression now flows out of all of these other emotions. "I have lost my home, and there's no way to get it back. I feel wretched."

It is easy then for the depressed person to slide into withdrawal and isolation. The emotional circuitry is over-stressed. The person can't handle the overload and just disconnects. He pulls the circuit breaker and shuts off the power. This is nature's way of protecting us when we have an overload. But it's unfortunate that the adult child of divorce pays the price for the parents' divorce and dysfunction.

At some point very early in my life, I decided I needed to protect myself. I felt emotionally abandoned. I felt safer if I trusted no one. I believed that somehow I would have to muddle through life on my own.

Many adult children of divorce express the same insecurities and lifelong damage to their self-image. One woman told me, "I expect abandonment as the natural outcome of any relationship with a man—and that's what I get. My parents' relationship set the tone for my life."

INADEQUATE BOUNDARIES

Low self-esteem is directly tied to our understanding of where our territory stops and someone else's starts—boundary issues. Adult children of divorce not only have low self-esteem and therefore become perfectionists prone to depression; they also don't know how to establish their own boundaries or to honor another person's boundaries.

One of the best discussions of boundaries is found in the book *Facing Codependence.* The author, Pia Mellody, says, "Boundary systems are invisible and symbolic fences." She points out that they have three purposes: (1) to keep people from coming into our space and abusing us, (2) to keep us from going into their space and abusing them, (3) to give each of us a way to identify who we are.

Then she talks about two types of boundaries, external and internal. Our external boundary is a combination of physical and sexual "distance." Our external boundary controls how close we let people come to us and whether they can touch us or not.

Our internal boundary protects our thinking, feeling and behaviors. It separates *our* thoughts, *our* feelings and *our* actions from those of other people.

Pia Mellody says, "Our internal boundary also stops us from taking responsibility for the thoughts, feelings, and behaviors of others. These boundaries keep us from being manipulated by other people. Boundaries also keep us from controlling those around us."

Very small children have no boundaries to protect them from abuse or to keep them from being abusive toward others. To develop properly, these boundaries need time and a positive family environment.

Parents need to protect their children by not allowing others to cross over the child's boundary. Parents also need to confront children about crossing the boundaries of other people. Protection and confrontation by the parents teach children to develop healthy and firm but flexible boundaries by the time they reach adulthood.

Parents who are less than nurturing produce children who have no boundaries, damaged boundaries or walls instead of boundaries.[1]

Manipulated by People

Because young children have no boundaries, they are easily abused emotionally, physically and sexually. They don't know what is inappropriate. A dysfunctional adult easily can become an offender or abuser in the child's life.

A divorced or dysfunctional home damages a child because boundaries are not yet in place to protect the child. The child may take on adult responsibilities or believe that wrong is right.

Incest is a topic not discussed in most polite circles. Frequently it consists of an older relative fondling a young child and telling the child that what is happening is all right. Because the child doesn't have boundaries established and because the older person is respected by the child, the child pushes down all of his or her natural feelings that this is wrong. The child is coerced into tolerating the situation.

One time, as a young pastor, I was calling on people who had recently visited our church. As I entered one home, I was shocked by how poorly the home was kept. I was invited to sit on a couch that was strewn with dirty clothes, candy wrappers and an open box of cereal. I pushed some of the debris aside and carefully sat down.

The father of the home was putting on his shirt as I explained to him that I noticed he and his family were in church Sunday, and I wanted to encourage them to come back. He apologized for the way he looked and continued to get dressed.

His next statement knocked me speechless. Red lights went on all over my brain. He said, as he buttoned his shirt, "Usually I go around the house naked. Eight hours a day is long enough for any man to wear clothes." I stumbled around, trying to talk about our church and what we had to offer to his family.

Just then some of the kids came running through the living room. They were scantily dressed, and I assumed that it was just because they were a poor family. The thirteen-year-old girl had obviously entered puberty. She and her eight-year-old brother were playfully chasing each other.

It Was Unbelievable!

I politely said to the father, "You have some good-looking kids." Without blinking an eye he looked lustfully at his daughter and said to me, "Yes, and I'm going to be the first one to have her."

I was stunned. This wasn't real life. Certainly this couldn't be America. Did I have the right address? Did this family really attend our church last Sunday? I was a twenty-eight-year-old pastor, and I had never in my life been exposed to such a blatant statement of incest by a father.

If that happened to me now, with the understanding that I have of the destructiveness of incest, I would report that man to the police and try to arrange some sort of protection for those children.

I never saw the family again, because shortly they moved out of the community. But I have often wondered what happened to those children, especially that thirteen-year-old girl. Maybe if she wrote to me today, her letter would sound the same as one I received from a forty-five-year-old woman from New Mexico who is exactly the same age as that girl would be today.

This woman said, "I still have trouble seeing God as my father because mine was so bad.

"My father not only molested me, he rejected me and never cared enough about me to have a normal relationship.

"I have been married fifteen years, yet I still have problems trusting my husband.

"I am constantly having to unlearn those old self-defeating behaviors. Because I didn't feel loved or accepted early in my life, I still haven't felt loved and accepted for who I am."

Men and women whose boundaries have been violated feel inferior and are "people-pleasers." They do not understand that it is okay to have their own boundaries and to be respected for having their own personhood. People-pleasers tend to see themselves as an extension of another person or as responsible for other people's happiness —always at the sacrifice of themselves.

Who Holds the Power?

Other writers have described the boundary issue by thinking of themselves as inside a tent with a zipper around the door. The question is asked, "Is the control for the zipper on the inside of the tent or on the outside?" Individuals with boundary problems tend to allow other people to control the zipper.[2]

People with inadequate boundaries also tend to accept too much responsibility. When they are overloaded, they tend to burn out and feel guilty that they let someone else down. Their feeling of failure in turn reinforces their sense of inadequacy.

They have accepted too many responsibilities that really belong to other people. For many years they have kept deeply buried inside themselves the family secrets about marital conflict, alcohol abuse or sexual sins.

Typical adult children of divorce have boundary problems because they are never quite sure they can trust themselves; they can never say with certainty, "This is what I think, and this is who I am." They are easily manipulated by stronger people who themselves have boundary problems.

Often adult children of divorce do not know how to honor the boundaries of other people. Because we adult children of divorce feel inadequate and because we are perfectionists, we try to control situations to make things work perfectly. It's easy to take the next step by trying to control other people—in order to make life work perfectly. As soon as we start controlling other people, we generally are intruding into their space, crossing over their boundaries.

Violated Boundaries

Many homes have a domineering mother or father. In my parental home my father did the thinking for everyone. Neither my mother nor any of us children were valued as individuals who had unique insights and contributions to make to the world. My father was always right.

My family practiced "group think"; that is, everyone is allowed only to think like the leader. Only my father was right. My mother and I reacted by being quiet. My brother fought back, but he was no match for my father. He was always in trouble and was labeled the black sheep. My sisters turned to each other for companionship and affirmation. Because they were girls they also had a natural link to my mother.

At a family reunion, after all of us were married and our own children were well on their way to maturity, we together asked Dad to stop trying to dominate our lives. Even though we were successful adults in our careers and with our individual families, he still thought he knew what was best for each of us. We asked him to accept us as adults and stop controlling us.

He totally rejected what we had to say. His response was to leave the family gathering and drive to a distant city to escape us. He had learned that when conflict comes, it's best to either fight or run.

All of the children felt, and continue to feel, that our father views himself as a benevolent person and, in fact, he is in certain circumstances. However, when his wife or one of his children does not totally agree with his perception of life, he treats that person with disdain and usually punishes that one by stopping contact with him or her.

(I realize now that even my father's most hurtful behavior was never meant to harm his family; he himself had learned some very destructive patterns in childhood, and he didn't know how to be different.)

Look Who's Talking

Now the kicker. Without realizing it, I began to duplicate my father's patterns with my own wife and children. Many times in our marriage, Sally has been afraid to voice an opinion for fear of making me angry. In essence, I was using my anger to manipulate her. I was crossing her boundaries by not giving her the right to be a person or to have her own valued opinion.

I did the same thing with our three daughters. I sometimes impressed on them that they needed to behave a certain way because they were "my kids." Sadly, our daughters were not always as free to be individuals as they needed to be. Sometimes they were afraid to displease me. As a result, some of the process of their becoming unique people in their own right did not happen until they were in their twenties and out on their own.

Ideal boundaries are not rigid walls, but are definitions of a person that continue to change as the individual desires to change in relationship to various people. Even in the most intimate relationships, there should be flexible boundaries. Sally and I are married, but still I am Jim and she is Sally. We have three daughters, three sons-in-law, and several grandchildren. Each individual has his or her own boundary definition. Fortunately, we are now learning to better respect each other's boundaries.

In the next chapter we're going to see why children who grow up in divorced or dysfunctional homes tend to reproduce that same kind of dysfunction in their own marriage and homelife.

6

Dysfunction
Breeds
Dysfunction

THINK OF A CHILD'S LIFE AS A CUP. THE PARents' role is to help fill that cup with love, trust, acceptance and guidance so the child can enter the world as an adult with something to offer to other people, rather than as a desperate person always trying to get the cup filled. The sickness of the divorced home is that it produces children who become adults with empty cups.

Tragically, these adult children of divorce *don't even realize they are dysfunctional*—with empty cups.

Barbara is a forty-year-old woman from the Midwest. Her parents divorced when she was nine. That started a lifelong nightmare of feeling cheated out of life.

Even after thirty-one years she feels that her parents abandoned her because they were too preoccupied with their own lives. Her father turned his back on the family and focused all his attention on his new wife. He just didn't have time to look back to see a nine-year-old girl emotionally shivering all alone.

An Instant Adult

Barbara's mother also ignored her. She had too many things to do, starting back to school and going back to work at the same time. Her mother felt like a fish out of water, both at school and at work. Yet in order to support the family, she did what she had to do.

The sad reality was that Barbara became an instant adult. She took over some of her mother's jobs at home, cooking some of the meals, cleaning the house and doing some of the laundry. She tried to stay out of the way so that her mother wouldn't have any additional pressures besides working, going to school and raising three kids as a single parent.

Unfortunately, Barbara did have needs—the needs of a nine-year-old kid who shouldn't have had to feel responsible for helping her mother survive the divorce.

Barbara lived with her mother for the next few years. As she came into puberty, her mother was still too busy. Her mother told her, "I need to have a life of my own. I need time to date." So Barbara's mother dated, trying to solve her problems, and Barbara entered puberty, trying to solve *her* problems.

Barbara was drifting through life. She knew she was missing something, but she couldn't put her finger on it. Even if she had been able to spot her problem as a lack of parental involvement and coaching, she would not have been able to force her parents to change.

Will I Ever Escape?

As a result, she was a miserable student. But neither of her parents knew how bad things were. Occasionally they would see a note from a teacher or a report card. Their response was not to give Barbara concrete help but just hurried harassment. "Why don't you do better in school, you dummy?"

Barbara felt so lost and abandoned living with her mother that she decided to see if it would be better living with her father. Unfortunately, as she tersely sums it up, "My father gave me no family life, no direction, no guidance, no nurturing and no attention."

Barbara's hopes for a normal family life and the opportunity to be a normal teen-ager were again smashed. As a result, she started searching for love in all the wrong places. She became sexually active and was known in junior high and high school as an easy mark. She desperately wanted someone to love her and to help her gain that sense of family. But again and again she found herself just being used and then abandoned. She was growing up physically, with a frightened little girl inside.

Barbara did get married and have three children. But at age thirty-six, she was divorced. Barbara firmly believes that her marriage failed because of the negative training she had received from her parents. They were never able to work out their problems, and after being divorced for many years, they still hate each other. She says remorsefully, "I vividly learned how to show disrespect for my husband, and I followed my parents' pattern of giving up when the going gets rough."

Now she is alone—again—caring for her three teen-age children. Even as a mid-life woman, Barbara carries deep feelings of abandonment. Her parents' dysfunction and divorce have now produced dysfunction and divorce in Barbara. She worries that the pattern will damage her children. She says, "I worry about my children having the same anxious feelings that I had all my life. Sometimes I become overwhelmed, knowing that I can't *ever* escape the hurt of divorce."

Search for Security

In a book entitled *Adult Children: The Secrets of Dysfunctional Families,* John and Linda Friel say,

> In a healthy family, children's needs for security, warmth, nurturance, and guidance are met most of the time. These children enter adulthood with a sense of security and trust that is *inside* of themselves.
>
> In dysfunctional families, these needs are not met enough or at all, and these children enter adulthood with a sense of incompleteness, mistrust, and fear *inside* of themselves, along with a strong need for some kind of security *outside* of themselves.
>
> As adults who grew up in troubled families, we constantly seek to fill up the empty parts inside of us that were never met while we were

growing up, and it is the *external* search for our unmet needs that leads us into addictive lifestyles.[1]

Most people who grew up in emotionally or legally divorced homes have blocked out some part of their past. They have found it less painful to forget the dysfunction of their parental home than to acknowledge it and work toward solutions.

Do We Value Bicycles or Girls?

What does the dysfunction in an emotionally divorced home look like? The answer is found by watching how a family handles a disappointment, tragedy or embarrassment in the life of a family member.

Karen had an accident with her new bicycle. Since she is being raised in a healthy family, she will be allowed to talk about her accident and to verbalize her feelings, including her anger at herself and her disappointment that her bicycle is scratched. The bicycle incident really did happen, and it becomes a part of Karen's history.

Because her family members are loving and affirming, the incident will be just that—a piece of history that reminds her when other disappointments come along that her family is supportive and understanding. As she experiences new losses, Karen will have warm feelings about her family and the confidence that she can handle whatever problems come her way.

If, however, Karen had been raised in an emotionally divorced, dysfunctional family, they would forget that bicycles aren't as important as little girls. So a great deal of anger would be focused on Karen as if she had destroyed the bicycle on purpose. The dysfunctional family would not allow Karen's feelings to be ventilated; in fact, she would be forced to take a protective stance and cover up her feelings.

Karen may totally internalize the anger she feels toward herself along with the anger she is getting from her family. She may try to block out the incident. But it will never leave her memory! In fact, this bicycle incident may become larger than the event itself. The accident will repeatedly remind her of all the other times she was misunderstood by her family—of all the times she was told that she was incompetent and stupid.

Every time Karen has a loss or disappointment in her future life, all the unfinished business from her past, such as the bicycle incident, will be retriggered in her subconscious mind, causing self-doubt and probably anger toward other people—perhaps her own daughter when she has a bike accident.

Generations of Dysfunction

Dysfunctional homes are characterized by some or all of the following traits:

- ☐ perfectionism
- ☐ inability to express feelings
- ☐ inability to have fun
- ☐ emotional abuse—"you're stupid," "you're a bother"
- ☐ rigid rules
- ☐ no talking to anyone outside the family
- ☐ tolerance for relational pain—don't try to work out problems
- ☐ neglect—not helping children to become normal adults
- ☐ physical abuse
- ☐ sexual abuse
- ☐ no personal boundaries—each intrudes on the others[2]

The dysfunctional family wounds the very core of the person. Tragically, *dysfunctional families don't recognize that they are dysfunctional.* These families don't deliberately plan to ignore each other's needs or purposely neglect giving the children what they need for normal adult development. They generally just do what they learned from their parental family.

Frequently, as the family history is traced back, we find that the parents in a dysfunctional family were also raised in dysfunction. The children parent a new generation, unaware they are trying to catch up on their own childhood needs—to fill their own empty cups. Since they probably don't know they are dysfunctional, they don't understand how to break the cycle of dysfunction they are perpetuating.

In the past decade the idea of the "child within" has been picked up most prominently by the self-help group called Adult Children of Alcoholics (ACoA)—and with good reason. Children raised in alcoholic homes often grow up to be wounded adult children. As adults, their sense of deprivation is deeply buried. The insistent call of the "child within" frequently goes unrecognized. Instead people seek quick emotional fixes to drown out their internal pain.[3]

The Fix

Adult children of divorce or dysfunction also often seek quick "fixes" to solve their inner emptiness. Many become addicts as they turn to alcohol, food, prescription pills, illegal drugs, gambling, illicit sex, shallow serial relationships.

These addictions of adult children of divorce follow typical downward spiraling patterns:

1. An individual feels a deep internal lack of fulfillment and profound loneliness.

2. Then the person enjoys the ability to alter the empty feeling with a drug, food, alcohol or new relationship.

3. The addict starts looking forward to the next opportunity to have his or her mood altered. At this stage the person begins to think obsessively about the mood-altering experience.

4. Dependency follows. Now having the mood altered is not just fun, but it becomes necessary in order to survive. Without the substance or experience, the person does not feel "normal."[4]

Adult children of divorce frequently become addicts as a compensation for what they missed or to forget what happened to them as they were growing up.

Father Hunger

In the last half of the eighties, our society began to have a growing awareness of the father's importance in being involved in his children's lives for their total healthy development. Movies such as *Mr. Mom* began to appear. Television and magazine ads showed fathers caring for children. We began to see fathers alone with their kids in the park or shopping malls.

Earlier generations pictured the husband as the distant breadwinner, as the authors of *Leaving the Enchanted Forest* describe him: "the hardworking achiever in the business world—competent, competitive, out of touch with his feelings, preoccupied with material success, tough, 'one of the boys,' business first.

"Men who grew up with such typical American fathers— physically present, but psychologically absent—often suffer from 'father hunger.' "[5]

"Father hunger" is a subconscious yearning for an ideal father. (The term *father hunger* was originally coined by psychoanalyst Herzog and referred primarily to the physically absent father. Today this concept is commonly understood as emotional absence as well.) For example, if a man does not have his father hunger met, he may become either a wimp, unable to make decisions, or a macho man, afraid to be intimate.

Intimacy can be learned only by being in a close relationship with a real person. Andrew Merton is quoted as saying, "This is why father hunger tends to be passed from generation to generation—why the son of a father-hungry father will be father-hungry himself."[6] Merton reminds us of another important correlation: "A man who fails to develop an intimate relationship with his wife has an extremely poor chance of doing so with his children."[7]

The mother's role in the past was to be at home, caring for the needs of the family by keeping the home running smoothly. However, as massive numbers of women moved into the work place and women's rights movements started to affect society, the role of men was re-examined. It was discovered that men have the capacity to be warm, caring and intimate in relationship with their children. We also learned that children in previous generations had been desperately hungry for their fathers.

The Unconnected Father

Samuel Osherson, author of *Finding Our Fathers: The Unfinished Business of Manhood,* tells about a father and son who are typical of divorced and dysfunctional families:

> The forty-two-year-old doctor talks about a recent visit with his father. His parents are divorced, as is he, but the whole family was recently brought together in St. Louis by a younger brother's wedding.
>
> Tears well up in his eyes as he admits: "Actually, I was scared of what he thought about me, of how much time I spent with my mother rather than him at the wedding . . . just like growing up." He cries, then anger masks his sadness and yearning when he concludes, "but what difference does it make? It does no good to try to talk to my father."[8]

The Empty Father

The typical pattern in divorce is that the father disappears. Generally the only information the children receive about him is from their angry mother, who uses negative information to recruit the children as her allies, to verify her innocence and to prove the father's abominable guilt.

But the adult children of divorce ask themselves, "Who is the man? What was he like as a young man? Do I bear any of his traits? Will there ever be any emotional connection between the two of us?" The adult children of divorce are dysfunctional for many reasons, but part of the reason is that they have a deep, unresolved father hunger.

In the play *Death of a Salesman,* Willy Loman is a shoe salesman in his sixties. He is a broken, worn-out man who has traded his energy in life for the benefit of the company. He asks for an easier job, but is fired instead. Willy's response is, "I put thirty-four years into this firm, Howard, and now I can't pay my insurance. You can't eat the orange and throw the peel away—a man is not a piece of fruit."[9]

There is a sad moment at the end of the play as Willy Loman is confronted by his oldest son, Biff. The son is trying to make some kind of connection with his father. He leans down and hugs his father, hoping that his father will hug him back. But Willy sits there immobilized. He shrugs his shoulders at his wife, hoping that somehow she'll explain to Biff what's happening. Willy never hugs back. There is no link between father and son.

Later Willy takes his own life through an intentional car accident, because he cannot live with his deep sense of failure. Unfortunately, Biff will live out his life with a deep sense of his father's failure, suicide and lack of connection.

The Dead Father

Father hunger is felt not only by adult children whose parents were legally divorced, but also by many adult children whose father was physically at home but emotionally uninvolved. Yes, he provided the income. Yes, he made some of the major decisions about the town to live in and which house to buy.

Perhaps he also mowed the lawn and kept things repaired around the house. But he never connected with his children in a meaningful way. Even though they lived under the same roof, he was emotionally divorced from his wife *and his children.*

One son wrote a letter in the form of a poem to his father who had died five years earlier. Pain drips from this poem:

Do you see now that fathers
who cannot love their sons
have sons who cannot love?

The poem ends with a bitter thrust:

It was not your fault
and it was not mine
I needed your love
but I recovered without it
Now I no longer need anything.[10]

But that son *does* need something. He still needs his cup filled—he needs the love, trust, acceptance and guidance that his dad was unable to give him. Until someone is able to fill that empty cup, the pain will continue.

Intervention

A dysfunctional family always produces a dysfunctional person unless some person or some event intervenes to provide hope and help to rescue or redirect the child. Sometimes intervention comes from a grandparent, uncle, aunt, friend, neighbor, schoolteacher, pastor, priest or youth worker. Sometimes the help comes in the form of a week at camp, a wilderness survival experience, going off to college or moving away from the dysfunctional family and setting up an independent life.

For a significant number of people I have worked with the intervener was God himself. These people came into a relationship with God where they saw him as a healthy father, someone who loved them, thought well of them and wanted only the best for their lives. For others it was professional counseling or a caring small group which brought a breakthrough.

The point is, *dysfunctional families produce dysfunctional people unless the links in the chain of dysfunction are broken.* The family environment is so powerful through the developmental years that children will be the product of their home—unless someone or something intervenes.

In my own life, my loving grandmother and a personal, vital, daily relationship with God became the intervening factors. The dramatic change God made in my life is probably the major factor for my choosing to enter the ministry. I have come to see God as the most powerful ally any adult child of divorce can have for stability. In the second half of this book I'll talk about how a person can have this meaningful relationship with God and specific steps you can take to break the cycle of dysfunction.

In the next chapter, however, we'll learn how the child from a divorced home is trained by that home to be an unhealthy adult.

7
Missing: Normal Life Development

ONE TIME I THREW MY WOOL SWEATER INTO a washing machine and then into the dryer. It came out child-sized. I pulled on it and stretched it every direction, but it was impossible to make it adult-sized once more. I never wore that sweater again.

Likewise, a child growing up in a divorced or dysfunctional home is permanently damaged. The child will become a fragile adult. The basic, normal developmental patterns are distorted. All of the future life will be affected.

Don't Leave Me!

The year was 1939 and I was seven. It was about seven-thirty in the morning. I was in the back seat of my father's four-door 1936 Pontiac. We were on Miles Avenue, coming from Maple Heights, Ohio, heading toward

Cleveland, and we were racing the morning train. The train tracks paralleled Miles Avenue, and each morning it was my father's personal challenge to beat the train through the crossing at 131st and Miles.

My father was on his way to work. He would drop me off at my grandmother's home, and later I would walk to school. Our family was in the process of relocating, and I had started to school in Cleveland before we actually moved.

As we raced along Miles Avenue at about fifty miles an hour, I was eating an apple, which was my breakfast. I was still very sleepy. When I finished the apple, I intended to roll down the right rear window and throw out the apple core. Instead I pushed on the door handle.

Since this was a 1936 four-door in which the rear doors opened from the center post, the door was snapped to a full open position by the force of the moving air. Because I was hanging onto the handle, I was jerked out of the car and sent tumbling onto the shoulder along the highway.

I immediately jumped up and started running after the car. When my father heard the rushing wind, he turned around to see that the door was open and I was gone. He glanced into the rear-view mirror and saw me running down the highway after the car. He stopped the car and started backing up. I was skinned all over but had no broken bones.

In a few minutes we arrived at my grandmother's house. She started washing the dirt and cinders out of my skinned-up areas. I remember lying on her couch in the living room and enjoying the process of being cared for. This was one of the experiences that bonded me to my grandmother to whom I felt very close all through my life.

Why Are You Afraid?

Some years after Sally and I were married, I told Sally about the incident of falling out of the car. Her first reaction was, "Why did you get up and start running after the car?" Right away I said, "I was afraid he would leave me." Until she asked me that question, I never had fully recognized the fear I had felt that day.

Sally looked at me and said, "Why were you afraid your father would leave you? If I'd fallen from a moving car, I would've known my dad wouldn't leave me." It began to dawn on me that I have always been afraid of being abandoned. The insecurity of my parents' bad marriage caused me to feel uncertain about whether they loved me and would take care of me.

I'm sure that my parents never intended for their marital dysfunction to affect me. In a sense, they put their marriage and me in two separate compartments: their loveless relationship in one, and me whom they loved in the second.

Unfortunately, children don't put things into neat little boxes. Because my parents' marriage was unstable, my whole world was unstable and every part of my developmental process was negatively affected.

My father *did* come back for me. He *didn't* leave me. But I ran after the car because I *felt* I would be abandoned. And to this day I'm afraid people will leave me.

Stages of Growth

From the time of birth a developmental process takes place that includes both the visible physical changes and the less obvious social, psychological, moral and spiritual ones. These less visible developmental processes have been categorized and defined by a number of sociologists, psychologists and educators such as Piaget, Erikson, Kohlberg, Fowler and many others.[1]

Many of these experts have viewed this growing-up process as strictly developmental, meaning that each new stage or development builds on a previous stage, and happens primarily in childhood. I would like to suggest, however, that many times during our lives we experience new circumstances or a fresh sense of our own development or aging. These events cause us to relearn, as we reintegrate our new life stage with our old understanding of ourselves, other people and the world.

We don't learn everything by age twenty-one and then coast the rest of our lives. Rather, we have "seasons" of experiencing new levels of trust, becoming more independent, gaining a deeper appreciation of our identity and learning new dimensions of intimacy.

Growing Up Dysfunctional

Children of divorce, however, experience gaps in their developmental stages. In some homes, children receive so much wrong treatment and faulty information that their whole adult development is severely damaged.

Healthy human development includes accomplishing certain tasks. Erik Erikson's list gives a good framework; let's use it to look at how life's basic developmental skills are hindered by the divorced home.

Trust

Erikson suggests that one of the first development tasks is learning to *trust*. If a strong bonding occurs between the parents and the child, with affirmation from the parents, the child believes that these parents are trustworthy and can be depended on.

In dysfunctional families, however, the parents are frequently preoccupied in competing with each other. They themselves may not be able to trust, or they may feel they are not trustworthy.

Sometimes parents use children to meet their own needs which are not being met in the marriage or which were unmet when they themselves were children. Children from such a dysfunctional family enter adulthood unable to trust people because their parents failed to develop this cradle of faith and security that we call "trust."

Autonomy

Another task in the progression of the child toward adulthood is acquiring a sense of *autonomy*. The child comes to understand, "I am not the same as my parents; I am unique." Healthy parents grant the child freedom to explore this uniqueness. All the while, the parents provide the security or "safety net" that gives a child the ability to test new limits without the fear of going too far.

Dysfunctional families, however, frequently don't tolerate autonomy. Children are taught, "Don't think. Just do as I say." Children are exposed to "group think," with the major originator of the "group thought" generally being a bossy, controlling parent.

Or the children may be ignored, especially if the parents are preoccupied with their own needs. The children then feel there is no safety net: "How do I know I can venture out, if no one is going to be there to protect me?"

In either scenario the children are afraid to be individuals, and so they become "people-pleasers" with a driving need to be in relationships. Yet their relationships are never deep; and, ironically, these adult children are unable to survive emotionally if forced to be alone.

As these children become adults, relationships are marred because they are never sure if what they feel and think is right. They have never had the secure base they needed to become independent individuals. They generally enter marriage as leaning, dependent people who end up sucking their mates emotionally dry, which often results in a marital collapse.

Mastery

Erikson discusses two other tasks, *initiative* and *industry*. I believe these two can be grouped together because they focus on acquiring a sense of mastery, such as achieving new things at school, in the community or later in a career.

This is a crucial developmental step in life. People experiment with their native gifting from God. They can ask, "What am I able to do?" A functional family will stand with children or teens as they experiment with many different directions and abilities in their lives. Many of these experimentations will help a child discover, "That's not really where I want to go or be." Healthy parents help children understand that this is a sorting-out time, and children aren't inherently bad if they keep experimenting.

However, the dysfunctional home is preoccupied with the stress of a potential divorce. It doesn't have time or tolerance for childhood experimentation.

Frequently, these children or teen-agers are pushed by their parents to fulfill the parents' unfulfilled goals. Or, because the parents are consumed with their own conflicts, the children are not encouraged to explore or not supported when the explorations are unsuccessful.

In dysfunctional homes the discovery process reinforces the children's inability to trust themselves or other people. The result is that the children or teens may be afraid to try new skills. They may be afraid to risk, because risk was punished in the dysfunctional home. Or they may take really harmful risks, either because no one has helped them see the possible consequences or because they feel, "What's the difference? My folks don't care what happens to me, anyway."

Self-Identity

Another major developmental task, which I believe begins at birth, is that of *discovering and appreciating who I am.*

This sense of identity, or self-image, is formed as important people give us information about ourselves. In some sense every interaction we have with any other person shapes our self-concept. We discover what we can do and what our gifts and abilities are. We then have a sense that we *are* somebody—somebody who is worthy of having a place in this world.

The dysfunctional family not only inhibits the development of a positive self-image but shrivels its children or teen-agers so that they will function far below their God-given potential. In the dysfunctional family the children may never come to the point of self-knowledge, because they are not encouraged to explore who they are.

These children learn early not to trust other people, their environment or themselves. So, although they may begin to understand their potential, they *will not believe* their potential. They will not trust themselves, and they will not trust people in the larger society around them, even if those people give them positive affirmation.

Because adult children of divorce have not learned to trust, affirmation from other people comes across as manipulation. They believe that people who compliment or encourage them are trying to get something for themselves, or they believe that the affirming person is distorting reality.

The dysfunctional family is raising blighted children who have repeatedly been told verbally and nonverbally that they are extremely inadequate. These damaged children have accepted a *life direction of mistrust* — mistrusting others and themselves. We can understand why it is so difficult for a teacher's affirmation to be believed by a school child from a dysfunctional family.

If someone doesn't intervene in this child's life, all these negative assumptions and directions may ultimately force him or her into antisocial behavior, inadequate career choices or escape into an unwise early marriage.

It's important to point out that every positive contact or affirming word has an impact in a person's life. But those positive expressions must come from people who are admired by the child or teen-ager. The affirming person also may experience many rejections before being believed.

Intimacy

Another developmental task is that of achieving *intimacy* with other people. To be intimate is to give and accept love. To love someone is to understand that person so well that you can care about him or her and enable that one to become all that he or she can be. Being intimate also means allowing other people to love you—to care for you and encourage your growth.

Intimacy requires vulnerability as well as trust. It calls for a willingness to be open, allowing yourself to be known and to know someone else at a feeling level where hopes, dreams and fears are fully known to each other. Intimacy is learned by children and teen-agers as they watch and relate to the people around them.

The dysfunctional home in which there is conflict—open or under the surface, an attitude of competition, words used to cut people down—teaches the children to withdraw from people and to be afraid of vulnerability.

Children in dysfunctional families learn that relating to people is a battle. They decide it's best to "play your cards close to your chest." They catch on that if they share their feelings, it's a sign of weakness. And those exposed feelings may get trampled!

Children and teen-agers are supposed to be learning how to relate to people as they grow up. The key to a successful marriage and the proper raising of children is learning how to be intimate with other people, especially one's mate. But the young adult from the dysfunctional home starts the search for a mate with all of the wrong preparations—preparations that will almost certainly guarantee that this new marriage will reproduce the dysfunction of the parental home unless intervention occurs.

Generativity

The next developmental task is *generativity*; that is, moving beyond being self-absorbed and beginning to care for a younger generation. I believe this task needs to be learned very early in life and should be continually refined as we age. Children, instead of being absorbed with their own rights and their own toys, need to be socialized to share with and care for other people.

As teen-agers develop, their focus needs to be larger than their clothes, possessions and small group of friends. They need to see the needs of a broader world and begin to accept responsibility to care for the larger world.

Sharing toys with a playmate may be the child's beginning stage, whereas a one-week trip to work with children in a Mexican village may help teen-agers develop the ability to use their life energy to benefit other people.

Integrity

The last developmental task is that of *integrity*, which often is thought to come at the end of life when a person evaluates all of life and accepts life "as is" without major regrets. I would suggest, however, that we should accept life "as is" throughout our lives.

As children start to school, they leave the past in order to enter a whole new era. When children move into puberty, they leave childhood. All of life will now be viewed through the eyes of sexuality. As teen-agers or young adults leave home for college, career or marriage, they leave one era and move to the next. Each time we leave the past we should have few regrets because of a settled sense of "that was a good era." We should feel "together" at each stage.

The dysfunctional home, however, makes each of these transitions painful and incomplete. Children going off to school for the first time may look forward to leaving home only to get away from conflict. They may come to hate their preschool days and use school as an escape. They have no integration of their earlier years into the school years. They may even unconsciously blot out their pain by suppressing their horrible home memories.

Children from dysfunctional homes going through the stages of puberty and separation from the home will likely have difficulty accepting themselves as sexual beings. They may learn to use sexuality as a weapon of power rather than an expression of healthy intimacy and mature love. They probably will not integrate their past life as part of the present. At each stage the individual may view the growth tasks chiefly as opportunities to escape the past with its pain and regrets.

Lifelong Dysfunction

Gary, a college junior from a divorced family, wrote to me, "I have turned inward. I am unsure of myself. I'm timid and bashful. Fear is a big part of my personality. I know it shouldn't be, but it is."

Later he said, "Dating is scary; in fact, I haven't dated much. I have trouble letting myself be myself. I tend to be possessive, yet I hold back on my personal self, and rely on a girl too much. For me, a girl tends to fill a gap. If she's taken away, I'm a basket case for a while."

Notice that Gary is passive in his dating relationships, depending on the woman to take the lead. He also refers to breaking up as "she's taken away." Life is happening *to* Gary; he is not making his own decisions.

Gary reacts this way because his father was very domineering and repeatedly told Gary he was a failure and dumb. Because of his parents' constant fighting, Gary tried to stay out of the way—be invisible—just let life happen.

Gary essentially has decided to isolate himself from meaningful relationships; then he won't be disappointed. Sadly, he has put God in the same category of not being able to help him.

"In my relationship with God, I have taken the 'I have to take care of myself attitude.' It's wrong—I'm trying to change. But surviving is the key. Never give up. Keep striving."

It's easy to understand how adult children of divorce like Gary will have problems such as:

☐ not trusting themselves or other people

☐ not feeling independent or sure of themselves—not daring to take risks

☐ not accepting and appreciating themselves

☐ not knowing how to love themselves or other people

☐ not being interested in other people's success, but being self-absorbed instead

☐ not being able to accept all of life's experiences as part of the positive total

Tomorrow, Tomorrow, I Love Ya, Tomorrow

Children from a divorced home will likely be very future-oriented, always hoping to escape the past—hoping that the next experience will somehow take away the pain. They are like golf players: "Well, that wasn't a good shot, but on the next hole, I'm really going to be great—maybe a birdie."

In addition, these people usually have a great deal of difficulty as they reach mid-life or move toward retirement. The new experiences are not gains and achievements, but are seen as dreadful losses—friends die, jobs end, their nest empties, and physical aging advances. Therefore, older people from dysfunctional families are trapped. As they move forward in the aging process, they feel they don't have much positive to look forward to and, if they look back, they see only the hurt and dysfunction of their childhood home and its damage all through their lives.

As you look back over the tasks that need to be accomplished as people grow up, you'll notice that all these tasks are somehow connected to getting along with other people. Individuals coming out of a divorced or dysfunctional home are at a great disadvantage. They have not learned people-relating skills, as we will see in the next chapter.

8
Distrust
and
Role-Playing

SOME YEARS AGO SALLY AND I WERE HAVING dinner with the acquisitions editor and the vice president of a major publishing house. We were in an elegant French restaurant, and every part of the meal was absolutely wonderful. Sally and I would not have gone to a restaurant of this class on our own, because it was light years beyond our budget. But these folks wanted us to sign a contract with them for a book we were writing, so they took us to this great restaurant.

By the time dessert was served, we were deeply into discussions about editing, marketing and financial proposals for the book. I kept asking dozens of questions, trying to make sure that every contingency was covered and that there would be no fuzzy areas that might be misunderstood at a later date. With each of my picky questions, the vice president was becoming visibly more and more irritated.

Finally, in desperation and with a degree of anger, he looked me squarely in the face and said, "Jim, you don't trust anybody, do you? You really believe that everybody in the world is out to get you."

Then he caught himself, realizing that the purpose of the dinner was not to correct me but to get me to sign a contract. He quickly apologized, and I didn't say anything. Silence shrouded the table.

That *was* why I had all the questions—I really didn't trust this man. At the same time, a little voice within me said, "Listen to what he has just said. It's true, you really don't trust *anyone*."

Adult children of divorce don't take a special class entitled "Don't trust people." They just absorb from their family the feeling that people are not to be trusted.

I absorbed from my mother not to trust people because she couldn't trust her father or her husband. I learned from my father not to trust people because he felt that no one ever did anything absolutely perfectly.

My father was head of a service business while I was in high school and college. When I would come home from college, I'd ask him how many men he had working for him. His standard and automatic reply was, "About half of them." Then he would laugh. At that age I thought it was a joke, but in reality, he never felt he could trust any of his employees. He didn't directly teach me not to trust people; I just absorbed it from him.

Unfortunately, my three daughters have struggled with trusting people because they, in turn, unconsciously picked up my inability to trust people. Our hope as a family is that we will all become more healthy so that our grandchildren will not have to wrestle with the same problems of distrust.

This inability to trust is related, many times, to the defensive roles these people took within the family during their childhood years—the play-acting they learned as a coping device. Let's look at how this all works.

INABILITY TO TRUST AND BE INTIMATE

Adrian was an attractive, well-educated mid-life woman, who by all outward standards seemed to be a success in her part-time career, her mothering role and her marriage.

Even though her life seemed quite well put together, I always had an uneasy feeling whenever I saw Adrian and her husband, Willis, in a social setting. Most of the time they would be in different parts of the room, visiting with friends as if their mate were not present. Sometimes they never linked together visually or conversationally as a couple during the entire evening.

You Want to Do *What* ?

One day Adrian settled uncomfortably in a chair in my office. Even though she had come for my help, this was a very difficult and humbling act for this "has-it-all-together" woman. Asking for my counsel was a serious violation of the sufficiency mystique she always presented. The very fact that she was sitting in my office was a clear indication that she was in trouble and needed assistance.

She started by asking my opinion: "What do you think about open marriages? I've been talking to Willis about the idea. He's hesitant, but he's willing to think about it."

I was startled at her question, because Adrian and Willis were very traditional types. I didn't think of them as people who would be willing to consider an open marriage, in which each person is given permission by their mate to date other people and, if the relationship develops, to have sex with that other person.

For the next several minutes we discussed the concept of an open marriage from a theoretical point of view, but it was obvious that this very unlikely woman was thinking of something more than theory.

But We're Both Christians!

In a few more minutes she seemed to have reached a plateau and dropped into silence. I looked at her and said, "Adrian, is there some particular male friend in your life that you'd like to get to know better?"

She looked at me with a sense of surprise, a touch of indignation, and a little bit of shame, and said simply, "Yes." But she followed it quickly with a flood of questions and statements. "But why would it be so wrong? We're both Christians. We seem to have a lot in common. Neither of us has any intention of leaving our mates nor damaging our marriage relationships. We just don't want to sneak around. We want to be able to be friends in public."

For the next several minutes she told me about her new friend and how much they were adding to each other's life. Again she came to a plateau of silence, indicating clearly that she didn't know what to do.

At that point I said, "Tell me about your relationship with Willis." Her head dropped, "Willis and I have never really been close. I guess I've never been able to trust him, even though we've been married for more than twenty years and he's given me no reason at all not to trust him. I've just never been able to give myself fully to him.

"It's strange as I think about it. I guess I really don't trust men. It's easy for me to have short-term relationships with people, but long-term is hard. I've always kept Willis at arm's length emotionally and sexually. Maybe that's why I think an open marriage would be good for him as well as me. Then he could finally get some of his sexual needs met."

I didn't say it but I thought to myself, "How is this new friend going to be different from Willis? Is Adrian just going to start into a pattern of short-term, surface relationships? How can I help her to see that the problem is not really Willis, nor is it a question of an open marriage? Rather, it's probably something from her childhood that is continuing to block her ability to trust people and to be intimate with her husband."

The Painting of Her Life

"Adrian," I said aloud, "tell me a little bit about your childhood. What were your parents like? Which parent did you relate to the most? How good was their marriage?"

In a few short sentences she filled in the gaps. Sure enough, the problems with her husband were really problems from her childhood.

Adrian grew up with fighting and conflict all around her. Her mother and father promised each other and Adrian again and again that things were going to be better—but they never were. Finally, when Adrian was in the third grade, her parents divorced.

Adrian's mother, in her anger, repeatedly told Adrian not to trust her father or any man, because "they'll always leave you and disappoint you."

Adrian told me a little about her relationship with her mother while she was in elementary school. Every sentence she spoke was another stroke of the brush on the canvas of her life, clearly showing a frightened little girl who desperately needed people but was afraid to trust them. Adrian's description was almost a duplicate of what another woman had written to me: "In elementary school I would pretend to be sick so that my mom would have to leave work and come to get me. That way I knew she was still around. When I came home from school, I would wait on the steps for my mom to return from work. If she was even a few minutes late, I would get scared and cry until she arrived."

Adrian had trouble with friendships all the way through grade school and on into adult life. She said, "I don't remember having a close friend throughout my childhood and high-school years because I was afraid to be open. I also had a hard time staying in an intimate or open relationship with boys. When they got too close, I dumped them.

"The reason I didn't have close friends is that I was afraid they would leave me. So I would leave the relationship first—there's less hurt that way. I guess I've always lived with the constant fear that what I love most will be taken away from me. I'm always waiting for the second shoe to drop."

Close—But Not Too Close

There was a moment of insight as Adrian sat quietly for awhile. Then she lifted her head and looked at me. "Maybe that's been my problem with Willis. He has never given me any reason to think he would abandon me, yet I've always been expecting it, so I've kept him at bay. I didn't want to get too close because then, when he left, it wouldn't hurt so much.

"But at the same time, I needed him. I wanted somebody close—but not too close. I guess I want people to love me, but I don't want to invest any of my feelings in them."

Then she chuckled and tossed her head in a playful sort of way and said, "But I guess that's not really possible, is it?"

Tragically, it was not only Adrian's human relationships that were affect-ed, but also her relationship to God. "Isn't it strange?" she said. "I go to church, but I'm afraid of God. It is difficult for me to even understand the concept of 'father.' Mostly I view God as cruel and judgmental. I both love and fear him, but it is fear that drives me to always try to be a 'good Christian.' "

Because Adrian felt she was unsuccessful in her relationships, she poured herself into activities. "My self-image and pride stemmed mostly from my accomplishments. I worked hard for recognition by joining all the high-school clubs. I was valedictorian."

If I Love—I'll Lose

Again she sat quietly, looking at the trees outside my office window. I wondered what was going on in her mind, what thoughts she was processing. Finally she said pensively, "I guess I've lived my whole life in reaction to my parents' divorce. I've always felt that anything I loved too much would be taken away from me—so I just didn't love."

Adrian had learned not to trust as a very young child in her insecure home. When her parents divorced, it was verified for her that people cannot be trusted.

We non-trusters look at life and people as unsafe. We need to be in control, to make sure things will turn out right. If we trust someone else, then we may not be able to guarantee the future. We might be abandoned, rejected or exploited by them. Therefore, it is easier for us to skip to another surface relationship, as Adrian wanted to do, where we are not expected to be open, vulnerable or trusting. In surface relationships, we can maintain our power position. Adrian's visit to my office that day led to the start of her working on inner healing. Instead of considering short-term relationships with other men, in a few months she chose to deepen her intimacy with her husband!

Non-Trusters React

In recent years over 90 per cent of the people Sally and I counsel are people in their mid-life years, ages 35 to 55. More than half of these mid-life people have come from legally or emotionally divorced homes and are still having trouble with relationships.

Frequently their marriages—the most intimate of relationships—are coming apart at mid-life. Through our ministry organization, we try to help these mid-life marriages stay together and become satisfying relationships. Many times the core issues we are dealing with are trust and intimacy. We have noticed several common patterns.

☐ *Blame.* For example, suppose the husband is from a dysfunctional home and has difficulty with trust and intimacy. Over the years of marriage any wife will point out some of his weaknesses or inadequacies to him. The husband doesn't see this as an opportunity for growth through the help of a trusted friend; instead he feels misunderstood and rejected by his wife.

As a defense mechanism, the husband retaliates by pointing out all of his wife's weaknesses. He hopes that by belittling or blaming her he can make her back off from what he feels as rejection and unjust criticism. This situation can easily escalate into a full-blown war of blame, which over a period of years can lead to a divorce.

☐ **Run.** Another common reaction to marital conflict is that one mate leaves. Sometimes the person who leaves thinks, "The only way I can be sure I'm in control is to leave first." Quite often the one who leaves is the person who has also been withholding love as a way of maintaining power.

The withholding of love is, however, a conditioned response learned through the parental family dysfunction. These adult children of divorce say to themselves, "Don't give too much love to anyone—then you can't be hurt. Don't trust anyone. Don't be open or vulnerable—then you will always be safe." So the "runner" leaves as a way of maintaining control. "After all," that person thinks, "there isn't any great loss in leaving, because I never had a very deep love investment anyway."

☐ **Cling.** A third response we see frequently is clinging. Strangely, while non-trusters want to stay aloof from any deep relationship, many times they themselves become "clingers," living in sheer terror that they may be abandoned. Tragically, in a close relationship such as marriage, when one person begins to cling, the other partner feels smothered and tries to escape.

Sometimes clingers become relationship addicts. They are so terrorized by the potential of abandonment that they become emotionally parasites on other people. When one person shakes them off, they must quickly latch onto someone else.

For relationship addicts, the focus is always on the other important person in their life. Their own choices and preferences are ignored. They are unable to say "no" to that person, because they are terribly dependent and fearful that he or she will reject or abandon them.

Often these people become mimics or duplicates of the people they depend on. They lose their own identity, fearing that being an individual will bring rejection. "I'll be whatever you want me to be—just tell me."

Unfortunately, the person who becomes a relationship addict clings to and depends on the other person so much that the relationship fails. The other person is smothered. All the fears of abandonment from childhood get draped on this new person. The new friend is supposed to meet all of the romantic-love needs, give excitement, and provide a sense of self-worth, as well as take away all the childhood feelings of loneliness and abandonment.

Only God is able to handle all of this emotional overload caused by our dysfunctional families that we now try to force on every human relationship.

As relationship addicts lose their sense of perspective, fearing that their close friend or mate may abandon them, their self-esteem is diminished. As the other friend tries to pull back from this overwhelmingly smothering experience to maintain his or her own identity, the addict's self-esteem drops and feelings of depression and worthlessless set in.

A terrible downward spiraling of thoughts and emotions follows. Relationship addicts may then begin to realize they are really dependent on the other person. Frightened by this fact, they may flop to the other extreme and say things such as this imagined conversation:

"This is crazy, so I must be crazy. Something's wrong, so there must be something wrong with me. I haven't got love, so I must be unlovable."

Now suppose both people in the relationship or marriage come from dysfunctional families. Both have needs for closeness. This may trigger a roller-coaster ride with intense inclinations to blame, run, cling or be an addict. These adults will react with childhood reflexes. Suddenly they are in the sandbox, throwing verbal sand at each other and yanking on the same toys.

Adult children from divorced families who have learned not to trust or to be vulnerable look "all grown up," but they still have trouble with relationships and frequently feel frightened, alone or abandoned.

DEFENSIVE ROLES TAKEN IN THE PARENTAL FAMILY
Closely tied with the inability to trust are the roles that children assume

in their parental homes as a way to protect themselves. When any family is under stress, each member in the family system takes on protective roles in order to survive personally and also to ensure that the family unit will survive.[1]

It's commonly known that children assume greater responsibilities after the family breaks up. After all, they now have to pitch in and pick up the slack for the parent who is gone from the home. Taking on extra work is a way of making sure that what's left of the family stays together.

"Ryan, age 9, was not happy that he had to do extra work since his dad left. 'I have to take out the garbage and mow the lawn,' he says. There is only a vague understanding that he has to pick up the extra work because his mother is taking courses so that she can get a better job. He goes on to say, 'Divorce makes you have to be more grown-up. You have to do more grown-up things, and you have more grown-up feelings.' "[2]

Faulty Family Roles

In addition to taking on extra jobs to keep the family together, children often assume other roles that help them survive in their troubled family. Claudia Black, author of a number of articles about the children of alcoholics, has observed that many children try very hard to look good or to be people-pleasers, while other children become delinquents. Most children adopt one or a combination of the following roles: *the responsible one, the hero, the adjuster, the lost child, the placater, the scapegoat, or the mascot.* [3]

The *responsible one* acts very mature and responsible beyond his or her years. As Claudia Black suggests, "These children will set their own alarm clocks for the morning, get their younger sisters and brothers up and make sure that the other children get breakfast. They may even be the ones who are in charge of getting their parents up for work. They are the children who will come home, fix dinner, and then do the laundry."

These children, referred to by others as the *hero* type, are usually the firstborn in the family and compensate for family weaknesses. These kids appear to be well adjusted, high achievers, and overall very successful.[4]

A second role many children play is that of the *adjuster.* This child adjusts by detaching. "This child can sit in a room watching TV while there is screaming going on and continue with whatever he or she is doing no matter what is happening, apparently oblivious to the environment."[5]

Sometimes the adjuster is referred to as the *lost child*. The lost child spends a lot of time in his or her room, playing alone, and feeling lonely. This child is the forgotten child. He or she tends to be shy, withdrawn and quiet. These children will follow anyone's suggestion. They seem afraid or incapable of making decisions. They think, "It doesn't matter." They have no sense of themselves and they believe that they cannot change their environment or their own lives.[6]

Some children are also *placaters* who are very sensitive and automatically try to reduce tension in any situation. They work hard at taking care of everyone's feelings and needs—everyone's except their own.

"At school they are Mr. or Ms. Congeniality. They seldom have an enemy in the world because they are continually pleasing, pleasing, pleasing. The only thing that you might notice is that at least a dozen times each day they say, 'Excuse me! I'm sorry! I didn't mean to do that.' They even apologize for apologizing," says Black.[7]

The *scapegoat* absorbs all of the family faults and may become the black sheep of the family by getting involved in drugs, alcohol, illicit sex, stealing and overall failure. Unconsciously, the dysfunctional family projects all of the family guilt and failure onto this person. The scapegoat is often the second child.[8]

The purpose of the *mascot* is to reduce tension by doing or saying something funny. Typically, he or she is the family clown or goof-off. The responsibility is to distract people from the family's dysfunction.

Unfortunately, mascots are marked by avoidance, hyperactivity, the inability to wrestle with hard problems. They usually are very uncomfortable if they are required to share their feelings or to be with people who are sharing their feelings.[9]

Children take on these roles as a way to find a secure place in a chaotic environment. Acting out a part gives a feeling of reality and identity. But many of these children don't find out for many years that they have been only playing roles, not living life. Whenever a person plays a role, it indicates a problem with trusting people.

Child Roles Become Adult Roles

As these children become adults they continue unhealthy roles. Often the adult child of divorce assumes more than one role or will change roles as the family needs dictate. Tragically, these roles duplicate the parental problems. Without realizing it, parents have passed on to their children indelible imprints that will follow the children into their adult lives.

The child who is the responsible one, or hero, will carry that role into adulthood, protecting other people, and covering up for the family weaknesses. The adjuster will ignore adult problems or will live out the family shame by an adult lifestyle which the family views as disgraceful.

The lost child will continue to work alone and feel like a forgotten person, even as an adult. The placater will become a very popular adult, because he or she always pleases everyone at the expense of his or her own identity and abilities. The scapegoat will become the adult who is always at odds with society—and society will let him or her be that way. Society will then feel free to dump its sins on the scapegoat.

The mascot will become the adult clown. With humor, this person will attempt to diffuse problems and reduce tension. The mascot will do almost anything to keep away from the deep sharing of feelings or confronting problems. When mascots have trouble in their marriages, they will reject help, brushing off problems —until their mate finally walks out. These role-playing children will become adults who still are play acting.

I'm in Charge, But I Feel Lost

In my parental family I tended to be the responsible one. I protected other people. At one point, when I was kindergarten age, my mother couldn't figure out why I stayed in bed and claimed to be sick when there were none of the usual signs of illness. After a couple of days I finally explained to her that my shoes were worn out and it was not my turn for new shoes. I stayed in bed so my father could get the shoes he needed.

I also took the role of the placater. I tried to keep peace. Recently one of my sisters reminded me that often when we kids were fighting and one of our parents would come into the room asking, "Okay, who's responsible for this?" I would accept the blame and the punishment rather than hear the arguing: "It's not my fault. He started it." "No I didn't, she hit me first."

I couldn't stand that kind of fighting, so it was easier for me to take the blame and get the punishment over with so life could settle down to normal.

The placater and responsible one were the two major roles I *acted* in my family; however, the role that I most *felt* was that of the lost child. In reality, I'm a shy person. It's easy for me to be alone. I live with the dreadful feeling that I am an outsider and that people like me only because of what I do. I feel, "If I stop doing good things for people, they will abandon me."

Role-playing indicates a basic problem: the child has not learned to trust people and tries to control the world or protect himself or herself by taking on a role.

Hope

But there is hope! In the last half of this book we'll talk about how to deal with some of your painful past. I know it's painful to keep reading about yourself and your family, but let me assure you, I have not been hiding in your closet, listening. I just happened to come from a family similar to yours.

In the next chapter we'll look at the marriage and family problems of adult children of divorce.

9
Unsuccessful Marriages and Fear of Parenting

GEORGETTE WAS EVERY MAN'S NIGHTMARE. SHE had phoned for an appointment, but I was totally unprepared for the woman who walked in my office door. She was beautiful—about five-foot-five, 110 pounds, radiant blonde hair, a flawless face, deep blue eyes, a magnificent tan, and an extremely sexy body poured into a tight sweater and short skirt.

As she sat on the chair, she crossed her legs and arranged her body so that the total image she communicated was, "I'm a sexy person."

I opened the conversation in my usual manner by saying, "What can I do for you?" I was thinking, "I hope she doesn't say what it *appears* she wants!"

I was glad she responded simply, "We're having trouble in our marriage."

"Tell me about it," I said.

A Dream Come True—Or Was It?

Georgette told me that she and Ron met while she was singing at a summer conference grounds where her parents were the conference musicians. They had a whirlwind romance. They did so many fun things together. She was treated like a queen, and he was an absolute gentleman who never pressed her sexually.

Their relationship developed very rapidly, and in six months, when she was just twenty and he twenty-one, they got married.

Right from the beginning there was trouble. Georgette described her husband as a sexual animal. He never seemed to get enough. In fact, sometimes he even wanted to have sex three or four times a week. "How normal," I thought to myself.

For the first few months she put up with sex by gritting her teeth and digging her fingernails into her hands. Each time after they had sex, she would have to wear bandages because her fingernails had made her hands bleed.

At first Ron thought she just needed time to adjust to being married. But before many months passed, he realized they had a greater problem. He thought it was his fault. Maybe she didn't really love him. He responded by not pressing her on the sexual issue, except on those rare occasions, about once a month, when it became marital rape.

Georgette and Ron settled into an uncomfortable truce and an unhappy marriage. They each found more reasons to criticize the other as every week went by.

I Want Control of My Life

About three years into the marriage Ron began to press Georgette to start a family. He thought that having children was a very separate issue from having sex. He kept raising the subject over several weeks. Finally one day Georgette exploded, "I don't ever want to have children! I would never condemn a child to being raised in this hell. Neither of us are fit parents, and I would be afraid to have a son turn out like you or a daughter have to go through the hell I have endured."

Soon after Georgette's explosion, she started making plans to have a hysterectomy. Even though Ron argued and pleaded, she would not be dissuaded from the operation. She kept saying to him, "I must have control of my life. I will never bring a child into this world."

After her hysterectomy their marriage really fell apart, but they had to keep up a pretense because Georgette's parents were nationally known musicians. They didn't want to damage her parents' image. So they continued to play their games in public while at home they fought tooth and nail.

The Threat

I asked Georgette, "Why did you come to see me now?" She responded very directly, "Because my husband wants a divorce. I think there's another woman, and I'm either going to kill him or kill myself."

Georgette was deadly serious. The instability of her marriage was very evident. I told her I wanted to help her. Even though she felt hopeless, I assured her that many difficult problems did have solutions and many seemingly hopeless relationships could be restored.

I asked her to tell me about her parental family. She was surprised at my request and wondered what that had to do with her failing marriage relationship. But she went on to talk about her family.

She told me again that her father was a famous Christian musician. At first she didn't want me to know his name. She didn't want her marriage problems to cast a shadow on her parents' lives and work. Eventually, however, she did tell me her father's name, and I instantly recognized it.

In our second session together I asked Georgette to give me more detail about her family. Again she was very defensive and, essentially, wanted to talk only about the positives in both her mother and father. After a few more sessions, though, more of the story began to unfold.

Her mother had been repeatedly raped by an uncle when she was a teen-ager. So when she married Georgette's father, they immediately had sexual problems. Each time her father attempted to have sexual intercourse, her mother saw the ghastly image of the uncle.

The Great Disillusionment

Georgette was the only child born to the family. Her parents came to a sexual truce after Georgette's birth. They would not have sex, but it would be permissible for Georgette's father to discreetly get his sexual needs met by the constant flow of women around him as he traveled.

Because Georgette was the only child, her parents spoiled her. She learned she could get her parents to do anything by looking pretty and being nice. She especially learned to manipulate her father, who frequently called her his "little princess."

By the time she got into her teen years, she was easily able to control her parents for essentially anything she wanted. About the same time she learned that her father, whom she deeply loved and admired, had repeated sexual liaisons with many different women.

This revelation about her father led to a love-hate relationship with her parents. She loved the admiration and gifts she got from them, especially her father, but she also hated her parents because they only pretended to love each other. Georgette came to see that she was the glue holding them together. They were actually emotionally divorced from each other and living out a marriage farce before their religious audiences.

So Georgette came to the end of her teen-age years as a beautiful, sexy, manipulative woman who despised men, hated sex, but knew how to use men. Her marriage with Ron never had a chance.

When Georgette told Ron she wanted a hysterectomy to avoid having a daughter who would have to endure the hell she had, she was referring not only to her relationship with Ron, but also to her childhood with emotionally divorced parents. She hated them but needed them. Now, tragically, she was duplicating her parents' phony marriage.

I told Georgette that the problem, as I saw it, was not so much Ron or her fear of being a parent, but the unresolved problems of her childhood. Those were the issues we needed to work through.

Unfortunately, Ron came home the next day and told Georgette he'd been seeing another woman and having fantastic sex with her for the last six months. He said he was moving out that night and intended to divorce her.

Georgette was frantic. She pleaded with Ron not to leave. She followed him out to his car, but he drove away.

She came back into the house in a state of hysteria, went to the bath-room medicine closet and collected every pill that could in any way help end her life. She grabbed her coat and went to her car.

She drove to a nearby drugstore and bought a bottle of alcohol. She then drove out into the country.

She found a dirt path between two farmers' fields and drove down the path for about a quarter of a mile. Then she turned her car into a field of uncut corn and drove to the center of the field so that her car could not be seen from the road or from the dirt path.

Georgette carefully wrote a note to her husband and pinned it to her blouse. Her final step was to use all the alcohol to swallow the pills.

Nobody Wins

Two days later I received a call from the county coroner. He asked if I would be willing to meet him at the county morgue to identify the body of a young woman whom he thought might be Georgette.

This was the first time I had ever been to the morgue. I was surprised to discover that it was in the bowels of our local hospital. Even though I had made hundreds of visits to the hospital, I never knew of the morgue's existence. Now I was standing outside the doors, wondering what I might find in there.

The coroner took me inside, and I stood before a body on a gurney, covered with a clean white sheet. I had been a pastor for many years. I had conducted scores of funerals, made hundreds of visits to people who were dying, and, on a few occasions, had been with people at the very moment of their death. But I was unprepared for what I saw when the coroner pulled back the white sheet.

It was Georgette—but her face was a sickening black color. Gone was all the beauty: the pampered tan, the attractive blue eyes, and the coy, sexy, princess look. Now there was just the ugliness of death.

Georgette was the product of generations of failure, resulting in failure as a person, failure as a parent, and failure in marriage.

The coroner continued to pull the sheet down so that I could see the note pinned to her blouse. It said simply, "Ron, you win."

I'm Fearful, Yet Desperate for Love

It's common for people like Georgette who come from such painful backgrounds to have a desperate need to be in close relationships but not know how to pull it off. Without help, they probably will fail.

Neil Kalter, psychologist at the University of Michigan, says that adult children of divorce "constitute a population at risk for developing particular emotional, social, and behavioral problems that either persist or first appear years after the marital rupture. Prominent among these are aggressive and anti-social problems; sadness, depression, and self-esteem problems; and difficulty establishing and maintaining mutually enhancing heterosexual relationships."[1]

Adult children of divorce have the cards stacked against them. They came from bad homes, so they desperately want a solid, happy home of their own. But they have been conditioned by their parental home to fail. A study done at the University of Wisconsin pointed out some of the difficulty that adult children from divorced families have as they try to start their own families. "Women who spend part of their childhoods in one-parent families are likely to marry and bear children early, to give birth before marriage, and to have their own marriages break up."[2]

How Am I Supposed to Act?

A forty-eight-year-old woman named Connie helps us understand why these marriages are so stressed. She said, "When I was newly married I feared being left by my husband. I also transferred my unsolved father/daughter 'junk' onto my husband. I frequently caught myself being afraid of what his reaction would be instead of remembering that he loved me and wanted my best interests. I've never really been able to be open in my communication with my husband for fear of being rejected by him."

Later I asked Connie what would most help her handle the stress she is currently facing because of her parents' conflict and divorce. She said, "I wish I could think of my husband as a friend—not as a parent figure."

There is a great deal of confusion about how people are supposed to relate in a family. Men repeatedly say, "I don't know what a husband is supposed to act like, and I'm not sure how husbands and wives are supposed to relate."

Women tell me, "I've always wondered what a real family must be like. I'm not sure how to be an effective wife and mother. I'm frightened about raising our children, because I want them to know happiness, love, joy and a feeling of being wanted. But I never had an example to follow."

A woman named Laura told me, "A few years ago I was in the hospital near death because of a ruptured spleen. My husband was physically abusing me, but I felt it was a normal occurrence, since my father had done the same to my mother. I guess I somehow felt it was my fault and that there must be a good reason for him to do this to me."

It's All My Fault

These adult children of divorced or dysfunctional families almost universally seem to believe that in "good families" relationships are perfect, without conflict. When their marriage relationship sours, they invariably blame themselves instead of seeing that the dysfunctional environment of their parental home has caused them to relate this way.

The typical pattern of self-blame sounds like this: "Everything is going wrong with my relationship. I know it's all my fault. Yet I try everything I know to fix it, but nothing works. I am not even sure if I love him or her. Maybe I don't know what love is. I'm so confused. It's hopeless."

But Do I Have to Have Children?

Not only have these adult children felt ambivalent about dating and getting married, but they're also afraid, as was Georgette, to have children. If they do have children they're confused about how to raise them.

Anne from the Midwest said, "I didn't think I would ever marry. After I finally got married in my late twenties, I put off having children for another seven years because first I wanted to make sure our marriage would work out. Now that my children are four and six, I'm continually anxious about whether I'm doing a good job in raising them. I'm absolutely repulsed by the way I was raised as a child, and I get very angry at myself because I notice some of the same traits coming out in me that I hated in my own home."

Adult children of divorce have a very clear-cut idea about what they do *not* want to happen if they have children of their own. However, they don't seem to have even a glimmer of understanding of how to provide the positive experiences their children will need. They repeatedly talk about having "no models" or "not knowing how a mother or father should interact with children."

Chuck from Colorado said that when his wife became pregnant, "I seriously thought of leaving her." He was not afraid of the increased financial responsibility, but he said, "What if the child was a boy. What would I do? What do kids need? Where would I even start?"

Every time he started thinking of the responsibilities of raising a boy, he would come to that ultimate question, "What if he turned out to be as messed-up as I am?"

Nan, a thirty-seven-year-old woman from the eastern United States, said that she never expected to get married. She dated frequently, was involved in several long-term relationships, but did not marry until she was thirty. Her fear of failure and her deep hatred toward her parents ("because their messed-up marriage ruined me") caused her to pull away from earlier opportunities to marry.

When Nan finally married, she and her husband had an agreement not to have children. However, her husband and friends pressured her about having a child so that in her middle thirties she thought it might be worth the risk. When she became pregnant, though, she experienced a violent anger toward herself. She despised her enlarging breasts and spreading abdomen. She repeatedly spoke of wishing she could "chop off her fat breasts and stomach."

At that point Nan sought counseling help and came to realize that she didn't hate gaining weight or seeing her body change so much as she hated the implication of these changes—becoming a mother. She abhorred the awesome responsibility that was being thrust on her. She kept feeling that her parents had given her the poorest foundation possible for the task of raising a child.

I Might Get Divorced

A frightening truism is commonly accepted in counseling circles: *Children whose parents divorce are themselves likely to get divorced.*

During their early teen years, children of divorce say, "I will never marry." However, they're just as likely as anyone else to marry and, in fact, they usually marry, at an earlier age. Their early marriage and immaturity might account for some of the reasons they are more likely to divorce, but there is an additional reason.

These children from divorced homes tend to have a "lower commit-ment-to-marriage concept," as authors Glenn and Kramer point out: "Thus, they seem to be strongly impelled toward marriage while at the same time often feeling highly apprehensive about it. It seems likely, there-fore, that when they marry they often hedge their bets against failure by withholding full commitment to the marriage."[3]

Another study reports: "Adult males whose parents ever divorced/sep-arated had a 34.7% greater chance of themselves divorcing than males who were raised where the home was still intact. For females their per-sonal divorce rate was 59.3% greater for those girls whose parents had divorced than for those from intact families."[4]

These studies *should forever shake us of the delusion* that divorce has no long-term impact in the adult life!

It is very important to understand that children react differently if they lose a parent through death than through divorce. If children lose one or more parents to death, even though they may have lived in a one-parent home or a step-parent home, "they do not seem to have experienced the same long-term negative effects on their psychological well-being."[5]

Is It Inherited?

People magazine, May 29, 1989, had as its cover story, "Learning to Live with a Past That Failed." The article was written on the information from the longevity study of Judith Wallerstein. In addition, the magazine inter-viewed a number of adults to assess the long-term impact of divorce.

One of the people interviewed was a young man named Blake. His parents divorced, and he dropped out of Berkeley in his sophomore year. Some of his comments reveal his own divorce-proneness.

Blake has had three girlfriends in the last six months. "I get tired of them," he says. "I'm very passive. If there's a problem, I feel like they are unreasonable, and I don't feel much like seeing it their way. I don't feel much like fighting it out. I'd just rather leave and forget the whole thing."

Blake is reacting to these relationships as his parents did. Then he adds an insightful comment. "Maybe it's inherited."[6]

We have found the same willingness to consider divorce as an option to solve marital conflict in many adult children of divorce from all over the United States.

Denise, twenty-six, said, "I postponed or canceled serious relationships throughout my teen years because of my lack of faith in the sanctity of marriage."

Denise is now married. I wanted to know how she intends to handle problems in her marriage, so I asked, "What problems do you anticipate facing in the future because of your parents' conflict and divorce?"

She responded, "When trouble starts, I automatically think of divorce. I remember my parents' divorce—instead of remembering my parents working out problems. I don't remember them solving *any* problems."

A forty-year-old woman named Lou put it very bluntly: "Don't love a man or he'll hurt you." When I asked her to tell me about her worst problem resulting from her parents' conflict and divorce, she said, "I have no patience with men. I feel very self-confident and I don't trust that they can do anything as quickly or as efficiently as I can do it myself. I can do it all. I don't need a man."

Later Lou confessed what I expected: "I'm divorced, myself. I have three children, and I don't understand the role of a father in the family."

I Won't Let It Happen

Many people who had indicated they were likely to consider divorce as a solution to marital problems were still married for the first time. They said, "It's a constant battle, and many times I've wanted to run—just as my parents did." But they held to their commitments as they remembered how it felt to be a child from a divorced family.

These people had promised themselves that they would *never* duplicate their parents' marriage breakup. They didn't want their kids to go through the same pain in which they are living. Yet, almost involuntarily, they found themselves thinking the same way as their parents—tempted to act out the same divorce scenario.

Is There Hope for Anyone?

I don't think we fully understand how very, very deep is the imprint that parents make on the lives of their children. Young minds are like plastic. After plastic has been put through the molding process, it will flex and bend, but it always returns to its original form.

A Rubbermaid ad makes that point. They build a plastic product so it will keep its shape. You can kick it, drop it, step on it. Kids can run into it with their tricycles or a garbage truck can back into it, but it still bounces back to its original shape.

So it is with children of divorce who later become adults of divorce. They have been molded into a dysfunctional shape by their parents' divorce. That shape can be temporarily changed, but *unless a very strong, warm reshaping of their lives takes place*, they are likely to snap back to the same dysfunctional shape and repeat the patterns and escapes of their parents' divorce.

But such reshaping *is* possible!

That's what this book is all about. Let's together start to remold *your* dysfunctional childhood so that you can take on the shape of a healthy adult.

In the next chapter we'll look at the problems adult children of divorce have with the outside world. Then, in part three, we'll deal with healing the hurt.

10
The Outside
World

JANE'S PARENTS DIVORCED WHEN SHE WAS ten-and-a-half years old. She was just starting puberty, so all of her life was taking on new meaning. She needed the insight of *both* her father and mother during this important transition time of looking at herself and other people through her growing sexual awareness.

Instead of giving her the wisdom and stability she needed, her father abandoned the home. Because he was going through his own mid-life crisis and was involved with another woman, he was too preoccupied to worry about Jane. Jane's mother was consumed with her anger at her husband and the added responsibility of a new full-time job, so she too had no time for Jane.[1]

Jane was the last of three children. Her older brother and sister didn't have any emotional energy to give to her because they were wrestling with their own reactions to the divorce, which came during their late teen years. As a result, Jane stumbled along through puberty, through her teen years, and then out into the adult world.

How did Jane react? Very much as we would expect. At age ten-and-a-half she decided she had to take care of herself since no one else was. She became a very controlling person. She didn't trust people but continually sought male approval. She was unwilling, however, to let men get close to her. She felt different from other people and became a very serious person at an early age. Jane also had surges of hostility, becoming very critical of herself or verbally attacking others.

She went off to college dysfunctional in several areas of life and, unknowingly, carrying all of her unresolved childhood baggage with her. Later she took the baggage into her career and then into marriage at age thirty-one. Now she is afraid she is passing on to her children the dysfunction she inherited.

The Ripple Effect

When parents divorce, everyone pays a price—parents, children, future mates, grandchildren and coming generations. Many other people also are affected as the child moves out of the divorced home into higher education or a career.

Earlier I mentioned the book *Second Chances,* in which Judith Wallerstein summarizes fifteen years of research on children of divorce who are now adults. At one point she says, "Almost half of the children entered adulthood as worried, underachieving and self-depreciating."

The young people wanted family structure and protection. They yearned for clear moral guidelines. An alarming number of teen-agers felt abandoned, physically and emotionally.

Wallerstein sums up her findings with a frightening prophetic statement: "As these anxieties peak in the children of divorce throughout our society, the full legacy of the past twenty years begins to hit home."[2]

A Mixed Bag

Not all of the effects of the parents' dysfunction and divorce are negative as these adult children enter the outside world.

For example, Carla, a twenty-nine-year-old single woman from Michigan, mentioned positives along with negatives: "My sisters, brother, and myself grew up faster than most kids. We had more responsibility placed on us at an earlier age. When my parents divorced, we learned to do the cooking, cleaning and laundry, and to take care of ourselves." She felt that this additional responsibility helped her to mature faster and learn how to manage her own life.

Paul, a twenty-eight-year-old from Minnesota, told me about a positive aspect of growing up in a divorced home. He said,

I began to stutter at the time of my parents' divorce. As I moved into my new step-family, I was teased by my step-brothers and sisters. My parents kept telling me that I would never succeed.

But my parents underestimated me. They said I would never get a job because of my stuttering. I had to prove them wrong—and I did.

I have been employed for four years now, supporting myself. I've been trying to follow Robert Schuller's statement of positive thinking, "You never fail until you fail to try" and "What the mind believes, the mind can achieve." My stuttering has improved through positive thinking and prayer.

Negative Fallout at School and Work

Tragically for others their parents' divorce has been totally negative. A thirty-one-year-old man from Missouri said, "From the time of my parents' divorce and throughout high school, I couldn't concentrate on my studies. I had little determination to get good grades, and I didn't care about the future." He continued, "Regarding work, I didn't want to get a job, and when I did work, I had no ambition to learn more or to advance."

My insides cried out as I read comments like these. I knew firsthand how these adult children of divorce felt about school and their jobs. I felt their shame, anger, frustration at never succeeding and terrible loss of self-esteem.

Basically, I was a failure at school. I always felt stupid. I tried to sit where the teacher couldn't see me. I knew I was going to fail every test I took, even before I started taking it.

As I look back, I think teachers felt sorry for me. They each hoped the next teacher could help me. So, although I was a marginal student, I was passed from grade to grade with about a D–minus average until I got into junior high school. Finally, I saw my first A's. They came through a mechanical drawing class and a woodworking class.

My parents ignored my schooling process except to send me off to school. They didn't even know that because of a long morning paper route, I was late to school nearly every morning during junior high and was kept after school every day to pay the penalty.

My mother had attended school only through the eighth grade, and my father, who was dyslexic, also had trouble with school. The important thing in our family was simply to attend school, not necessarily to achieve.

My parents didn't realize I was such a failure, because I learned to forge my father's name on report cards. The reports and memos to my parents never reached them. I had learned to be "in control" of the situation.

Third in the Class?

Several years ago I was invited to become a trustee for Sterling College, the college Sally and I attended in central Kansas. On one occasion I was invited to speak to the chapel service. The president introduced me as "one of our more famous alumni" and embarrassed me by telling about my degrees, books, travel and other accomplishments.

After he had impressed the students, he said, "However, there is a little-known fact about Jim that might put all that he is going to say into perspective." He continued, "I dug out Jim's college record and noticed that when he was admitted to Sterling College, he ranked third in his high-school class." Then, with a sly grin, he added, "Third from the bottom."

Growing up in a dysfunctional home doesn't make it easy to go to school. And if you don't succeed at school, you will probably have trouble with any job that you take. It wasn't until I came into a personal relationship with Christ at the time I began college that my grades began to change.

Losers or Winners

Adult children of divorce seem to take one of two very distinct directions as they move out into the world:

1. They will become **super-achievers** whose success becomes a way

of compensating for all the loss they experienced in their parental home.

2. They will become *failures* in their relationships with the outside world, not able to live up to their full potential educationally or in their career.

Many adult children of divorce fail as they move into the outside world because their parents' attention was focused on their own problems rather than on the child's development. And often the parents' money was spent on the divorce and separate housing, so funds were not available for college or career training.[3]

Mona was a fifty-six-year-old woman from Florida whose parents were divorced when she was fifteen. Mona described herself as not knowing how to establish relationships and lacking the self-confidence and self-esteem to 'get ahead.' She said she is rigid, legalistic, lacks spontaneity and warmth, and feels lonely and insecure.

Then Mona said, "I did not expect to be liked or succeed, so I seldom tried. At home I tried not to 'make waves,' to do what I was told, 'to keep lightning from striking!' " Her goal was to "stay out of the way and out of sight by being in a book or out in the fields or woods with a friend."

Mona continued, "I married a man I thought would love me and take care of me, but he doesn't. I became a person who thought everyone else's wants and needs came ahead of mine. There was no self-development, nor could I know what I wanted to do, let alone allow myself to do it.

"Because of all the stress and pressure, my box that I lived in became smaller and smaller. I came very close to losing my mental stability and my will to go on living."

Mona did eventually take employment, but it was not easy for her. Nor is it easy for her to assert herself in her job now.

Successful, But . . .

Other people are very successful at work, yet their external success is not the full measure of how they feel.

Noreen said, "Because of my parents' problems, I excelled at work and school, and I became the kind of friend who could always be counted on, primarily because I did not consider my own needs or welfare as important. I never expected anything in return. I maintained an aloofness to avoid possible pain. This gave people the illusion that I was strong, and, therefore, it was okay for them to do anything they wanted—after all, I could 'take it.' "

This woman is a success. Yet the dysfunction she carries from her childhood also makes her a continued victim in her relationships and at work. To be successful in education or at work, a person must practice a high degree of trust. As trust breaks down, people do not function effectively. As we have already seen, adult children of divorce—even those who are very successful—frequently come into the workplace with a low level of trust.

Super-achievers know what they need to do to arrive at their goals. They have learned that people can be manipulated, that success always means looking out for number one, and that you don't trust anyone.

A thirty-five-year-old single woman from Southern California expresses an interesting contrast. She says, "I have a very low trust in men or male relationships." Then she goes on to discuss her relationships with men at work: "I have a good working relationship with men—because of my logic, reasoning, and extreme independence. But it's very difficult to socialize, apart from work."

This woman has learned how to work with men, even though she does not know how to relate to them socially. She is successful at her job because she understands that men are goal-oriented, and she is willing to relate to them on that level. At the same time, she thinks of herself as a dismal failure in dating relationships, describing herself as "never even being close to marriage."

Hostility on the Job
Paul Amato reports that adult children of divorce feel a sense of "powerlessness and helplessness."[4]

Frequently people who have difficulty trusting others have been burned in the past. Sometimes they feel cheated, hostile, or that people owe them. On top of all that, they often feel hopeless or helpless, because they don't have the power to control the situation and achieve their goals. Therefore, they may be angry at everyone around them.

A thirty-year-old teacher from Kansas told me her biggest problem was being angry at school. This anger finally caused her to seek counseling. Her first counselor did not seem to move fast enough to accomplish the goals she wanted, so she quit. The second counselor tried to ignore her anger. She felt that no one, including her husband, understood her anger.

Later she said, "My husband's lack of empathy over my problem was deeply frustrating. No one seems to understand that there is something deep inside of me that's angry. I am not choosing deliberately to be angry, it's just there." Her anger, it was finally discovered by another counselor, was because of the way she had been treated and ignored years before as her parents' marriage fell apart.

No One Measures Up

More than 50 per cent of these adult children of divorce are still judging themselves too critically.

A twenty-six-year-old counselor said, "I believe that my fear of being hurt in a relationship has had a significant impact on my life. I think it makes me highly critical of both myself and others. Consequently, I am often disappointed by others' actions. So I withdraw quickly for fear of repeated disappointment."

There's a logical flow in these faulty work-personality traits. The person who has difficulty trusting or feels cheated will find it easy to be hostile. Because adult children of divorce tend to be perfectionists—critical of themselves and others—they justify their lack of trust, hostility and critical spirit as being someone else's fault.

Keep Everyone Happy

Almost 60 per cent of adult children of divorce are constantly seeking approval. That's a startling number. They are reaching out for affirmation, even on their jobs. The potential danger at work is that coworkers or bosses will manipulate or misunderstand them or violate their boundaries.

Bette, a forty-six-year-old legal secretary from the West Coast, said, "On my job performance reviews, the usual 'needs improvement' comment has been, 'needs to be more assertive.' I have read several books and have taken classes over the past ten years. Intellectually I believe in being assertive. But if I think it will 'make waves,' I'll bury my needs for the sake of peace. Emotionally I can't take a fight. I hate it when anyone fights or argues. I want to run away!"

When I read what Bette had said about trying to keep everyone happy, I said to myself, "She's taken the words right out of my mouth. I also hate it when anyone fights. I want people to be at peace with each other."

Over a period of twenty-four years I was the pastor of three different churches. Each of the churches had experienced a split or had a strong divisive element before I came to them. My role was to be a healer, helping people to get along with each other even though they disagreed. My childhood dysfunction, in these cases, helped me to be gentle and seek reconciliation.

On other occasions, however, this overpowering desire to have people get along has led me to not speak up when I should have. I repeated a pattern of not giving regular feedback to my employees or staff workers. So little problems sometimes grew to become such irritants to me that finally I would explode, venting my anger on the offending person and taking him or her totally by surprise. Then I would swing in the other direction, away from hostility toward a "peace at any price" mode. As I've gotten healthier, it's easier for me to function at a midpoint. I can chat with people in a friendly way about their job performance, not allowing the problem to become so severe that it produces hostility in me.

I Feel Walked On

In chapter five we discussed boundaries. They are important in both social and work relationships. John and Linda Friel describe three types: *Rigid* boundaries are those that are too strong or too fixed. *Diffused* boundaries are too weak, allowing too many people in. *Flexible* boundaries are a healthy balance of being able to maintain personal identity, yet allowing people into our lives.

The Friels then discuss what happens with the typical person from a dysfunctional family. If boundaries are too weak, a person will always let people do whatever they want. The person will never say no. He or she gets walked on. A person who does this long enough will develop serious emotional problems and eventually swing to the opposite extreme and set up rigid boundaries. Then that one loses all contact with people, becoming an emotional hermit.

John and Linda Friel say, "It is our belief that the underlying reason that we can't set these healthy limits is that we are desperately afraid that we will be *abandoned* if we say 'no.' "[5]

As adult children from a divorced family go to school or enter the workplace, with boundary problems, they either isolate themselves from people or accept too much responsibility. In addition, they feel guilty if they try to meet their own needs instead of the needs of the workplace or people around them.

Retreat from Burnout

When people with diffused boundaries are overextended at their job because of increased responsibilities, or because their coworkers see them as a wonderful dumping-ground for personal problems, they burn out. When exhaustion comes, they don't retreat to a middle ground with normal boundaries. They retreat into rigid isolation, and then feel guilty for doing so. This only reinforces the fact that they're inadequate, they are not like other people.

More than 50 per cent of adult children of divorce feel very different from other people. They do not feel in control. Everyone else seems to be able to manage life. They always seem to be either overly stressed-out or overly withdrawn.

Too Much Responsibility

These adult children often feel a desperate need to do something, to help someone, or to contribute something to society, so they can verify their existence. Then they plunge head-over-heels into work. They are easily manipulated by the pressure of the job, requests from bosses or authority figures, or the personal and emotional needs of coworkers.

Jana was a twenty-eight-year-old secretary whose parents divorced when she was a child. Her husband was a full-time college student who also worked about twenty-five hours a week in an outside job. Jana worked full-time in a drug rehabilitation center and was deeply enmeshed in the people's emotional problems. Frequently her workload was more than fifty hours a week because of the additional volunteer time she gave to the center.

Then she had a baby, but there was no slowdown in her pace. In fact, she also volunteered to serve as a resident dorm supervisor at the college her husband attended.

In addition, she was taking college courses herself—"on the side." Repeatedly two different employers would call her for emergency help. She'd say, "Sure, I can come. How about if I come straight from my main job and work till 9:30 or 10:00?"

No end was ever in sight. Enough was never enough. Her marital relationship became more and more tense as her husband kept asking, "When is there ever time for the baby and me? When is there time for you? Why are you so driven?"

Jana's story illustrates how personal and relational dysfunction shows up not only in dating, marriage and family, but also in the outside world of education and career.

For several chapters we've looked at the problems. Now, in the next part of the book, we'll look at the positive side: how to heal the hurt.

Part Three
Steps for
Healing Your
Damaged Past

11

Step One:
Deciding
to Be Healed

IF YOU PICKED UP THIS BOOK, LOOKED AT THE
table of contents, and then skipped to this point in the book, let
me encourage you to go back now and read the early chapters.
Even though we are going to offer steps for healing, this is not
a process you can jump into quickly. The purpose of the first half
of the book is to help you think through your own development
by identifying with some of the people who shared their stories.

Those first chapters are an important part of your healing
process. As you read them you will understand that you are not
alone, you are not strange—you just came from an emotionally
or legally divorced home.

As you think back over the early chapters, let yourself feel
those moments when your life story matched the life story of

another person. Perhaps you can hear the exact words that your parents or some other authority figure said to you. Remember the feelings of a helpless little child which those parental words brought back.

Perhaps as you went through the first half of this book, you were tempted to cry, but your tough, adult exterior pushed down those feelings. Let yourself become soft, like a garden hose lying in the hot summer sun, rather than like the hose in your backyard when the temperature is zero. You are getting ready for healing.

What Is Recovery?

It took you a long time, perhaps most of your lifetime, to develop your dysfunction and to learn to tolerate your pain. Now we're going to start the process of healing, and it too takes time. This is not the same as dealing with a cold, where you swallow some extra vitamin C and a decongestant tablet and put a throat lozenge in your mouth. You won't be able to work through all that needs to be accomplished in a few days, a few weeks or even a few months. But healing *can* happen.

Let's look at what's involved in your healing.

1. Decide to be healed. Say to yourself, "This is the year I'm going to get better. This is the week I'm going to get started." Without a definite decision, you may keep putting it off, just as you've been doing for many years.

2. Commit yourself to time. It takes time to read, to think, to reflect. It takes time to remember and to walk back into your childhood. It takes time to be with God, to be with yourself and to be with close friends. It takes time to be in a group or to visit a counselor. It takes time to talk with family members so that you can learn the truth. The process of healing takes time. Part of your decision to be healed is the decision to make room in your schedule, among all your responsibilities—for *you.*

3. Prepare for pain/anger/grief. Imagine that you are working in the yard and step on a board with a rusty nail sticking out of it. The nail goes through the bottom of your tennis shoe and into your foot. The pain is terrible. Quickly you wash off your foot, but in the midst of your pain you don't notice that a little tip of the nail has broken off in your foot.

Hours later the pain is still intense. Your foot is swelling. You notice red streaks on your leg. You're frightened and decide to go to the emergency room. The doctor tells you, "A piece of nail has lodged in your foot; you'll need immediate surgery."

It's difficult to imagine that you would walk out, get into your car and say, "I'm going to forget it." Neither would you say to yourself, "Hey, surgery hurts too much! I don't want to go through this." Rather, you would probably think, "This is going to hurt like crazy. I don't want to do it, but if I want to live, I have to go through this procedure. That bit of nail has got to come out so my body will have a chance to recover."

The process of your being healed from your parents' divorce is also going to include times of intense pain, anger and grief. But you will also have times of great joy and freedom, plus a growing sense of hope.

4. You are not the Lone Ranger. Even the Lone Ranger had Tonto. He wasn't out there on his own, and neither should you try to resolve all of the junk from your past on your own. If you think you can do it on your own, let me ask, "Why haven't you done it by now? Why do you have trouble with trust, anger, and control? Why are you still full of lust and perfectionism? Why are you afraid to be known? Why do you experience depression? If you don't need any help, why are you still dysfunctional?"

I'm sorry to be so direct, but let me assure you that you do need help. Let other people help you. Let God help you. Decide now that you're *not* going to try it on your own. Take advantage of *all the help you can find.*

5. Healing means that you resolve the problems that plague you. Is your problem anger? depression? lostness? perfectionism? These areas will need to change. By now, as you've read the first ten chapters, you should be able to identify some of your problem areas. Each time you identified with one of the stories, you were discovering a problem you will need to work out.

6. Live your new life. The process of healing requires not only receiving a new insight, but also putting it into practice. As you gain new freedom and learn new ways to relate, use those areas of growth in the normal flow of your life.

7. Healing is lifelong. An alcoholic is always an alcoholic. However, a recovering alcoholic has made a decision to go through the growth necessary to be dry. You can't escape the fact that your home was what it was, but, day by day, you can live out new patterns that are very different from what might be expected from a person with your background. Healing is a lifelong process. *Welcome to the first day of your new life!*

Congratulations

Deciding to be healed from the impact of your parents' divorce and dysfunction is your first major step. Making this decision is not easy, because you've learned to live with or ignore your past pain. Your entire personality is a reflection of and a reaction to what went on with your parental home. All the other major parts of your life, such as the way you relate to people and the way you think of yourself, have been tainted by your parents' dysfunction.

Dozens of times during 1989 I told Sally and other friends, "This is my year to be healed." Now I want to congratulate you for joining me and millions of others who have decided that "enough is enough." It's time to be healed.

I know that deciding to be healed is frightening. Many people choose just to live with life as it is instead of going through the process of healing. We absorbed our tolerance for pain from our parental homes. Someone made us feel it was our fault that our parents fought and their lives were unhappy. Some of us firmly believe we were the cause of their divorce. So your decision to be healed may lead you to face the scary, but false, feeling that you're to blame for all of the trash in your background.

I've got good news for you. You are not to blame! You are not responsible for your parents' unhappiness! Even today you are not responsible to make them happy. You may choose to do things for them, but that choice must be a healthy choice by a healthy adult who has been set free from the tyranny of the parents' divorce.

A Growing Pressure on Me

Several times in my life I came close to making the decision to get whatever help I needed for the healing process. But each time I felt too ashamed or too embarrassed. It also sounded like too much work. It was easier to pretend that my parents didn't exist. Yes, I had obligations to them, and occasionally we would drop into each other's lives, but the rest of the time—they just didn't exist.

Finally I decided to come out of hiding, stop pretending, stop covering up for my parents.

My decision was triggered by a recurring physical problem. I was continually exhausted. When I sat down in a chair, I didn't even have the energy to lift my arms or to get up again. If I worked in the yard, within a half an hour I would start trembling and be forced to rest. I was only able to work by sheer will power. I had no physical strength, no emotional drive, no enthusiasm for anything. I kept thinking how wonderful it would be to die and to be gone from this stress and exhaustion.

Of course, I didn't link this at all to my parents' emotional divorce. I assumed it was all my fault—something I had done wrong. Perhaps I wasn't eating or sleeping right. Maybe I wasn't getting enough exercise.

One day on the car radio, I heard a nutritionist talking about food, stress and fatigue. When I came into the house I told Sally, "This has gone on long enough. I'm going to that nutritionist to see if I can get some answers." There followed a series of blood tests and diet changes to strengthen my natural immune system.

At the same time, I started seeing a doctor who prescribed extended antibiotic treatment for a chronic low-grade infection. The result of paying attention to my physical body, eating right, taking a vitamin supplement with heavy B vitamins, and getting over my infection was that I began to have more energy and an increased capacity to handle problems.

Forced to Decide

The awful feeling of being dragged down had gone on for a couple of years. During those same years our daughters were having intense conflict with my father. I was caught in the middle, feeling obligated to both my father and my daughters. Their conflict continually reminded me of my lifelong conflict with him. All of my life I had smarted under his dictatorial way of relating. I was forced to remember my parents' sterile marriage. They were married legally, but they ignored each other, each wishing they had married someone else.

As the conflict between my daughters and my father continued, he tried a power play. He verbally attacked my daughters and my wife, and tried to draw me into his corner, hoping I would agree that he was never wrong and therefore the conflict must be the fault of my daughters and my wife.

At that point, enough was enough. I was shaken into the reality of my father's lifelong distorted way of relating. I decided that I wasn't going to cover up or feel guilty anymore. I was going to stop pretending, stop trying to keep the peace, and stop defending him.

I experienced a great deal of freedom as I made that decision. I also began to realize how many of the things I didn't like about myself had originally come from my dysfunctional home.

Digging Up My Past

Another factor in my personal decision to get healed was the invitation to write this book. I've already told you that as I began to do more reading and research on the topic, I began to see how dysfunctional I was personally. I was especially influenced by people writing about adult children of alcoholics. That wasn't my family's problem—but the patterns were the same! I was also greatly freed up by John Bradshaw's book *Healing the Shame That Binds You.*[1]

The more reading I did, the less I felt able to write a book on adult children of divorce. Suddenly, the problem was not about "those people" out there, but about me and my painful childhood that I had kept buried.

I experienced great freedom by deciding to stop covering up for my father. And then I also began to see that my dysfunction came from my father's and mother's dysfunction. Their problems were being passed down to me. It was not my fault. What a relief!

I also began to realize that some of the things I constantly struggled with—distrust, control, anger, lust, perfectionism, competitiveness, depression, and always presenting myself through my accomplishments rather than as a person—were all out of my dysfunctional parental home.

As a result, I felt encouraged to further expand my commitment to be healed. Besides my medical doctor, a physical therapist and the nutritionist, I decided to see a psychological counselor.

I started looking for the right counselor by asking trusted friends for names of counselors with a proven track record of working with adults from dysfunctional families. I narrowed the choice down to three. Then I interviewed each of them over the phone to see how we would get along and to hear of their experience. Meanwhile, Sally and I made this choice a matter of prayer. I finally settled on a counselor who himself came from a dysfunctional family of alcohol and divorce. It's great to talk to my counselor, Earl. He understands me not simply because of his theoretical training, but because he has been there himself.

I Don't Have Time

About five months before I started seeing the medical doctor and the nutritionist, I was dragged into a small group by John, who has been a friend for several years. John didn't say, "You need to be in this group." Neither did he remind me that I had taught several small-group development courses. He simply said, "I need a group to talk with, to help me be accountable, to keep me sane."

John was also working on another guy named Dennis. So the three of us began meeting every other week. I was so exhausted and discouraged that I didn't have the energy to contribute anything. But these guys just carried me emotionally. It was in the fall of 1988 that we started meeting, and I've experienced tremendous growth and healing. I hadn't realized how much I had missed since I had moved away from my last group in Illinois seven years earlier.

Deciding to be healed was difficult for me, because it has always been easier to have people know me by my successes and activities rather than my weaknesses. However, allowing my weaknesses as well as my strengths to be known to these trusted friends has been releasing.

These men know some of the worst facts about me, and they still accept me. This is, by the way, the very genius of the Alcoholics Anonymous organization. When a person introduces himself to the group he says, "My name is *(first name only)*. I'm an alcoholic." This personal identification with the individual's key problem reminds the person that he or she is powerless to control alcohol—he or she needs the help of God and the group.

Years ago Jesus used a simple illustration to point out that we win by surrendering. He said, "I tell you the truth, unless a kernel of wheat falls to the ground and dies, it remains only a single seed. But if it dies, it produces many seeds."[2]

John Bradshaw says, "We must give up our delusional false selves and ego defenses to find the vital and precious core of ourselves."[3]

I needed to come to the point where I would be willing to give up all my false fronts and let these two guys know what I was struggling with. I had to face my pain.

Enduring the Agony

I used to run track in high school and college: the half-mile, mile, and two-mile. When I was in training, I deliberately focused my mind and body energy on good running procedures and on overcoming pain. Training is a painful process. My lungs ached day after day, my feet were sore, and I had terrific pain alongside my shinbones. It took time out of my life to practice and to recover from practice.

Every time I ran a race, I also had to face my pain. When the gun went off for the beginning of the mile event, I was so charged with adrenalin that it felt as if my feet weren't even touching the ground. I literally floated around the track for the first lap, a quarter of a mile. The second quarter mile I settled down. It was just plain running: watching my stride and pace, paying attention to my arm movements, and concentrating on good breathing.

By the time I reached the third quarter mile, I had to work hard. I was running out of energy. A numbness settled over me. I knew I was running, but it was mechanical. I could hear my feet pounding the track, but it seemed as if I were in a dream. My legs hurt, my heart pounded, my lungs ached and I began to feel like a rubber doll. Now I was looking pain squarely in the face.

Then I started that awful fourth lap. Everyone realized this was the last lap. With a momentary sense of excitement, the pace picked up. At the same time, the pain in my body was beginning to overtake me. I was pushing my body—and my body was pushing back. Somehow I would make it two-thirds around the track. From that point on, the plan was to run as fast as possible—to give it everything I had. Invariably, my body and my mind had a ferocious argument. My mind said, "Okay, body, let's really pump it out now!" My body responded, "That's easy for you to say; you just sit up there and don't have to do any of the sweating or hurting!"

The debate would rage on—but, grudgingly, my body would give in. I would think, "If I quit now, I'll be disappointed with myself. The only way out of this is to face the blackness of these next few minutes, to confront my pain—to run for the finish line."

Just so that you don't wonder, I never was very great. I did, however, win the gold in the two-mile in our annual central Kansas small-college meet. (You need to underline the word "small" to keep my running feats in perspective.)

What's the point of that story? Simply this: you have to face your pain—whatever you most fear. Be willing to say, as the person in AA docs, "I am an alcoholic." For you it might be "I don't trust people," "I am angry," "I am a perfectionist" or "I am depressed." You may have to meet your painful past head-on, being willing to go through the near-death experience of remembering your childhood and how it affected you. Only then will you gain the release and the new life you want.

It's All in the Follow-Through

One more word about your decision to be healed. You've already decided that you need to be healed or you wouldn't have picked up this book. The very fact that you have read this far indicates that you've made some sort of decision for healing. Now go ahead, follow through on it. Say out loud, "This is the year I'm going to get healed." Telling a friend of your decision will also help to settle your decision and keep you on track.

After I made the decision to be healed, it was hard for me to find the time. (I forgot to tell you that I'm also a workaholic. We workaholics work so that we don't have to think or feel. If we can be preoccupied with lots of activities, we don't have to deal with our pain and our past.)

I had to back up my decision to be healed by taking time for doctors, lab tests, my small group, visits to my counselor and long talks with Sally.

At first it was easy for me to say, "I don't have the time for this. I'll just keep on living the way I've been living. After all, I've got things under control."

But another voice inside me kept asking, "Well, if you have your stuff under control so well, why are you angry? Why are you depressed? Why are you such a perfectionist? Why do you only want people to know you by your achievements?"

All those questions kept me committed to my decision to be healed. Confronting the truth about what I didn't like in me also helped me to be willing to invest the necessary time for healing.

Deciding to be healed, then, is saying out loud, "Yes, this is my year to be healed. I will invest the necessary time, and I will come out of hiding. I will stop pretending. Finally, I will break the silence."

As you resolve to be healed, you are saying, "I will look my pain and my past squarely in the face and work them through. I will stop trying to forget my childhood. I will stop trying to forget that my parents were divorced. I will stop pretending that it didn't affect me."

Yes, choosing to be healed is a *powerful* decision. So follow through by committing whatever time is needed for the process. Commit yourself, as well, to the next eight steps.

Congratulate yourself! You've made a life-changing decision. You've joined the rest of us who are in the process of being healed. Now let's press on to Step Two.

12

Step Two:
The Spiritual
Link

Larry had spent most his life in the midwest. At the time I got to know him he was forty-four years old. From all appearances he was doing well in life. His relationships with his wife and children were positive and he was successful in his career.

I learned that his father had been a building contractor until his retirement. Larry respected his father, and they had provided support for each other over the years.

Larry told me that his parents had divorced in his second year of high school. As he viewed the situation, it was primarily his mother's fault, although he acknowledged a combination of factors had pulled his parents apart.

As Larry saw it, his mother seemed to be searching for her own identity. She felt she wasn't important to her children or her husband. She enrolled in the local community college, hoping to finish the three years she needed for a college degree.

His father seemed to be preoccupied with making his business a success and didn't spend much time with his wife. Larry also felt that his mother was struggling with her aging. She hated getting older when there were so many things in life she yet wanted to do.

The couple's fighting, emotional isolation from each other, and preoccupation with their individual needs finally brought them to divorce. Larry was caught in the middle. He deeply loved both of them, but he felt totally lost. His parents pulled at him to take sides, yet how could he be close to one without denying the other?

The Lost Puppy

Larry's parents were so concerned with proving that the other parent was wrong that they didn't even realize their son was the one paying the price. He lost the friendship of both his parents. They were not around to give him the coaching he needed. His sense of "home" was gone and, in his words, "I felt like a stray puppy looking for someone to feed me."

Then something happened that drastically changed Larry's life. Some of his high school friends invited him to join their local church youth group. Even though Larry's family never attended church, the warm, caring friendship of the students and their youth leader began to fill the ravenous appetite that Larry had for a place called "home."

Within a matter of weeks, Larry made a personal commitment to Jesus Christ and began regularly to read the Bible. The result was that even though his home was falling apart, he had a solid stability because of God's love and the acceptance of his new Christian friends. Larry sums up the change by saying, "My youth pastor, a personal relationship with Jesus Christ, and a caring church enabled me to believe in myself and in God."

Larry's new spiritual home so changed his life that he decided to go into full-time ministry as a pastor. He wanted to duplicate for other people the sense of community and home that he had found in that local church.

Larry attributes his success in life to his spiritual link with God. Without God his life might have been very different. He says, "I have a sister whose life is a complete mess because of our parents' divorce. I imagine I would be the same if I hadn't met God. He has given me a wonderful wife and a wonderful ministry." The emptiness of the boy who felt like a stray puppy has been filled.

The Spiritual—Power for Healing

The best known and most effective program for treating alcoholics is Alcoholics Anonymous. Out of this program have come dozens of different types of recovery groups dealing with such issues as drug addiction, gambling, sexual addiction, and eating disorders, to name just a few. Each of these groups has followed, to some degree, the Twelve-Step program that is so well known and has proved so effective in Alcoholics Anonymous.

The basic thrust of the Twelve-Step program is to admit to ourselves and to a trusted group that we are powerless over our addiction. We surrender ourselves to a higher power (God, in whatever way we understand him), to give us the inner strength we lack.

The strong movement that developed in the eighties, Adult Children of Alcoholics, has continued to utilize the spiritual core and direction of AA. Gravitz and Bowden write, "Recovery from the disease of alcoholism is three-fold: physical, mental, and spiritual. Alcoholics Anonymous, the first effective recovery program for alcoholism, has a clear spiritual foundation. We believe that a spiritual side to recovery is applicable to children of alcoholics as well."[1]

Another writer says, "Spirituality is the last 'stage' in our recovery period. And paradoxically, it can never be a stage, since it is an on-going process throughout suffering, healing and serenity."[2]

The writers and therapists working with adult children of alcoholics clearly acknowledge the spiritual dimension as an indispensable ingredient in the healing process. However, most of these people place their discussions of the spiritual as the very last chapter of their book or as the culmination of the healing process.

I feel it is unfortunate to get a person involved in the process of healing before giving any consideration to God. In some recovery programs God is not brought into the picture until after the person has resolved a number of issues and experiences a degree of freedom. The original Twelve-Step program, on the other hand, introduces God as a major key in the beginning of the healing process.

Not Just Any Repairman

I would suggest that we not see God as an impotent, well-meaning old man whom we invite into our lives after we have brought things under control. Rather, we should see God as the powerful Creator who is waiting to energize and re-create our lives.

Some months ago our cuckoo clock stopped working. Each time the minute hand came to the eleven, it stopped. I thought it needed a little oil. So I took off the back, blew out some of the dust, squirted a little bit of light-weight oil around here and there, and put it back together. But it was not fixed. It would occasionally go past the eleven, but most of the time it would stop.

Finally I took it to a cuckoo clock repairman. He said the problem was that the music box mechanism was broken. Also some dummy had squirted too much oil inside the clock. (I wasn't about to confess that I knew the "dummy" who put too much oil in the clock.)

It strikes me that many of us who have come out of troubled homes are embarrassed to admit our needs, to seek counseling, or to find a recovery group. And we certainly are not about to admit our imperfections to God. So we try tinkering with our lives on our own—but we don't get better.

I say, "Let God get involved in your life as soon as possible!" That's why I've put "The Spiritual Link" as the second step in your healing process. As you invite God to come into your life to help you with the recovery process, you unleash his power at the beginning of your healing process—rather than stumbling along on your own.

I Have a Problem with God

At this point you may say, "Look, I've tried God. He doesn't work," or "I'm angry at God for allowing me to be raised in a divorced home," or "God and I never have communicated very well." It's true that growing up in a divorced or other dysfunctional family has often deeply soured people on God.

Losing hope in God is a gradual process. Archibald Hart describes his own childhood reaction to his parents' divorce and his prayers to God. At first, he says, his prayer was a simple " 'Please, God, make Mommy and

Daddy happy.' Slowly my prayers changed from simple requests to outright demands. 'God, you've got to make Mommy and Daddy happy.' Then they became angry prayers. I argued with God. I threatened him. 'Why don't You make them happy? What's wrong? Don't You love me?'

"About the time my mother told us she was separating from my father, I began to think God was using my parents' fighting to punish me. The reason he wasn't answering my prayer was that I had been naughty, so I tried to find ways to atone for my sin."

After Hart's parents separated, he slowly came to realize that nothing he could do would change the situation or influence the outcome of the divorce. Hart felt hopeless. He says, "I distinctly remember coming to the conclusion that the reason God wasn't answering my prayers was that God didn't exist. Or if he did, he was too busy with other worlds, or other parts of this world, to care about me."[3]

Angry Accusations

When we are hurt our natural response is to hurt back. Sometimes when a child is hurt by a brother or a sister, or when a parent disappoints a child, the child becomes very angry, hitting any person or anything nearby. We understand that the child is deeply disappointed. The child is retaliating by lashing out at whatever is handy. Adult children of divorce have been hurt, and frequently these adults lash out at God.

I've asked myself thousands of times, "Why did I have to be born in a family where the parents didn't like each other? Why did I have to be born in a family where they pretended to be religious, but did immoral things to each other and with other people? Why was I ignored as a child?"

Adult children of divorce want everything to work perfectly. I have reasoned many times, "Because God has all power, and he can do whatever he wants to do, why didn't he make my life normal like others?" I have blamed God and wildly struck out at him. The problem is that when I think those thoughts, I am living in the past. I am failing to live in the here and now. Those thoughts are actually feeding my perfectionism and my need to be a controller.

Bad things happen to everybody. The Bible says God "sends rain on the righteous and the unrighteous."[4] I have to keep forcing myself to remember that God doesn't promise to take all the pain from our lives. He only promises to transform our pain by transforming us—if we'll allow him to do that.

Tell God You're Angry

Suppose you're driving your car and the oil warning light comes on. It would be too bad if you say to yourself, "Something's just wrong with the warning system. The motor's okay." No! The warning system is telling you that the motor is *not* okay. Something needs immediate attention.

If you ignore it, the motor may burn out and you'll have a dead car and big bills! If you are angry with God, that's your personality telling you, "Something is wrong with your basic emotional mechanism." I encourage you not to ignore that anger. Face it, and start talking to God.

Perhaps you've identified yourself as an atheist or an agnostic. Rather than continuing to hide behind a label or behind your anger, acknowledge your disappointment with God. Tell God that you're disappointed, and ask him to help you to deal with your anger. Ask his help to handle all that has happened as a result of your being raised in a dysfunctional home.

Many of the people I have worked with were raised in religious homes and regularly attended church. When their parents were divorced, their relationship with God was hindered. Sometimes people coming from religious backgrounds have even more trouble with God than other people when their parents divorce.

A thirty-two-year-old man said, "When Dad first left home, my quiet time with God went from half an hour every day to zero. I just *could not* spend time with God. I felt that he didn't do what he could have done to prevent the conflict and divorce of my parents. Yes, I continued to study the Bible in preparation to teach my Sunday-school class, but God and I never met. I was not able to be intimate with God."

Wherever you are in recovering from your parents' emotional or legal divorce, I urge you to include God—even if that means expressing your anger, bitterness and confusion to him. You can even tell him it's hard to talk to him. But until you are healed spiritually, you will not be fully healed.

Misplaced Focus

It's easy for adult children of divorce to focus on externals such as money, health, relationships, power and status, instead of focusing on their spiritual interior. But trying to compensate for the wounds of the past through outward successes and achievements is absolutely a dead-end street.

Instead of putting your energies toward making yourself look good on the outside or trying to convince yourself that you don't hurt on the inside, why not admit that you hurt and reach out to God for his help. Your escapism will only lead to certain disappointment. An open relationship with God, on the other hand, can accelerate your healing.

Benefits of a Spiritual Link

Our minds are very powerful. The architect imagines a building. The artist envisions a scene. The playwright mentally sees a drama unfolding. In the beginning none of these things have tangible reality. They only exist in the mind of the creators. But the mind envisions the form, and soon reality results.

As we link with God, we allow the Creator of the universe to enter our minds and help us envision ourselves as new people—unshackled from our parents' emotional or legal divorce. We are able to live pro-actively instead of re-actively. We decide what we want to do and think, instead of just reacting to all of the hurt and bondage from our past.

A thirty-nine-year-old woman from the South told me that her marriage broke up because of some of the characteristics she carried from her parental home. Then she talked about the benefits of her spiritual link:

"After I was divorced, I attended some Twelve-Step group meetings and learned a lot about how to love myself, whether or not anyone else loved me. That was a turning point in my life, and I am most grateful. I have gone from dependence to independence to interdependence. God helped me learn these skills; they didn't come from my parents."

A California woman said, "Six months after my parents separated, I was tired, angry, hurt and frustrated. I went to a conference and heard a talk on bitterness. I realized I was becoming bitter, so I gave it over to God and started forgiving both my parents. I asked God to give me supernatural love and wisdom as I related to my parents. Unfortunately, my brothers and sisters spent eight years being bitter and angry before they asked for God's help two years ago."

God wants to give you peace now so that, while you work through the other steps of healing, you'll have a deep sense of settledness and confidence—you *are* going to be healed.

The Good Old Days Are Still Here

When Sally and I were in Kansas one fall, attending the inauguration of Dr. Roger Parrott as the eighth president of Sterling College, we were reminded of our spiritual heritage and roots. It was a chance to be quiet, to slow down and remember where God had found us.

We both had been students at Sterling College and had grown spiritually because of the environment there. In addition, we had fallen in love and decided we would get married after I graduated.

At Sterling we had both sensed God's call into full-time ministry. During my last two years in college I was a student pastor for two different small churches. I had the great opportunity to speak every week about God's power to change lives. My Sterling College years were wonderful, with daily quiet times with God while reading the Bible or walking the gravel roads on the edge of town. So Sterling is a special place for Sally and me.

During that recent trip back, we were driving to the Wichita airport when we saw two large flocks of Canadian geese flying majestically in their "V" formation. We stopped the car along the quiet, rural Kansas highway, rolled down the windows, and listened to the friendly honking of the geese.

My heart felt a wonderful peace and quiet. It was more than a touch of nostalgia or getting in touch with nature—it was a touch from God. He reminded me that I needed to pull off the busy road of my life more often, allowing him to speak to me and give me his peace.

Right now, before you go on to read any more—please stop and talk to God as a friend. Say to him, "I want to know you better. I want to experience your spiritual peace. I need you to heal my troubled past."

Cautions about the Spiritual Link

Even though I've placed the spiritual link as your second step of healing, and even though I encourage you to give your life and problems to God, I am not at all suggesting that you do not need to complete the rest of the steps.

Surrendering your life and your past hurts to God does not eliminate the need for the healing process. Just because you've become friends with a dentist in your neighborhood doesn't mean you can skip getting your cavities filled. God wants to help you through the other necessary steps of healing.

Remember, each person comes to this spiritual step in the healing process with a different readiness. Don't give up if you're not as ready as you'd like to be. Don't be discouraged if you don't become close to God as quickly as you'd like.

Just as healing is a *process,* so is developing a relationship with God. It's a process that is started when you choose to start it, but it will continue to expand as you maintain a sustained contact with God.

Diverted from the Spiritual Link

Another caution: When you start to link with God, notice if certain things repeatedly take your mind away from focusing on him. Do you continually feel unworthy to talk to God? Is your mind filled with your anger at your parents? Notice those thoughts that distract you from communicating with God. Stop yourself from following those rabbit trails. Come back again to focusing on God. Ask God to help you focus on him and not on those stray thoughts that lead you away.

One of the frequent blockages that adult children of divorce experience are the negative thoughts about their parents. When your parents pop up in your mind, say, "God, I'm giving my parents to you. I can't handle them anymore. I can't handle the injuries they have caused. I'm surrendering them to you, and I'm giving my hurt to you." As you release your parents to God, you begin to pave the way for your healing from the damage of the divorce and dysfunction.

How to Link with God

Your spiritual link with God is an admission that you're surrendering control of this whole hurtful situation to him. You are admitting that you do not have the ability to change your own life.

I've found it helpful to think of this linking with God in two separate ways: the initial contact and a sustained contact.

1. The Initial Contact. As I teach people how to link with God, I suggest that they repeat a simple prayer. First, find a quiet place alone and allow your body to slow down and your mind to become restful. For me it's helpful to imagine that I'm sitting on an empty beach, looking out at the ocean and the endless horizon. I'm conscious of the waves continuing their march to the shore, but I deliberately block out all the city life and my own business, and I let my mind become quiet. Some people find it helpful to think of sitting in front of a fire or looking into a moonless sky at night. Whatever it is, first let yourself become quiet.

Now in this quietness, visualize the friendly face of God. Then speak directly to him, "God, I am powerless. I've tried unsuccessfully for years to overcome these hurts. I need your help.

"I'm sorry for keeping you out of my life. I'm sorry I didn't even think about you as being able to help me with this situation.

"Please forgive me. Come into my life. Be God in me, instead of just God to the outside world. Please increase my sensitivity to spiritual things. I do intend to follow the spiritual directions and insights that you give me. I'm open to you—lead me—heal me."

Use your own words. Enlarge on my suggestions in any way you want.

Next, you may want to pour out some of your frustrations, or talk about the inadequacies of your life and your inability to cope. It is extremely important that you tell God whatever comes to your mind. This is not the time to pretend. This is the time to let it all hang out. Be honest; God can handle whatever you want to say.

After you've spent some time talking to God, return to just being quiet and visualizing God's face. Keep your mind in that same open state and allow God to care for you, to love you, to warm you.

Finally—the Creator of the universe has been invited into your problem and into your life. Let God bathe your life with his presence as you sit quietly.

Experiences with God vary from person to person. Some feel an instant sense of relief, even euphoria. For others it is a matter-of-fact conversation. Whatever is your experience, remember you're not competing with the experience of someone else—only communicating directly and privately with God.

2. Sustained Contact. Linking with God is not a one-time experience. It should be repeated each day. In your daily conversations with God, follow the same format of quieting yourself before him and visualizing his face.

Then thank God for the privilege of this spiritual link. Thank him for whatever peace you are experiencing—for insights that are coming. Thank him for your increased sensitivity to spiritual things, even though sometimes you have pain when you're confronted with areas that need change.

Sustaining your contact with God will help you to live in the here and now. It will help you to link your childhood with your adult life so that both parts of your life will be healed.

Talk to God about the group you're in, books you're reading, insights you're getting from other people, and insights you're getting as you spend time quietly meditating with him each day.

Remember, you are not looking for perfection as you sustain your link with God. You are looking for his presence and peace as you continue to go through the healing process. You are looking for truth—the truth about your parents. They were not all bad. You are looking for truth about yourself—yes, some things need to change, but you are not all bad. The healing process can only go forward as you know the truth. Jesus said, "You will know the truth and the truth will set you free."[5]

God is more concerned about your emotional health than you are. His plan is to give you a deep sense of peace and the strength to face your painful past. Keep in focus the two aspects of your contact with God. Prayer is your side of the conversation with God, while the Bible is his way of speaking to you.

Let me suggest a little assignment as you finish this chapter. Start reading the Bible, a chapter a day, beginning with the Gospel of John. Use your daily reading as part of the process of sustaining your contact with God.

13
Step Three: Joining a Recovery Group

IN THE LATE SIXTIES I WAS IN A MASTER OF ARTS in psychology program. One of my professors encouraged me to join an elective course about small group development. He said the main purpose of the course was for students to become part of a small group, get to know each other in depth and learn from the inside out how small groups work.

This made me sick to my stomach. A terrible wave of panic swept over me. He was one of my favorite professors, and I was honored that he was encouraging me to join this class, yet I was terrified of being exposed. What if they found out about my family background? What if they learned about my insecurity, my inability to trust people, my manipulation and control? What if they learned about my lust, my perfectionism, my competitiveness? What if they began to mess around in my motives or to suggest that my call into ministry was really a way to control people rather than to care for them? The risk was just too great; I did not join the group.

I had been caught in a dilemma that I've often experienced in life. I desperately wanted to please this professor, yet I was too terrified for someone to know me on the inside.

Vulnerable, But . . .

In the seventies, as my confidence in my ministry began to grow and as I saw how small care groups were helping people, I became increasingly willing to be vulnerable. Much to my surprise, I discovered that my openness and vulnerability in groups, as well as when I preached, was not a negative, causing people to turn away from me or think I was weird; rather, it drew us closer.

They felt I was more believable because I really did have human problems. My vulnerability helped people to see that my pastoral leadership and teaching was not theoretical, "ivory tower" stuff but came from real life experiences and hurts.

In spite of increasing openness as I related to people, my position and visibility as a leader still made me afraid at times to be involved in small groups. One of these times came when I was working on a doctoral degree at Fuller Theological Seminary in Pasadena, California. I was on campus for a two-week period, studying small group development. During the three months previous to the on-campus time, I had read over three thousand pages from twenty-five books on the subject of small groups. I had assumed this course would be like previous ones—primarily classroom lecture, followed by three to six months of work back home.

Honking Geese

I was surprised on our first day when the professor, Dr. Roberta Hestenes, divided us into small groups of five people. She told us to spend the afternoons of the next two weeks using any methods we chose in order to get to know each other in our group as deeply as possible.

It was a wonderful setting. On some days we sat around the pool at the hotel with the warm, winter Southern California sun beating down on us. We thought this would be an easy assignment. But we failed to take into account that we were all strangers—and we were all afraid to be vulnerable.

One man was senior pastor of a church of 6000; another pastored a church of 2000; another was vice-president of a seminary; another was a missionary executive, responsible for half of his denomination's missionaries. I was senior pastor of a church that had grown to a Sunday morning attendance of over 1500 at that point. All of us were successful professionals.

When we introduced ourselves to each other, we talked about our external successes. We didn't talk about our weaknesses, our fears or our problems—we hid all those from each other.

That first day we sounded like a bunch of geese in a barnyard, each honking away and vying for position. It reminded me of so many of those "ministerial assassination" meetings I had attended, when ministers got together under the pretense of mutual encouragement. Tragically, they usually were occasions for each person to honk his own horn about how things were going in his church.

As I listened to our group of professionals sharing in that small group in California, I had the same feelings as in those earlier ministerial meetings. We were impressing each other—competing. We had no sense of cohesiveness, vulnerability or investment in each other's lives.

After we introduced ourselves, we decided the safest way to start the group would be to share some of our earliest remembrances. So we each told what it felt like to be three and four years old. The problem was that we continued every day for a week in those childhood memories. Yes, we were doing our classwork assignment, but we were not really getting to know each other in the here and now.

I'm Not Coming Back!

On Friday of that first week, when we had spent almost half our afternoon again discussing our early childhood, I had had enough. I jumped up abruptly and said, "I'm leaving this group. I feel like we're just playing games. We're never going to get to what is going on in our lives now. We're not going to become a group. I don't want to waste any more time in this process." I turned and walked away from the group.

As I started off, one of the group members came after me. He put his arm around my shoulders and said, "What's happening, Jim?"

So I told him that I almost hadn't come to this course. Ten days before, my sixteen-year-old daughter's left leg had been amputated because of cancer. I had truly believed that God would perform a miracle and heal Becki. But he allowed her to lose her leg. In the process I lost God! That was the darkest day of my life![1]

Then I started to sob as I said angrily, "I tell people that God loves them and has a wonderful plan for their lives, yet God didn't answer my prayer. How am I supposed to continue being a pastor if I can't believe what I'm saying?"

I almost shouted at my classmate through my tears, "What I need now is some men who will stand around me and help me in this terrible double crisis—my daughter has lost her leg and I've lost God. I don't want to be part of a group where we're just play-acting and talking about what was going on in our lives thirty or forty years ago. I need some help *today*."

Finally We Become a Group

He urged me to come back and tell the group what I had just told him. Reluctantly, I went back and shared my agonizing story with them.

Then one of the other men said, "I haven't told you the whole truth. Yes, technically, I'm the pastor of a church of 6000, but I've been given a year's leave of absence because I'm going through an emotional breakdown."

One by one the men began to share. Another pastor was experiencing deep conflict in his church, but he had no one to talk to—no one whom he could trust with his heartache. The missionary executive became emotional, and with great vulnerability he blurted out, "My missionaries are at each other's throats. I'm trying to hold them together, to keep the rebellion from spreading, and to keep the news from the home churches that these people whom they have idealized are sometimes extremely mean and selfish. The truth is, the mission is about to split apart."

The seminary vice-president told us he'd received a call from his wife during the week. While we were talking about what it felt like to be three and four years old, one of his daughters had been picked up on her high-school campus and booked by police on a drug charge.

It was as if a dam had broken! Suddenly we were a group of men committed to each other. We were no longer polished professionals, competing and impressing each other. We were now a group of vulnerable men with desperate needs. Yes, we were successful, but all of us had terrible hurts, and we needed to share our stories and pray for each other.

Everyone Is Afraid

When you saw the title of this chapter, did you have a sinking, uneasy feeling? If you did, you're not alone. In fact, most people from a divorced home have tried all their lives to keep their "family secrets" from other people. So the thought of joining a group where we might have to talk about these problems is very frightening to people like us. When I say that I understand your fear about joining a recovery group, those are not idle words. I have been part of many small groups. I have taught people how to start small groups. I've written articles about small groups, but read this next sentence slowly: *I have never met any person who is not afraid to become part of a small group.*

The only people who seem to have their fear of groups somewhat under control are people who have been in other small care groups. Once you've experienced a successful recovery group, you have more courage to go through that natural fear barrier when you start into another small group. Still, every person is somewhat afraid.

Let me assure you, however, that joining a recovery group will be one of the most helpful and important events of your life. You will—even though you may experience fear and stress as you listen to other people's stories and share your own—wonder what took you so long to get into a group, and you will wish it would never end.

Why Am I Afraid to Join a Group?

I am currently in a group with two other men. Even though I have been a part of dozens of different groups, I experienced a rush of emotions, including fear, when I was invited to join this group.

As I mentioned before, John said to me one day, "I feel I need to be in a group. It's one of my high priorities since I have just moved here." Then he asked, "Would you be willing to be part of a group with me? I need somebody to hold me accountable, but in a safe environment where I can be vulnerable. I need to be in a group where we can develop deep friendships."

He continued to talk about flexible time schedules, keeping the size down to maybe only one or two other people, and other details. All the time he was talking, I was running over my list of fears. On the other hand, I kept asking myself, "Why am I so afraid to get into this new group? Groups have been such a help to me in the past. Why am I afraid now?"

My first comment to John was, "I don't have time. I'm flattered that you want me to be a part of your group, but it's just not going to work out."

But that was all a smoke screen to cover my fear. I've found that some of my fears are common to many other people. Maybe some of my fears are also yours. Let's look at my list.

1. I don't need help. I can handle my own problems.
Coming out of an emotionally divorced home, I've learned not to talk about my problems. I don't go for outside help. After all, my parents never did, and they let me know in no uncertain terms that we didn't talk to people on the outside about our internal family problems.

So now I'm an adult, but I carry with me this sense that I must solve all the problems in my life by myself. I don't need anyone else. I don't need a group. After all, what can they do for me that I can't do on my own?

I found myself mentally repeating those words that were so common in childhood, "I'm in control. I can take care of my own problems."

2. I don't dare risk.
My inner voice said, "If I do decide to join this group, what will they do with me? Will these men really accept me? Maybe as they learn about my background and what's going on in my life right now, they will reject or abandon me."

An adult child from a divorced home has felt abandoned. Truth was distorted. Parents were preoccupied with their own problems and didn't have time for nurturing their children. These people don't have any extra "love dollars" to lose in a risky situation.

"Love dollars" are what I call those experiences in life when we have been encouraged, built up, affirmed and appreciated. Our personality is like a bank. Either people are making deposits into our "love dollar" account or, by criticism, rejection, abandonment and a thousand subtle put-downs, they are taking money out of our bank.

If your account doesn't have many extra love dollars, you will do everything possible to keep from losing any. You won't enter into risky situations. People who have experienced affirmation, appreciation and acceptance can afford to risk losing a few love dollars here and there. They have lots left over. But the child of divorce may come into adulthood with a bank account in the red.

I found myself saying to John, "I have too many commitments. I'm exhausted all the time. I just won't be able to work it into my schedule." I didn't want to tell him I was also very depressed. Sometimes I was so discouraged that I felt that life was not worth living.

Here was a man offering me an opportunity that could help me cope with depression and my nagging sense that life was not worth living. Yet I was turning him down because the risk was just too great.

3. I don't want old wounds opened.

I was so emotionally exhausted that I didn't want to hear anybody else's troubles. I didn't want the obligation to pray for someone else. I didn't want to become someone else's friend.

In addition, I didn't want their problems to remind me of my own. Neither did I want to be pushed to explore some of the hurts of my past. You see, I've developed this great mechanism called denial. If I deny that something exists, then it doesn't hurt. At least that's what I kept telling myself.

John was patient. He kept asking. Finally about two months later, after he had cornered me several times, I reluctantly said yes. But I wanted him to know up front that it needed to be a small group with no more than three people, flexible meeting times and no homework. And I also let him know that I was doing this as a favor to him, not for me!

Some months after we started meeting, I told two of the guys I was sorry for being so negative about forming the group. I felt they had contributed far more to my life and stability than I had contributed to theirs. I was glad that we really had become brothers over these months.

Why Do I Need a Group?

As you've been reading this chapter, you may have been wondering what a group could do for you. Let me suggest a few reasons why I need a group. Maybe my reasons will also fit you.

1. To Help Me Recover from My Damaged Past

Millions of people are meeting around the world in various recovery groups. These people report that their lives are changing. They are being freed from their past or from current addictions. They're experiencing a new capacity to love, to express their feelings, and to hope. They've learned to forgive the past and accept themselves. They're realizing a new sense of creativity and purpose for living. My care group is helping me recover in a way I could not ever accomplish on my own.

2. To Help Me Come Out of Hiding

If you've been keeping secrets about your childhood, you've probably developed a lifestyle of keeping secrets. Remember that *we are in bondage to the things that we hide.* All our secrets are part of what weighs us down. You'll never truly experience freedom until at least one other human being knows your secrets. My small care group has helped me come out of hiding as it has given me a safe environment to talk about those shameful secrets of the past. These guys understand. They've been there. They too are in the process of coming out of hiding. To come out of hiding is not a one-time event; it happens over many months as I gradually talk about where I came from and how I got the way I am.

Coming out of hiding means you're willing to stop denying your past and to claim it. You can finally put your arms around your past, with all of its ugliness, and say, "That really was and is part of me." It's much the same as when alcoholics learn to introduce themselves in AA meetings: "My name is _____ . I'm an alcoholic." They identify with their shameful past, and this enables them to experience a new freedom so that they can begin to handle their alcohol addiction.

3. To Help Me Get Unstuck

In isolation it's easy for me to believe that my situation is hopeless, that

I have no choices, that things will never be any different. Sometimes the trap is that since I feel so awful, I don't want to look at my past and I don't want anyone else to see it either.

Only by looking at your past, preferably with a group of people who care, can you come to realize your feelings and reactions are normal. Finally you'll be able to break the bondage and come to see that it was your past—not you—that was bad. You are lovable and acceptable.

4. To Help Me Feel Again

An adult child from a dysfunctional family may say, "I don't hurt because I don't feel. I don't feel because I don't remember. I've blocked it all out." However, our negative feelings from our childhood cannot simply be locked up in a closet. They keep beating on the door. They continually express themselves in other forms such as anger or depression.

You may have hated the lying and deception of your parents, yet now you are in bondage to the very things you hate. You lie when you say, "It doesn't hurt. I don't feel." You're deceiving yourself when you try to keep all those secrets tucked away in your closet.

The group will help to bring together your feelings and your intellect. A person may say, "Yes, I know I had a tough childhood. My parents were divorced. There was lots of fighting. I know that intellectually, but I don't *feel* any of the pain." A person who says that is really two people—the thinking person and the feeling person. Unfortunately, the feeling little child has been stuffed in the closet.

Your care group will allow you to touch all the feelings associated with any event or remembrance of your past. The group will accept you when you're angry or feel hurt or grieve over your lost childhood. They also will help you work through the healing of those bad memories.

5. To Give Me a Link with God

Some people have a deep-seated problem with God. They're angry. They feel God has let them down, so they want nothing to do with him. For people like this the group may become, spiritually speaking, a halfway house. They learn perhaps for the first time that people can be trusted. It was their home that was at fault, not God. When the "feeling door" starts to swing open, people often experience a spiritual rebirth as they meet God and realize that he has been a loving friend all along.

What Should I Look For in a Group?

Let me suggest several important characteristics for a great group.

1. A Safe Group of Fellow Strugglers

You need people you can trust. This is no place to make a good impression! Honesty must be the agenda. Start out by looking for a recovery group that is specifically for adult children of divorce or adult children of dysfunction. Don't be embarrassed to ask the general background of the people in the group and the experience of the leader.

Try to find a group that works with Twelve-Step principles. Additional qualities to look for in choosing the group: nonjudgmental, non-perfectionistic, not rigid, free expression of all emotions, and warm, caring people who will give an appropriate hug.

2. The Right Purpose

Groups form for lots of reasons. But you are looking for a very specific kind, so other groups will not meet your need at this point. You are not looking for a Bible study group, a social gathering or a hobby club. You need a group whose purpose is *support*—adult children helping each other recover from the trauma of divorced homes.

Look, too, for a group that is doing more than just sharing war stories. It's very important in the healing process for people to share what has happened in their lives and how they're currently processing life. But sometimes groups focus *only* on sharing the past and no one ever lifts them out of the pit. In a sense, they're just pooling their pain.

Look for a group which gets input from other sources. It could be from books, tapes, videos or outside speakers—resources that will help steer them toward health and healing.

3. A Closed Group

A support group that continually admits new people tends to be shallow, because it takes several weeks for people to develop trust and be willing to be vulnerable. A group that is closed to new members will more likely be intimate and supportive. This may sound unfriendly, but it's necessary for the special purpose around which you are organized. You may agree to open it up to new people at the end of a half-year or so, but be aware that the dynamics will change. Don't allow a constant shuffle of members, or the safety and depth of sharing will disappear.

4. Structural Details

The group may be a great match for you in many ways, but it may not fit your structure. Ideally, look for a group that matches your life in many of the following areas: where they meet, the time, day and length of meetings, and goals. It's also important to ask: How is the leadership handled? Will there be outside homework? Are visitors allowed? And how does the group view confidentiality?

Be Realistic

There are no perfect groups and no perfect matches. But look for a group that comes close to what you want. Don't expect perfection—you'll never find it. On the other hand, don't get stuck in just any group if it doesn't fit; move on and try another group. (Appendix B lists organizations that can help you find a support group in your area.)

I really believe it's impossible to heal ourselves. We need other people to help us in a variety of ways. We may need a medical doctor for a good physical checkup. We may need a counselor who can steer us through some of the most difficult areas of our recovery. We need the support of several individual friends who love us and care for us. In addition, we need a small sharing group of people who are traveling the same recovery road we are, willing to listen to our stories of anguish and disillusionment, able to accept the worst within us, and wanting to encourage us to keep on going in the healing process.

Should I Start a Support Group?

"Whoa! Wait a minute," you say. "You've barely convinced me that I should get into a recovery group, and now you're suggesting I should start one."

I don't mean that everybody who reads this book should start a support group. I do believe, however, that everyone can be trained to lead a group. Part of that training means you have participated in a recovery group, you know how a good group works, and you have seen from the inside out how people can be healed through a recovery group. So these next comments are really directed toward people who have already been a part of a successful care group.

Isn't it great that someone had the vision and concern to provide a recovery group for you to experience? Wouldn't it be great if you could give that opportunity to some other person who is looking for healing and hope? Many organizations would be glad to train, coach and support you so that you and a second trained person could launch a support group.

In appendix A, I have provided some basic coaching about how to start a support group. In that section you'll find information about how to get started, covenants, structures and potential problems. It certainly is not a complete training manual on how to start and run a small group, but perhaps it will whet your appetite and reduce your fear, so that you might be willing to offer yourself to some organization as a future leader for recovery groups.

Perhaps the strongest reason for you to start a group is that you know several other people like yourself who would benefit from a group. Maybe you could take the first step by giving them each a copy of this book. Ask if they would like to talk about the book on a regular basis. Then see what develops.

If someone has helped you toward healing, consider some way you might offer that gift of healing to some other hurting people.

14
Step Four:
Remembering
Your Past

IT WAS MY FIRST VISIT TO MY COUNSELOR'S OF-
fice. I'd chosen him because he specialized in helping people from dysfunctional families. He knew something about me because of my writings and
my teaching at a nearby seminary, but he wasn't aware of my family
dysfunction.

He asked what I hoped to get out of the counseling sessions. I explained
to him, "Most of my adult life I've been involved in helping people with their
problems. But now I'm not able to handle the problems in my own life."

I told him, "I want to control people, I don't trust people, and I have a
huge reservoir of anger inside me that I constantly 'sit on' for fear it will
explode." I continued, "I struggle with lust, perfectionism and competitiveness. I'm afraid to be known to other people other than for my accomplishments. From time to time I also struggle with life-threatening depres-

sion, and I've found myself growing increasingly cynical about people, life and God."

Then I grinned at him and said, "Earl, heal me!" He threw back his head with a hearty chuckle. He adjusted his massive, teddy bear frame on the couch, rubbed his hands together and said, "Well, let's see what we can do."

Earl is a warm, loving man about fifteen years younger than I am. He came from an alcoholic and divorced home. Dysfunction isn't simply theory to him. He's been there.

I said, "Well, let's get started. What do we do?" I jokingly went on to remind him that part of my problem is that I want to control everything, even during counseling. He looked at me with a big grin and said, "I understand. I can handle it."

Then he explained, "In order to heal your list of problems, you have to get in touch with your past—your childhood. You must work at remembering your family life and be willing to re-live some of those experiences."

You've Got to Be Kidding!

I covered the anger I felt by laughing. "Why in the world would I want to get in touch with my past? I've spent my whole life trying to forget it. In fact, I've so effectively denied my past, large blocks of time from my childhood and teenage years are totally gone. Now you're asking me to dredge that up? Why would I want to experience that pain? Isn't it better just to go on from where I am? Just heal me as I am, Earl. I want help, but I don't want to be dragged back through that slime."

I had been reading dozens of books about dysfunctional families, codependence, shame and various forms of addiction. All of a sudden the words of Pia Mellody reached out and grabbed me:

I tell every patient I treat, "The secret of your recovery is to learn to embrace your own history. Look at it, become aware of it, and experience your feelings about the less-than-nurturing events of your past. Because if you don't, the issues from your history will be held in minimization, denial, and delusion, and truly be demons you are not aware of."

More directly I tell my patients, "Hug your demons or they will bite you in the ass." In other words, "If you do not embrace what is dysfunctional, you are doomed to repeat it and stay in the pain."[1]

Meet Major Pain

I began to realize that I was in for major pain. I felt trapped. I was either going to keep on trying to deny the dysfunction of my emotionally divorced parents and all the damage that had resulted—or I was going to look at those childhood experiences and feel those feelings again. I felt like a loser either way.

I looked at Earl's face for a long time. I wasn't sure I wanted to do what he was asking me to do. Earl was kind. He waited quietly; his face said, "I understand your hurt. I know you're afraid to go back." I'm sure my sad face told him what I was about to say. Finally I pleaded, "Isn't there some other way, Earl?"

He shook his head and said gently, "Jim, you need to get in touch with the child that's in you. You need to look at those childhood experiences with your adult insight. Those unhealed childhood memories have to be healed. It's not going to be easy, but you've tried to handle those feelings by denial and that hasn't worked. You've attempted to block out your feelings, but they keep bubbling up in anger, in perfectionism, in your desire to control people."

We both sat quietly for a few moments. Then he said, "Let's go back and find that crying, hurt child within you and feel those feelings again. Let's work to heal those feelings."

I protested again. "Earl, I'm not sure that I want you to know me the way I really am. I would rather have you respect me for all my accomplishments rather than know about the hurts and imperfections in my life."

Again Earl's face took on that warm, caring, understanding look as he said, "I know. I've been there. It's frightening. But I won't abandon you. Let's try it."

The Terrible Saturday

"What I'd like you to do," Earl said, "is to close your eyes and let your mind wander freely through your childhood. Don't force yourself to think in any direction. Just give your mind permission to roam around in your childhood. Pick out any event where you were hurt, sad or lonely. Look for a specific time when the little boy within you needed to be understood."

I turned my mind loose and felt as if it were a giant computer, flipping through event after event to pick out some of the more painful experiences. Soon it picked out three or four. My mind kept going around and around those particular events, and then it chose one. Earl told me later that at that moment my expression changed. A look of grief spread over my face, and I flushed red.

"Now tell me what happened." Earl said. "With your eyes closed, describe the incident as you remember it—as a little boy."

"It was that horrible Saturday morning." I told him. "It had been coming for a week. It was the morning my brother and I were to get a beating from my father, with a one-by-two-inch board about eighteen inches long.

"I know the exact size of the board because six days earlier my father had put it on the corner of the kitchen counter right near the doorway. He said, 'On Saturday morning you're going to get a spanking.' Every time we went in or out of the house all week, that board stared us in the face. And we clearly knew that 'spanking' was not really the right word. It was going to be a pants-down-lie-over-the-edge-of-the-bed *beating*.

"The cause of the beating was that we had disobeyed our parents. They went off to church on Sunday night. We were left home with Mrs. Ranch, who lived with us. While she was in the living room, my brother and I took her flashlight and went out into the back yard to look for fishing worms. We knew that when the ground was wet, an hour or two after dark, worms would come up to the surface of the grass and were easy to pick up. We would store them in our dirt box for the next time we'd go fishing.

"But we had trouble making the flashlight work. Even though we tapped it and jiggled it, it wouldn't stay on. We decided maybe something was wrong inside, so we took it apart. It was very dark outside, and we needed the light of the flashlight to help us repair the flashlight!

" 'Oh, oh, I dropped something.' Each of us started feeling around, trying to find the part, but it was gone. We just couldn't find it. 'We better get back inside,' I said. 'Mom and Dad'll be home soon.' So we put the flashlight back together as well as we could and went inside to bed.

"Mrs. Ranch discovered that her flashlight didn't work when she went to bed that night. And our parents figured out that we must have been the ones fooling around with it since a part was missing.

"That's where the board comes in. We were brought into the kitchen that evening and confronted with the broken flashlight. After we'd confessed that we'd been out in the back yard, we had disobeyed our parents, and we had lost the part, my father got the board and said, 'I don't have time to give you a spanking now, but next Saturday morning you're going to get it. I'll set this board here where you can see it. I want you to realize what you've done wrong. Saturday you're going to get punished for it.'

"Saturday came, and I was the first one to get the beating. I was a compliant child, so I pulled my pants down and leaned over the edge of the bed while my almost six-foot, two-hundred-pound father, with the build of a football player, gave me his 'spanking.'

"When my beating was done, I stumbled into our big closet, sobbing uncontrollably. I screamed silently, 'I hate you! I hate you! I hate you!' I wished that my father did not exist or that I did not exist.

"By this time my brother was getting his beating. But my brother was not compliant. Yes, he pulled his pants down, but after the first blow smashed across his buttocks, he fought back. That only angered my father more, and so my brother was beaten all over his body.

"The eternity passed, and my brother was next to me in the closet where we had both gone for refuge. My father stood in the doorway continuing his lecture, as if we needed more convincing that he was the boss—he was in control."

Why Remembering Your Past Helps

It was a strange feeling. I was sitting in Earl's office, but I was also in that closet weeping. I was embarrassed as I sat before Earl with my eyes closed, crying. How could an event which happened almost fifty years ago still draw such emotion out of me? I could feel my anger again. I could feel the board hitting me. I could see my father's angry face. I could hear myself internally yelling, "I hate you!"

Then Earl gently said to me, "Now don't open your eyes. Keep that scene in your mind. You and your brother are in the closet, your father is outside the door, and he has just finished his lecture to both of you. I want you as an adult man to go into that room and tell me what you would do or say *now* if you were to walk into that situation."

I told Earl, "I'd go over to my father and say to him, 'This beating is totally uncalled-for. You are way out of bounds. There is no connection whatsoever between the degree of the offense and the punishment you just administered. You are absolutely wrong.' "

Then Earl said, "What else would you do?"

I responded, "I would turn my back on him, walk into the closet and comfort those two boys. I'd say, 'Yes, what you did was wrong, but the beating you just received was also wrong.' Next I would tell those boys, 'Jesus is not like this man at all. He loves you. He doesn't want you to do things that are wrong, but he loves you.' "

Then, with my eyes closed, I told Earl I saw myself putting my arms around the boys, hugging them and assuring them that I'm with them. "It's okay, I'll protect you."

Then I just sat, silently remembering the scene as an adult.

After a long time Earl gently said, "It's okay, Jim, it's okay. It's all right to feel the experience you've just gone through. The process is painful, but it's helpful."

I was embarrassed to look up at Earl. My face was flushed. Tears were running down my cheek. My emotions were going in two different directions: I felt so much compassion for the two little boys and so much anger at the man who had beaten them so harshly.

I told Earl, "You are the first human being to hear my feelings of what happened on that Saturday morning."

The Awesome Slide
Maybe some of you reading this book are saying to yourselves the same thing I said: "I don't want to go through that muck." But let me assure you, remembering your past and telling your story to another human being is transforming. You gain a completely new perspective on the event so that the fear, loneliness, sadness and anger are reduced. The pain of my "terrible Saturday" memory is much less acute since I faced it and talked about it that day with Earl.

Do you recall that giant slide at school when you were a kid? Remember when you finally got up your courage, or were taunted enough by the other kids, to finally climb to the top of that slide? As you looked down, your greatest fears were realized. That slide was *awesome!*

Finally the kid behind you pushed, and it seemed that you dropped straight down twenty feet before the slide began to level out, shooting you out into the sand pile. It was terrifying. The point is, if you've never seen that slide as an adult, the slide still holds that child's image of terror in your mind.

I remember watching our kids transform a slide in their minds. There was this awesome slide in a park in Newton, Kansas, where we lived when they were little. After a great deal of pain and fear, they all learned to go down that frightening slide.

Years later when the girls were older, we visited Newton again. The girls wanted to visit the park and see the huge slide. They were amazed. The slide was only six feet high, and the angle of it seemed embarrassingly tame. They all laughed and told about the fears they had carried in their minds. Until that very moment it had remained the awesome slide of their childhood, but facing it when they were older eliminated the terror.

The Truth Will Set You Free

When you remember your past and tell the story again, you are reducing that childhood definition and the fears. You have an opportunity now to step back into that scene and give an adult perspective or correction. You have an opportunity to comfort that child as I did little "Jimmy" and his brother.

In the process you as an adult are transformed. You move beyond the shame and secrecy that have kept you in bondage. You also move through the denial as you acknowledge the truth about what happened. Remember, "You will know the truth and the truth will set you free."[2] It is important to get adult truth about your childhood experiences.

Telling your story breaks the cycle of silence that keeps the hurt alive and publicly identifies you as a person working on your bad memories of the past. Telling your story makes it possible for you:

☐ to get understanding and help from other people
☐ to get in touch with your feelings

☐ to hear your story aloud for perhaps the first time
☐ to become more strongly in charge of your life
☐ to loosen the grip of old pains on your life

It's Not Easy to Remember Your Past
It's hard to tell someone else your story because children growing up in dysfunctional families have very poor models of communication. My parents talked about business, but they didn't talk about their marriage or family relationships. So it was absolutely unthinkable to me that I would ever tell anyone else how I felt about the beating.

Children from divorced homes have been raised in an environment of secrecy, denial, anger or fighting. There's an urgency to always keep a lid on things. Now you're being asked by your recovery group and your counselor to remember your past and talk about it. The very process of remembering and sharing is absolutely opposed to all of your background and training.

Prepare for the Result of Remembering
I walked out of Earl's office, got into my car and sat there for awhile. I was absolutely exhausted—totally drained. I felt as if I had vomited and had diarrhea at the same time. I felt empty inside. Yes, I was glad I finally had been able to tell someone, but I didn't like being so vulnerable. And I was still shocked at the impact that old memory had on me.

On the drive home I began to criticize myself. "Why aren't you stronger? Why couldn't you handle this problem yourself? After all, you're a trained counselor. You've read dozens of books on this subject." I went into a terrible downward spiral of self-recrimination. I really *was* as bad as I thought I was!

When I got back to my office, I began to realize how raw and naked my nerves were. Within half an hour I had picked a fight with Sally. I realize now that I was projecting onto Sally my anger toward my father and mother.

I was unable to go back to my writing tasks. I just wanted to be left alone. Finally I quit working and simply spent some time by myself.

It was about two days before I began to feel better. At first I didn't want to continue counseling because I didn't feel this process of remembering my past was worth the agony. Every time I found myself feeling grumpy with myself or anyone else, I became more angry at myself.

But after a few sessions with Earl, I noticed I wasn't continually depressed any more. Yes, I experienced a dip after every counseling session, but I could see the deep-seated depression was lifting between sessions.

So, prepare yourself. Your remembering will produce some changes. You will probably experience an emotional drop, and things may seem worse right after you've gone through an episode of remembering your past, but keep on encouraging yourself—you are healing.

Appendix C will give you additional help in how to choose a counselor.

Please, Just Try to Hit the Bowl

It's been helpful for me to compare my "remembering the past" process to going to the dentist. On my first visit, he tells me the bad news: "You've got some cavities. You ought to let me put on a crown to protect one tooth that is cracking."

Then he sets up the appointments. The next sessions with him are sheer agony. He jabs that "twelve-foot" needle into my gum. All the while he's assuring me this is not going to hurt. (Who isn't it going to hurt—him or me?)

I especially enjoy the needles that go in by my front teeth. It seems I have about a hundred million nerves there, and none of them want to be deadened. So he jabs me again and again, each time telling me, "You really have tough gums."

Then he starts drilling. He uses this giant drill that whirs like an angry bee. It feels as if he's going all the way through my jaw. Then he flushes out my mouth and tells me to spit.

Have you ever tried to spit when your lips are numb? I always feel like a stroke victim as I drool down my chin and all over my shirt sleeve, the arm of the dentist's chair and the floor. Then what's left hits the bowl of swirling water.

Why does the water have to be moving? My head is already spinning, and I have a combined feeling of wanting to vomit and wanting to go to heaven. Finally he stuffs my tooth with a temporary filling and says, "I want to see you in a week."

This process of being stabbed, drilled, ground and fitted goes on for several weeks. Then I get my last little bit of bite adjustment. I also get my teeth cleaned. Only then do I look in the mirror and say, "Well, it was worth it."

In a sense, that's the remembering process. You must keep saying to yourself, "It's worth it." As you go through each cycle of pain—experience it, step into it and feel it for all it's worth. Remember your adult perspective is going to change that pain. Also remember that your small care group, your counselor and God are all going to walk with you through that pain.

Cautions about Remembering
There's a fine line that needs to be drawn here. It's important to talk about an event as much as you need to, so that your feelings are fully aired. At the same time, be careful about "wallowing" in one particular experience. Sometimes telling the same story over and over again is an excuse for not going on to probe other areas, or an excuse not to work at a resolution of the painful episode. Sometimes people are so relieved to be able to remember certain painful experiences that they keep rehashing these incidents rather than moving on to new, yet undiscovered ones.

Another danger is that after children from divorced homes have finally been able to open up and share their feelings, they begin to share them with everyone. Not everyone can handle what you have to share.

Limit your first sharing to your support group and your counselor. If you start to share what you're feeling with people in the supermarket or the church foyer, they might feel that you are rather odd. And they will not know how to help you process those deep wounds of the past.

One further caution. A few days after you have gone through a remembering experience, you'll start to feel just great—almost euphoric—and you'll begin to think, "I feel so good, I must be healed."

It may be true that you are healed in that one memory area, but you are not recovered from the total impact your parents' divorce has had on your personality and behaviors. It's important, as AA says, to "take one day at a time." It may be a good day or a bad day, but just take it and live it. Tomorrow is another day with another opportunity for growth.

Refusing to Remember Your Past

Why would anyone deny that there was fighting and disagreement? Why would anyone ignore, as I did, that my mother was emotionally, verbally, and intellectually abused all of her married life by my father?

Very bluntly, denial has helped me to live—to survive. It has also helped me to live with my guilt. If I really knew what was going on, then maybe I should have stepped in and done something. But my mother was also denying. If she knew what was going on, maybe *she* should have done something. So it's a giant conspiracy of silence among all my relatives: "It didn't happen," or "It's not as bad as it looks," or "No one else needs to know that now."

Another reason for my denial: I feel that if I pretend it doesn't exist, then it doesn't exist. And if it doesn't exist, I can't be hurt by it—or so I believe. Unfortunately, that's not true. Every negative or positive thing that happens in our lives has a long-term effect on our personality and behavior.

Past Denial Is Linked with Present Lifestyle

Opening up your past links you to behaviors and attitudes in the present. As you remember pain from the past, you may need to change some of your behaviors in the present. This is not easy, but it is extremely helpful.

As I have stopped denying the truth of my parental family, I have been able to see that I have duplicated with my wife and our three daughters some of the same patterns I so despise in my parents.

I've been a controlling person with my family, so much so that I have stifled some of their individuality. I have always wanted to be right, always to be logical. Anytime there was a disagreement, it was always settled by my oppressive demands for being logical. I used logic to outmaneuver the rest of the family.

As I came to understand how my parents had shamed and neglected me, I saw those same patterns in myself. I confessed to Sally just a few weeks ago that all of our married life I have waited for her to make mistakes so that I could pounce on those mistakes to prove her wrong. Somehow that helped me feel superior. Yet I despised that trait in my father. (Let me point out that my dad was himself just following patterns his own background had taught *him;* he probably didn't even realize where his need to be right and to control came from.)

My mother was not built up or encouraged by my father. Instead she was constantly belittled and told she was inferior. Indirectly, I was sometimes doing the very same thing to my wife.

My Parents Will Get Together

Breaking the strangle hold of denial on your life does not happen all at once. Being in a secure environment with a trusted counselor and a recovery group will give your unconscious self the freedom to begin to let loose of denial.

Denial has been your protection. It may have saved your life. You pretended that your parents didn't fight, that your dad wasn't actually threatening to walk out. Even after they were legally divorced, you may have pretended that it never happened.

Almost all children from a divorced family believe that somehow, someday, their parents are going to get back together. That's denial. It is the protection that helps children make it through. Yet it blocks you from being a healthy adult. Denial also puts you in the position of keeping the family secrets—of protecting your parents. Only as you begin to get healthy will you realize that your parents should have been protecting you, not you protecting your parents.

Anger: Friend and Foe

Many adult children of divorce think in extremes, with no middle ground. People and events are either all good or all bad; they're all nice or all nasty. This extremism is part of our perfectionism. We know how things should be, and we know how people should act. When people don't perform exactly as we expect, we tend to label the situation or the person as hopeless. When things don't function the way we imagine they should, we feel cheated. We think life is totally unfair, and we get angry.

Because we've been raised in a home that taught us not to feel things and not to express anger, we have learned to push anger down. But the conflict between our parents has filled us with shame, and that shame continually feeds our anger.

So our little child within is left with a double message. On the one hand, we have these feelings: disappointment, loss, shame, anger. On the other hand, we are trained not to express our true feelings. When our emotions are stuffed down for a long time, our anger continues to grow. The only way we can handle the confusing and conflicting emotions and messages is to feel nothing. So we become numb.

I've told Sally on a number of occasions that I don't think I love anybody or anything. I feel like ground meat with no form, shape or identity. To cope with my anger, sadly, I've shut down everything, including feelings of love.

Anger has many uses. It helps us protect ourselves or our loved ones. It may provide us with the emotional energy and drive we need to make a decision or to finish a project.

Anger can also be used to control other people or situations. In my home my parents used anger to control the children. Sometimes anger is also used to bolster a low self-image or cover up emotions such as fear, guilt or depression. Anger can be used to divert attention from one person's problems by focusing on the shortcomings of another.

Anger can also be your friend. It is working *for* you when it gives you the courage to finally remember your past. You should go ahead and let anger help you express your true feelings. Your counselor can be trusted to keep confidential what you share.

As you begin to remember your past, you will experience a wide range of feelings. There'll be times when you feel sad, abandoned, lonely, depressed, happy, angry, proud or ashamed. Feel those feelings. Tell your counselor or small group what you are feeling and what particular part of your remembering causes you to feel that way.

For too many years you have been splitting yourself into two people by denying and repressing your feelings. One part of you has a wide range of feelings yet never gets to speak, while the other, more dominant reasoning part of you controls everything. It's time to remember your past, and let those two people within you become friends.

How to Remember Your Past

Because each person is unique, each of us will find different ways of remembering. Let's look at some common methods that have helped me and other adult children of divorce remember our past.

1. Verbally Tell Your Story. You may tell your story to a trusted friend, to your counselor or to your small recovery group. Wherever you do it, telling the story, as we've mentioned before, is an important method to get in touch with your child within and heal those memories which resulted from your parents' legal or emotional divorce.

2. Write about Your Experiences. Sometimes it's hard for people to get started, so you might begin by writing part of your family history. List some of the events and experiences as you remember them. Later on you might want to write about your feelings as a little child living within the family. Another time you might write about how you coped with life or about some of the family secrets.

As you're writing you may come to things that are very difficult, painful or humiliating. Keep on writing! You don't have to share them with anyone if you don't choose to, but writing them honestly will help the healing process.

When you get stuck in the writing process because the feelings or emotions are too sensitive, write about that. You might get unstuck if you write, "I don't want to write about this because I don't think I ought to be talking about my parents this way. After all, it wasn't all their fault. It was my fault too." Keep writing. Frequently, as you continue to write, you'll break through that area of denial into a new area of exploration.

3. Guided Regression. Your counselor can help you through the process of walking back into your past. It is called regression. I have described one of those sessions in my life as Earl walked me back into the Saturday when I was beaten.

The strength of a loving, supportive relationship with a trained professional can give you the courage and freedom to talk about childhood areas which you might feel unable to bring up with others.

4. Reading Books and Articles. Self-help books have been a powerful tool in my life. They have helped me understand that I am not some strange "weirdo." Rather, I am acting exactly as would be expected for an adult out of an emotionally divorced home. These books also trigger my memory and give me fresh insights that help in my journey of healing.

5. Normal Life Events. Sometimes a smell I despise will trigger off a memory of a traumatic experience when I felt sad or alone. Or someone touches me in a way that reminds me of a parental touch. Suddenly I'm transported back into my childhood.

Thousands of things can happen in your daily life to activate a flashback. You may see a movie, a TV program, a magazine cover, a child on a bicycle. Don't deny the flashback. Don't push it away. Let it teach you. Your mind is reaching out and asking for healing. Let the process take place.

Big Changes

Anytime you experience a major change in your life, no matter whether it is positive or negative, you are opened up in a new way for learning. You experience what is called a "teachable moment." If you move, lose a friend or family member through death, have a major illness or change jobs, you are ripe to learn.

If you get married, get a divorce, have a child, win the lottery or totally demolish your car—whatever the event—you must say to yourself, "I am now in a new learning curve. What can I learn now about my childhood? How can I move along one more step on my road to recovery?"

One final caution. Slow down and take time to think and feel. Let God, things you read, current everyday events, and life's changes probe your mind and feelings. Remember, this is a process. Your healing will be speeded up—as you slow down.

15

Step Five:
Grieving
Your Losses

IT WAS SIX-THIRTY ON A TUESDAY MORN-
ing. John, Dennis and I were sitting around my dining room table, sharing
breakfast and talking about life. These guys are my small group.

We had hugged each other and joked about how difficult it was to get
going in the morning. But now it was time for the serious stuff. "How are
things going in your life?"

I told them I felt I had been ripped off. "Why did I have to be raised by
a mother who herself was abused and didn't instinctively know how to
draw the best out of children? Why was I stuck with a father who never
loved my mother and arranged to be gone from us as much as possible
It was just so unfair."

Then, because they were listening with openness and caring, I decided
to really get honest and risk telling them some specifics.

I explained that when I was growing up my father always seemed to be at work. During World War 2 he worked twelve-hour shifts, seven nights a week in a factory. It was a tough time—the country was just coming out of the Depression and he had four kids to feed. Our paths didn't cross all week long. It was as if I were being raised by a single parent. The routine was disrupted only on Sunday when we went to church together.

All during my childhood I never felt a bonding with my father. To me he was an authoritarian figure whom I did my best to please. Mostly I did this by keeping out of his way. Unknowingly, I was following my father's pattern of avoidance. I avoided him. I avoided my mother. I also avoided thinking about how uncomfortable they were with each other. I simply thought, that's the way a family is. You just try to stay out of each other's way. Yes, I slept at home. I ate meals there. But there was no involvement in each other's lives. I felt we were strangers living under the same roof.

Who Was This Man?

When I was about fourteen, my father said to me, "It's time we got to know each other. I want to take you fishing in Canada." My reaction was very mixed. One part of me was extremely excited about the adventure of going to Canada, of finally getting to do what the men in our family had done each year for as long as I could remember. But the other part of me wondered, "Why the sudden interest?"

My father bought me a rod and reel and I spent every free moment on our long gravel driveway, practicing my casting. I got so good that nine out of ten times I could put my lead sinker into a two-foot circle seventy-five feet away. I practiced so much that I wore out the fishing line on the gravel.

It was a great trip with my father, mother and brother. My sisters were left at home because they were too young to enjoy it.

We stayed in a cabin on the edge of a lake in Ontario. The air was wonderfully clear compared to the factory smoke in Cleveland. And the night was without city lights. Wow, the stars were magnificent!

Each day we'd take our rented motorboat out on this very large lake, filled with hundreds of islands. We had to remember the landmarks because it was easy to get lost.

We fished around islands of magnificent beauty. Then at noon we would beach the boat on an uninhabited island, without another boat in sight, and cook our fish over an open fire for lunch. My father was more relaxed than usual and seemed proud of both of us boys when we landed a fish and helped with the work.

The trip was great. But soon it was over, and we were back home where life fell into the same old routine of avoidance. My father and uncle were starting a new business, so my father was gone from home even more than before.

Over the following years I realized that that week in Canada had been my father's attempt to make up for his absentee fathering of all the years before.

I asked my group that morning, "How does a one-week fishing trip make up for fourteen years of being gone?"

Why the Crying?

Then I told them what happened a few years later as I left Ohio to head off for college in Kansas. Strangely, my father cried when I went. I wondered why at the time. He hadn't seemed to want to be around me before. Why would he cry when I left? As I think of that moment now, I believe he loved me, but he didn't know how to help me feel loved instead of afraid of him.

College was great for me. I came into a new relationship with God, who became my Father. For the first time in my life I felt I was a person. I believed I had meaning and value, people accepted me, and life was worth living, not just enduring.

One summer day when I was home from college after my freshman year, my father and I started to talk person to person for the first time I can remember. I told him what was happening in college and how I was growing and changing. He was glad that college was a good experience for me. Earlier in his life he had felt called into the ministry but had not responded, so he was glad I was going into the ministry. It felt really good to be able to talk with him.

I also had been gaining insight into myself—and my family. But I didn't share that with him. I was afraid he would be angry. I realized that I had survived in the family by being invisible, by not making waves.

Cut from the Same Fabric

My brother, however, was always running up against my father. My father couldn't seem to control him and said he had "too much of his mother's blood in him."

In some ways my mother and my brother were the same. My mother did what my father wanted her to do outwardly, but she never yielded to him emotionally. It was the only way she could protect herself from his bullying, controlling tactics. She would pull back into her shell as if to say, "I'll do what you want me to do on the outside, but there's no way that you can control my inner person."

My brother had some of that same spirit, only he wouldn't even outwardly do what my father wanted him to do. So there was always war.

As my father and I talked that warm summer day, I said, "You know, you've missed it with me because you've never really been a father to me. Now you have a chance with my brother. Work on it, before it's too late."

That remark was not said in anger, but it stung him very deeply, especially because I, Jim, the compliant one, had said it. No one ever dared to tell my father the truth about himself. Surprisingly, he just turned and walked away from me. I saw his large body begin to convulse and shake. He was *crying*—for the second time.

I related all this to my two friends, Dennis and John, across my breakfast table. Their faces told the story. They felt my sadness and my grief. They felt the little boy within me wanting to have a loving relationship with a dad instead of trying to be invisible. They felt my fear of irritating a frightening authority figure.

John looked at me and said, "Then you felt alone all of your childhood, didn't you?"

"No, John, I've felt alone *all my life*. I've never really been sure that anybody in the world likes me for who I am and not just for what I do. In fact, I'm afraid right now that as I tell you this story, you guys might pull back and say, 'How disgusting!' "

But I didn't need to worry. When we finished talking and sharing that morning, we put our arms around each other's shoulders as if we were in a mini-football huddle and prayed for each other. These guys really did love me.

Why Grieve?

Whenever we have lost something very important to us or have not received what we expected, needed or wanted, we feel pain and unhappiness. Feeling this pain or loss is called "grieving."

When we allow ourselves to feel the painful losses and share those feelings with a supportive individual or group, we are doing what is called "grief work." So if you ask the question as I did, "Why should I grieve?", here are a few answers.

1. You need to grieve *so that your grief won't fester* like a deep wound that never heals. Unresolved grief is like a cancer that spreads to other parts of your body. You can't just forget cancer. Nor can you forget that you have experienced losses in your life. You can't simply dismiss your grief. You need to face it, feel it and talk about it—so that it can be resolved.

Unresolved grief produces such things as "chronic anxiety, tension, fear or nervousness, anger or resentment, sadness, emptiness, unfulfillment, confusion, guilt, shame or, as is common among many who grew up in a troubled family, a feeling of numbness or 'no feeling at all.' "[1]

2. As an adult, *you are able now to handle* the terrible feelings from your childhood. When you were a child you buried your grief because, if you didn't, you might have been destroyed by the intense pain of what was happening to you. It was a way of surviving in your dysfunctional family.

However, now you're an adult. You can go back and re-live those experiences you had as a child. You can feel those emotions again. You are re-living those feelings from the secure position of an adult who is not going to be destroyed by the memories. Now you can grieve as an adult surrounded by supportive friends and counselors.

3. By telling your story and allowing yourself to feel those feelings again, *you gain a new perspective* on your loss. A wonderful transformation is allowed to take place. That awesome slide of your childhood is now viewed with adult eyes. It no longer terrorizes you. So it is with your past. It was horrible. It is still painful. But facing those childhood griefs as an adult helps you to transform them because of your adult perspective. Now

you have the capacity to resolve that grief—no longer is it a terror to your life.

4. Grieving *enables you to relate to other people* instead of running from them. Adult children of divorce tend to condemn themselves whenever relationships don't work out. We feel it is our fault—something is basically wrong with us. We fail to realize it is the unfinished business from our troubled parental home that is causing our present problems. We bury this unfinished business, but repeatedly it erupts in our relationships as we try to control life, or we get angry over seemingly small things, or we basically mistrust people.

The way we adult children handle the problem is to say, "I'm at fault. It's never going to work with this person, so I'll try somebody else. Maybe I can make it work next time." We totally ignore the cancer that keeps spreading and destroying our relationships. Grieving with friends, then, becomes the road back to good relationships.

5. When you grieve, *you learn to feel again.* In an average family, people express a wide range of feelings—from deep discouragement and unhappiness to great exhilaration and joy. But in the dysfunctional family, children are taught not to feel negative feelings. Only positive feelings are acceptable.

Our range of feelings is cut down to about one-fourth of what the normal person feels. Our parents teach us in many ways, "Don't talk about negative feelings because that's a put-down on our family." All the while we're told, it's okay to feel anything that is positive—but not *too* positive because, "Who are you to enjoy life, when all the rest of us feel so miserable?"

Remember my question to Earl, "Why should I remember my past? Why should I feel those feelings again? Why should I grieve?" The answer is that, without grief, unresolved childhood anxieties continue like a spreading malignancy, gradually taking over all of our personhood.

What Is "Grief Work"?

Let's review a bit. Please remember that every loss, in whatever form, produces an unhappiness or pain within us. When we allow ourselves to *feel* those pains and unhappinesses, we call that "grieving." When we say we are doing "grief work" or "grieving," it means that we are identifying and facing our loss and allowing ourselves to feel all the emotions associated with it. "Grief work" also means that we are adapting and changing our adult life to include losses as part of our life.

It's also important to remember that every loss has a direct negative effect on our self-esteem. Loss causes us to feel crummy, to feel smaller, to feel cheated. Every time we ignore the feelings of our loss, we are building a larger and more putrid cesspool of negative self-esteem.

Much of this takes place on an unconscious level. And there is no sense of time there. Therefore, "An ungrieved loss remains forever alive in our unconscious."[2]

An additional point to remember is that all of these accumulated losses from the past set patterns for the future. For example, my parents neglected me as a child. Because I hadn't "grieved" that loss, I grew up expecting that everyone would abandon me sooner or later.

Stages of Grief

The grieving process is more than just saying to yourself, "Oh, yeah, my parents fought all the time." Or, "My dad was mean." Or, "My mother was a bossy, controlling person." Or, "My parents had a messy legal divorce."

You need to go through the following normal stages as you grieve your losses.

Stage One: Shock

Often, as adult children begin to remember what has happened to them, they say to themselves, "This is unbelievable!" You may be shocked at some of the painful memories which you have totally blocked out for years and years.

Stage Two: Denial

A shocking remembrance frequently is followed by denial. "That couldn't really have happened to me. My family isn't really worse than anyone else's. How can I even think such bad thoughts of my parents?" Sometimes a person will get stuck here because he or she fears that maybe even more dreadful things lie buried.

The denial barrier will be put up because it's just too much to handle.

If you get stuck for a while, it's okay; you're not a bad person. Just keep working on whatever you can. When your mind is ready, that memory will pop up again.

Stage Three: Grief

During this stage of feeling the loss, you likely will experience some of the following:

- ☐ being preoccupied with remembering losses
- ☐ wishing that it were different
- ☐ feeling aimless
- ☐ feeling lost
- ☐ being unable to function in normal activities
- ☐ feeling that time is suspended
- ☐ wondering if life will be worth living again
- ☐ feeling that life isn't real
- ☐ being afraid you're going crazy
- ☐ crying
- ☐ being angry
- ☐ feeling guilty
- ☐ feeling shame
- ☐ feeling helplessness
- ☐ being depressed
- ☐ feeling hopeless

Grieving is a process with many different emotions. Keep reminding yourself, "It's okay to feel these jumbled feelings." For a time you may feel you are emotionally moving away from your family and, indeed, you may need to disconnect for a time in order to have a healthy reconnection when you are stronger.

Stage Four: Integration

The loss, having been fully felt, is now absorbed, or integrated, into your personality as either a negative or a positive.

Positive Integration. If you accept your loss as a fact of life, you will have a deeper, more mature view of yourself. Those losses actually contribute to a positive uniqueness in your character.

Crying is now reduced. Self-esteem is more positive. The focus is on your present and future instead of your past. Life is now seen as more positive because of the lessons you have learned and the new growth you have experienced.

Negative Integration. In this situation, the person is unable to accept the loss as beneficial and has a continuing sense of depression and diminished self-esteem.

The personality now reorganizes around this loss as a persisting source of pain. There is an unspoken expectation that because the person has been cheated in the past, he or she likely will experience similar losses in the future. The stories are continually retold and the person is always waiting to be disappointed again.[3]

Feeling these many emotions of grieving, and then talking or writing about them, will drain away the harmful effects of the losses you've experienced.

Secondary Losses

In addition to the losses within my parental family, I also found it necessary to grieve the secondary losses that resulted from the first losses. I was jolted again and again as I realized that, unconsciously, I had been set up to be a controlling person, to not trust people and to be a perfectionist.

I was humiliated and depressed as I began to realize how I had let my wife and children down. Our marriage had experienced a series of losses because I came into the marriage as an adult child from an emotionally divorced home. In our early married years I wouldn't listen to get Sally's opinion. I knew what was right.

Everywhere I turned I saw the effect—in my job, my relationships with people, my evaluation of life events, my view of myself and my relationship with God.

My insides were a mixture of jumbled emotions. I felt sometimes as if my brain and my feelings were like tennis shoes inside a tumble dryer, banging and thumping, tossed and mixed with all the other clothes.

For me, grieving all the losses caused in my adult life was far more difficult than remembering my childhood pain. Many, many times, as I've looked at the pervasive results of my childhood deprivation on my adult life, I have wished I could just slip out of this life and go to heaven.

New Losses

Steps toward positive integration can introduce *new* pain! As soon as I became willing to criticize my father, he moved me into a lower level of acceptance with him. Previous to this, because I was a compliant child and the oldest son, I had been in the number one position. However, when I took a stand against my father—telling the truth and not covering up for him—I found myself suddenly moved to a very distant fourth position. Without telling me, he removed me from being executor of his estate and placed one of my sisters in that position.

In addition, some of the other members of my extended family started distancing themselves from me. They would say, "I hear what you're saying, but I don't feel the same way."

Sandra Wilson reports that adult children of alcoholics frequently feel disloyal for not honoring their parents. She also says that frequently they feel responsible or trapped. Their thinking goes like this: "If I see how bad it is, then I will really have to fix it." She also says that her "clients feel 'orphaned and abandoned.' If the adult child is the only one in the family who has come out of denial and entered recovery, he or she has chosen to construct a new reality based on truth, not denial and deceit. Thus, these individuals have lost their base of attachment to their families. They feel like orphans."[4]

I not only had my loss of a nurturing childhood to contend with, but as an adult I was now being pushed even farther away by my father and subtly pushed away by other extended family members.

Blocks to Grieving

Many of the blocks to grieving are not intentional. In fact, most adult children of a dysfunctional family would say that they are not blocking anything. We have falsely assumed that most people don't remember large chunks of their childhood.

This unconscious blocking process may be related to how the brain functions. A recent study reports:

The ability to tune out feelings like anger and anxiety is reflected in brain function. A recent study of stiff-upper-lip types found they had a lag in the time it took certain information to get from one hemisphere of the brain to the other. The lag was only for disturbing messages, not for neutral ones.

Although experts believe that the repressor personality is rooted in psychological experiences of childhood, the findings on brain function provide a tangible marker of the syndrome. In effect, the brain hampers the conscious registering of negative emotions.[5]
For protection, the child learns to block the intensity and anguish of the home situation, not allowing those negative feelings to be transferred in the brain. Unconsciously the child reasons, "If I don't let this event into my brain, then I don't have to feel it." Unfortunately, as we have said before, everything that happens in our lives is stored in our unconscious and, in some way, affects our life.

It's Easier to Hate

As a child I really liked animals. I felt close to them. I understood some of their moods and feelings. Perhaps that was a partial way of compensating for feeling invisible at home.

My father disliked animals. They were a bother, a waste, a nuisance. On one occasion a litter of kittens crawled into a drainpipe that ran under our garage and emptied onto the slope behind the garage. My father closed off the exit to the drain and turned on the water hose, filling the drainpipe so that all the kittens drowned.

My close feeling to animals changed one day as I sat at my second-floor bedroom window, watching the traffic go by on the street below. Suddenly Whitey, our magnificent long-haired, white cat, darted out from the curb. He never made it across the street.

The next morning before my brother and sisters were up, my father told me to take the shovel and scrape Whitey off the street. He had been run over hundreds of times. The temperature was in the teens. He was a large frozen disk. I carefully stuffed him into the garbage can—and I didn't feel a thing.

I had loved that cat so much. I vowed then and there never to love another pet. I decided I would be a "man." I would not feel anything. It was easier just to be like my father and hate all animals. My feelings toward animals were frozen for many years, until Sally and our three daughters helped me enjoy them again.

They Hurt—We Hurt

Human beings are designed to pick up the feelings from people around them. For example, think of a church nursery or a day-care center. All the children are playing happily. Suddenly one gets hurt or feels lonely and starts to cry. The pathetic crying causes all the other children to stop playing and look. Soon other lips begin to quiver and more children start to cry. They are absorbing the feeling of the first child and they join the crying process. Suddenly the whole room is in chaos as attendants rush around, frantically trying to calm all the children.

Absorbing feelings goes on constantly within the home. Children learn values and approaches to life mostly by absorption rather than direct teaching.

Parents think if they fight in another room where the children are not present the kids won't be affected. Wrong! There is an electricity of tension in the home. The child instinctively absorbs the anger, resentment, feelings of betrayal, mistrust, loneliness and isolation that parents think they alone feel. Obviously, the child also spontaneously absorbs the positive, good and happy—those gracious and generous feelings in a healthy home.

If there is an overload of negative feelings, children instinctively learn to block them out of their conscious minds so their lives won't be overwhelmed. Blocked from the conscious mind, these feelings live on timelessly in the unconscious, waiting for a time of grieving. This process of building a wall can continue into adult life, but now, tragically, the wall hampers full adult development.

Don't Feel It

Adult children of divorce frequently block their grieving process by intellectualizing. We talk about the losses as cold facts that occurred in our life, but we don't allow ourselves to feel the loss. Sometimes I'll joke about my past losses, saying to friends or my counselor, "It's better to laugh than to cry." But the intellectualizing and joking are part of a blocking mechanism to avoid the pain.

Sometimes adult children take an "I can handle it by myself" approach. "I'm an adult now, I don't have to feel those childhood feelings. There was bad stuff back there, but forget it; I'm moving on." Unfortunately, our unconscious won't forget it.

Other adult children use alcohol, drugs or over-involvement in a career or a hobby as a way to block thinking and feeling their past. My compulsion or addiction is to keep busy. I like to have my days jam-packed with activity. Then if sad feelings come, I can just bury them in my busy schedule and keep going.

In *Healing the Child Within,* Charles L. Whitfield suggests several thoughts that adult children from dysfunctional families use to block their grieving process. These include:

1. "Yes, my childhood may have been somewhat bad, but my parents did the best they could." So the problem is rationalized away.

2. "My therapist thinks that some bad things happened to me, but they really didn't happen." The loss is viewed as fantasy.

3. "I will be evil or a bad person if I get angry at them." Quoting an authority like the Bible settles the issue: "Honor thy father and thy mother."[6]

I want to comment on this religious blockage before we go on. The Bible nowhere implies that honoring your parents means you do not confront their incorrect ideas or that you must absorb their dysfunctional living.

Jesus as a young boy was in the temple talking with the elders. His parents were worried that he was lost. Mary said, "Son, why have you treated us like this? Your father and I have been anxiously searching for you."

Jesus didn't feel he was dishonoring his parents. In fact, he challenged their error: " 'Why are you searching for me?' he asked. 'Didn't you know I had to be in my Father's house?' "[7]. Mary and Joseph did not understand what he meant and they probably felt that he was out of place in saying what he did. But Jesus clearly shows us that you can speak the truth about your relationship with your parents and not dishonor them.

The adult child who is not dealing with the loss from childhood generally feels numb toward his or her parents. You may be afraid to think bad things about them. But you're never going to see the *good* in your parents until you've faced the losses. Through the grieving process you can finally come out on the other side and say, "Yes, my parents did things that were bad, but they also did some good things." Then you will have arrived at a position of genuine honor, not just numbness toward them.

4. "If I express my rage, they won't love me." This is the fear of abandonment.

5. "I'll just forgive them." Or, "I've already forgiven them." This assumes that forgiveness can be accomplished without grieving.

How can you forgive your parents if you've never fully faced how their acts or attitudes affected you as a child and are affecting you now? To forgive someone means a wrong was committed that requires forgiveness. We'll look at this issue in more detail in chapter seventeen.

6. "How dare you suggest that my parents could have been bad?"[8] Adult children attack the person who says something was wrong with their parents.

Most of the blocks to the grieving process are not intentional. However, to be healthy, we must begin to identify these blocks that keep us from continuing the grieving process.

I once saw a poster that read, "The truth will set you free, but first it will make you miserable."[9]

How to Grieve

Grieving is a *process* accomplished by allowing our inner selves the months or years needed to face our pain and to allow our past to be transformed.

Let's review the process.

Task #1: Recognize and accept the reality of your losses.

Task #2: Feel the pain, loss, loneliness, abandonment.

Task #3: Accept the reality that you can't go back and reconstruct your past to eliminate those losses. Childhood losses will have to be repaired in your current adult life. A poster motto says, Accept the truth of your past and the truth of the person that you have become.

Task #4: Invest your emotional energies, which have been consumed with your past, toward being a whole person now in your relationships and your work.

How to Get Started

Ask yourself these questions:

1. What are the two or three feelings that are easiest for me to share?
2. What are the most difficult feelings for me to experience and share?
3. What do I do to defend myself against experiencing those feelings?[10]

Answering these three questions will help you begin to discover those areas of loss which you have blocked from your consciousness, but which continue to fester and produce disturbance in your personality and relationships.

In *Healing the Shame That Binds You,* Bradshaw speaks of the importance of the support group to help the person resolve grief. He says,

> The reason people go into delayed grief is that there's nobody there to validate and support them. You cannot grieve alone. Millions of us adult children tried it. We went to sleep crying into our pillows or locked in the bathroom.
>
> All through your life there should have been lots of people saying to you, "I'm glad you're here. Welcome to our family and home. I'm glad you're a boy or a girl. I like being with you. Your feelings are absolutely normal. You're a special person to me."[11]

You can't heal yourself because you don't like yourself, and you don't have enough strength within yourself to affirm yourself or to validate yourself. That validation requires an outside opinion! That's why trying it on your own will result in going around in circles, and you'll reinforce your own personal defeat.

The Goal Is to Feel and to Share Your Feelings

Recently one of our daughters and her husband moved more than a thousand miles away. In the days following their move Sally's eyes would swim as she'd say to me, "I really miss them. It isn't that I want them to stay here with us. I'm glad they have this great opportunity to live in the city of their choice. But it really does leave a hole and an emptiness."

My response to Sally was, "Just don't think about it." Suddenly I saw the little boy in me, scooping up Whitey the cat and saying to myself, "I'm not going to feel anymore." Here I am fifty-eight years old, one of our daughters has moved away, and I'm still telling myself, "Don't feel anything."

After a couple of days Sally reminded me of my words. "Do you remember that you told me, 'Just don't think about it?' Well, I've been watching you. The last few days you've been grumpy and irritable. Almost anything that anyone does annoys you."

Then she gave me an important insight: "You know, I believe you feel the loss of their move as intensely as I do, but instead of talking about it, you get frustrated, depressed and crabby."

I put my arms around her and said, "I'm sorry. I need to keep letting myself feel and grieve the losses that come along in my daily life so, finally, I can truly be healed."

16
Step Six:
Shaking Off
the Victim
Mentality

MILLIE WAS THIRTY-ONE YEARS OLD, BUT SHE looked twenty years older. Her hair was stringy and unkempt. She wore no make-up. Her general appearance told the story. She really didn't care about herself or life in general.

As her sad story spilled out, I often felt as if my emotions would not be able to cope with the enormity of her problems. Beyond a doubt, life had been a hell for her.

She was the oldest child, born to a couple before they were married, a couple who fought continually. These folks didn't just exchange a few bad words; their fights were vicious physical battles. Police were frequently called to the various rented places they called home.

Millie's parents repeatedly told her and the other children, who were also unplanned, that they were not wanted. On many occasions the children were left for weeks with relatives or neighbors.

When Millie was about eleven years old, her father started regularly raping her. He said she owed it to him, because he was providing food, clothes and a place for her to live.

As the years went along, a brother a year younger also regularly raped her. On a number of occasions she asked her mother for help, but her mother would just push her away and say, "That's what men do. Just shut up and take it."

Millie's father had an increasing number of scrapes with the law. Finally the county stepped in and put the children into foster homes. At this point Millie's parents were legally divorced.

Millie bounced around from foster home to foster home as a pawn who was used as a means of income for the foster parents. Somehow males spotted her as an easy sexual victim, resulting in continued rapes by foster fathers and brothers and other neighborhood boys.

Freedom at Last?

When Millie was fifteen, one of these neighbor boys, Kevin, talked her into running away with him to get married. Kevin frequently was in trouble with the law and was in and out of jails for the next several years. Millie had two children before she was twenty. Neither she nor Kevin wanted either of these children, and Millie began to raise them in the same way she had been raised.

Ever since her early teen years she had used alcohol as a way to forget her horrible situation. In her twenties she and Kevin discovered drugs as a way to temporarily escape their miserable existence. Millie and Kevin worked at a variety of low-paying jobs, but it never was enough for their family along with their alcohol and drug habits. So Kevin started stealing. By their late twenties, Kevin was into mid-sized holdups. Finally, he was caught and sent to the penitentiary.

Millie went on welfare. Her children were taken from her and put in foster care homes. She continued her erratic pattern of working at low-paying jobs. At that point, she came to see me. She had heard that our church cared for people. Maybe there was hope for her.

Same Song—Second Verse

At the end of our first counseling session where this story spilled out, I encouraged her to join one of our small caring groups and to attend an educational class for young singles. Together we began exploring potential training and jobs for Millie. We agreed to meet together in a week to see how things were going.

At the second session Millie started her story right from the beginning as if we had never talked. I thought, "This isn't unusual; many people who have been as traumatized as she need to re-tell their stories." So I let the process continue. At the end of the session, I shared a few more ideas and gave her more encouragement. But I began to sense that she wasn't really interested in following up on any of my leads.

Sessions three through five were exactly the same. I couldn't believe it! I thought I was hearing a tape recording. It was exactly the same story, repeated almost verbatim.

I began to realize that Millie was not only a victim, but that she was continuing to *choose* to be a victim. She had learned that people would pay attention to her, feel sorry for her and reach out with emotional love if her story was bad enough. So she had carefully honed her story, which I had verified as true, in order to get people to love her.

Somewhere between sessions three and five, I began to get complaints from several people in the church who told me that ever since they had expressed concern for her, Millie had been coming often to their homes. She would spend the whole morning or afternoon, telling her story and embellishing all of the details. Each time she visited their homes, it was the same pattern as in my office. The story was repeated over and over again.

Loved for Being a Victim

In session number six, before she had time to start her story, I pulled my chair directly in front of her. I looked her squarely in the face and said, "Millie, I don't think you want to get better. You don't enjoy being a victim, but you enjoy what that victim status achieves for you. By telling people all the pathetic things that have happened in your life, you draw people to love you and care for you because your life has been so awful."

Then I said, "Millie, you are asking people to love you because of your troubles, but you never give them a chance to love you as a person. Your troubles are all they know about you."

She looked at me with fear in her eyes and said, "Without my troubles there *is* no me!"

Repeated Victimization—or Freedom

As I talk about this subject, I am in a very precarious spot. It's like the diamond cutter with a large uncut diamond. He carefully examines the stone so that he can cut it on one of the natural cracking lines. If he misjudges where to place the chisel, the blow from the hammer on the chisel could cause the diamond to break in many pieces and become a total loss.

It's the same as I talk with you about shaking off the victim mentality. I must be careful where I place the chisel to help you correct your life. Two things are true, yet they sound totally opposite.

1. Please don't conclude from Millie's story that I am trying to keep you from telling your story about your pain. You did grow up in a troubled family, and *you do need to talk about your pain.* You must allow your feelings of anger and grief to spill out.

2. On the other hand, you may have a tendency to continue the victim pattern. I'm urging you to *make positive choices* and stop letting your past victimization keep control of you.

Please understand that when I push you to make positive choices, it isn't that I don't feel the agony of your childhood problems. I do. But I know from personal experience and from working with hundreds of other victims that it's easy for victims to feel justified and to be unable to make positive decisions.

It all boils down to this: yes, you must feel your pain, but that pain must not keep you from the healing process. *You must get rid of that victim mentality or you may forever be trapped where you are today.*

Morgan Cryar sings a song entitled "Break the Chain":

Suzy's daddy just nags and shouts
She yells back, then they have it out

She wants to run away and get married real bad
But her boyfriend Joe is just like Dad.
Better break the chain

Billy is another kid right across town
His dad left his mom 'cause she held him down
To think about his father just drives him mad
But he uses his girlfriends just like Dad.
Break the chain, break the chain
Cut the cord, end the curse, stop the reign
Break the chain, break the chain
The family sin will do you in, so break the chain

Little Jan was a battered child
She used to hide out while her mama went wild
Will she raise the seed that her mama has sown?
What's she gonna do with kids of her own?
Better break the chain

I could tell Reggie was a preacher's kid
By the fire in his eyes and the things he did
He never heard his father say "I love you"
When Reggie has a son tell me what's he gonna do?
He better break the chain . . .

Sometimes sin is just a family tradition
But it'll burn the family tree to the ground
Nobody wants to inherit the flames
You sure don't want to pass 'em down
Break the chain[1]

Choosing Not to Be a Victim

The message of the song and this chapter is: don't let your parents' problems automatically become your problems. Stop perpetuating your victim identification.

Whenever we experience a teachable moment, that is, when we have a new awareness of who we are and what has happened in our lives, we are offered a choice. We can move forward, making the commitment to face the pain. Or we can move backward, hiding behind our victim status, building up resentments, blaming those who mistreated us, blaming ourselves, even blaming God.

If we don't choose to face our pain and grow, we only prolong the suffering, much the same as when we have a toothache. We can either go to the dentist and experience the pain head-on, or we can prolong the pain and suffering, hoping that magically it will disappear.

The Victim's Creed

I've discovered that victims mentally tend to repeat one or more of the following ideas, reinforcing their victim status.

☐ I'm waiting for something good, but it probably won't happen.

☐ If I work as hard as I can, I will just barely pass.

☐ No matter how hard I work, my insides say, "You could have tried harder."

☐ Change is impossible.

☐ I'll always be the same.

☐ I feel safest when no one pays any attention to me.

☐ I hate myself whenever I disappoint someone.

☐ People are out to rip me off.

☐ I'm insignificant and powerless.

☐ Rewards are earned, but I've never done enough to deserve any rewards.

☐ When I reward myself, I make bad choices—such as sex, food, drugs or alcohol.

☐ I hate my body.

☐ I hate myself.

☐ I don't think anyone will ever understand me, because I don't know how to tell them about myself.

☐ I'm always angry at myself and at everything and everyone around me.[2]

You may begin to feel, "I'm not cured, so it must not be working. I'm going to give up." Please don't retreat into a victim mentality. And don't get tricked by a perfectionistic view. It's true, you're not totally healed, but stop thinking in terms of 100 percent. Have you learned *anything?* Have you received *any* insights? Then focus on those successes. They may seem small, but more successes will come.

I know I'm being tough on you, but this is something that I myself continually fight. In fact, I recently told my counselor, "Earl, I want you to know how bad things were as a child so that you'll feel sorry for me. I need you to love me." Earl smiled. He understood, but he also didn't want me to remain a victim of my childhood problems. He wanted me to be healed, so he urged me to keep growing.

There will never be a time when you are *totally* healed, because you never will be able to wipe out your history or the fact that your parents were divorced and your home was dysfunctional. You will never be able to change the impact of your home on you.

You will, however, come to a time when you will use your pain as an energy source, not to destroy you, but to help you be more effective. That's the ultimate goal! When you arrive at that point, you're going to be at peace with your past.

The authors of *The Courage to Heal* speak of one woman who had spent years resisting and hating herself because of being sexually molested as a child. She said, "Finally, I had to realize it was part of me. It's not something I can get rid of. If I'm going to really love myself totally, then I have to love all of me, and this is part of who I am."[3]

Seek the Truth

The truth is, your home was dysfunctional and you may not even know the full extent of that dysfunction. The truth is, your parents were supposed to be parents to you, passing on health and wholeness, not transmitting their problems. But they were unable to do that job very well.

The truth is, it's okay to talk. You are not "just strange." You're not the only one. Millions of other people are just like you—adult children still struggling from the impact of their parents' divorce and dysfunction.

However, the truth also is that you need to move beyond the hurt and pain of your past. You need to fully grieve and leave the victim mentality behind. You must transform that pain into a powerful energy to make your life more effective now. Let me paraphrase for you an Old Testament proverb to emphasize the point: "As a person thinks, so he becomes."[4] The New Testament reinforces that idea as it urges, "Be transformed by the renewing of your mind."[5]

Search for the truth about your past, including both the negative and the positive. Listen to the truth from your counselor, your group, other friends and relatives. Let God as well as people tell you the truth. You are a valued and important person who has a unique contribution to make to the world—all the more so because of what you've experienced. You know realities about life and people that you never would have learned if you had not suffered.

A running debate goes on in psychological circles. Do we change people's behavior by changing their thinking? Or do we change people's thinking by changing their behavior? The truth is both. You will change as you think new thoughts. But you will also change as you redirect your actions by exposing yourself to reading, listening to other people, working on your problems and grieving your past. This process of thinking new thoughts and changing your actions will move you from being simply a victim of your parents' divorce to being a person utilizing your pain and your new insights to live a profitable and fulfilling life.

Surrender Punishment

In the next chapter we'll talk more about forgiveness, but for now I want to encourage you to give up your right to punish your parents. It will help you to get away from the victim position. The Bible says, "Vengeance is mine; I will repay, saith the Lord."[6] Let God take care of whatever punishment needs to be given.

But I hear you say, "I want to punish them. They deserve it. I'm not sure you understand. I was only a child. I was a victim. I didn't have a choice. They defrauded me."

Yes, all of that is true. But as long as you hold on to your right to punish them, you will continue to reinforce your victim mentality. You're hurting yourself more than you're hurting them! Let God and other people help you with this problem.

Live in the Now

I'm a very future-oriented person. I love the words from the musical *Annie:* "Tomorrow, tomorrow, I love ya, tomorrow." I continually hope that tomorrow will be better. I hope that I will get more pages written, that I will be more sensitive to Sally, that I will progress more in my own healing process and that I will be more successful with my children and grandchildren.

I don't consciously focus on the past. But unconsciously I am continually affected by it. I hate the reality that I still am reacting to my past. At the same time I'm looking to the future, hoping that things will be better.

The result is that I almost ignore the present. I keep putting off today's pleasures. I tend not to stop to smell the roses. I don't like being the age I am right now. I don't accept and enjoy the achievements that are happening right now. In a sense, I'm a rubber band pulled between two extremes—my dysfunctional past and my hoped-for, perfect future.

Focusing on the past or fantasizing about the future often keeps me thinking of myself as a victim. I say to myself, "Life is tough because of what I came from." I also say, "I hope life will be better in the future." And then my victim mentality comes through and adds, "but not likely." I focus either on the unreliable past or the unpredictable future instead of the present. Getting rid of the victim identification for me means that I need to live and enjoy *today.*

A Man for Everyone but Himself

"John Quincy Adams held more important offices than anyone else in the history of the United States. He served with distinction as President, senator, congressman, minister to major European powers, and participated in various capacities in the American Revolution, the War of 1812, and events leading to the Civil War period. Yet, at age seventy, with much of that behind him, he wrote, 'My whole life has been a succession of disappointments. I can scarcely recollect a single instance of success in anything that I ever undertook.' "[7]

John Quincy Adams was always looking for the next thing. His perfectionism kept driving him to some future event, service, act or deed which might somehow be worthwhile. He was never able to enjoy the here and now of his achievements.

Living in the "here and now" means surrendering the past. You'll never get the lost things back. You're not going to reunite your parents. That era of your life is over. You have been affected by it. Now it's time to live today, with all of today's realities.

Think of the glorious sugar maple trees in the fall with their leaves of magnificent red and orange. As the frosts come on, they let their leaves drop. The leaves then return to the earth and become part of the nourishment for another year. Oaks, however, seem to fight to hang onto their leaves. They don't want to let go. So winter comes along and has to whip the leaves off the oak tree.

Be a maple. Relax your grip on your past. Allow your past to fall to the ground and nourish yourself and others.

Recognize Your Addictions

Escaping your victim mentality also means identifying your addictions. Addictions can be anything you use to defend yourself against pain or difficulties in life. Addictions are walls we erect to protect ourselves from further damage or to help us forget that we have been damaged.

Therefore, addictions, by their very function, reinforce a victim mentality. If you use alcohol or drugs, you are continuing to say, "I had it tough. I deserve relief from the pain I've experienced."

If you're a sexual addict, you think, "I felt abandoned at home. I'm lonely. I need someone to care for me." Your sexual addiction then fortifies your victim status.

The reason it's hard to stop our addictions is that they are a help to us. They feel good. They serve us. They may have protected us as children, and we've carried them for many years into adulthood. We don't stop our addictions because we don't want to stop them.

But addictions keep us trapped. They keep saying to us loudly and clearly, "Poor baby, you've had it tough. You deserve your escape."

I told you this was going to be a tough chapter. It's times like this when all of us adult children of divorce say, "My addictions are the fault of my dysfunctional home." That's true. But it's also true that, to be finished with our victim condition, we have to make the choice, become proactive and change our behavior patterns as well as our thinking.

What Will Help?

Let's try to focus this chapter in a few sentences:

1. Soak your mind with the truth. Enjoy your relationship with God. Read more books like this one that will help you grow. Attend seminars or workshops for adult children of divorced or dysfunctional families.

2. Repeatedly question yourself. "How long am I going to think like a victim—for the next month, the next six months or maybe till my next birthday? When will I decide that long enough is long enough?"

3. Become proactive and break the chain of your past. You've already decided to be healed—keep reminding yourself of that decision. Each time you react to your past like a puppet on a string, pull out your scissors and cut the string.

Okay, it was bad. But if you follow normal patterns, everything in your life will be affected: your job, your marriage, your relationships with your children and friends. They will all be tainted unless you decide to break the chain.

In our family we've agreed to help each other break the chain. Yes, I've already passed down some bad things to my three daughters, but from now on I want to destroy the chain. I've apologized to them, and together we've agreed not to let it go on affecting them, or their children, or their children's children.

4. Share your intention to break out of the victim mentality. Tell your group, your wife or husband, your counselor or a trusted friend. Tell them you're trying to quit seeing yourself as a victim. Ask them to help.

5. Sum it all up. Ask yourself, "What will help me to be free from the victim mentality? Do I need more quiet meditation with God? More counseling sessions? More honesty in the group? Do I need to make some things right with family members? Do I need to confront certain people? Do I need to go back to school?"

Whatever it is, decide now! Tell yourself again, "I'm not going to be a victim—this is the year that I'm going to be healed!"

17
Step Seven:
Forgiving the
Past

I WAS ASKED BY FRIENDS TO FIND VALERIE AND do what I could to help her. Our friends said her father was a traveling evangelist, but she had totally disowned her family and any faith in God.

I located Valerie, and she agreed to speak to me. We spent about three hours in my office, intellectually debating the benefits of various world religions and the overall appeal of atheism.

I could tell that Valerie's reasoning was based not on logic but on anger. She wanted nothing to do with God, especially the God of the Christian world. Even though her anger was clear, I urged her not to turn away from God. She continued to denounce God, all religions and especially all Christians. In a burst of anger she jumped to her feet and started for the door.

I jumped up too and said, "Before you go out the door, let me say this.

God is not at all like the Christians you have known! I would like to talk some more about your relationship with God. Could we get together again?"

She angrily insisted, "I want nothing to do with God, ever!"

"Do you really believe those words?" I said. Her eyes flashed. Her jaw was firmly set. She almost snarled as she said, "Yes!"

"Valerie," I said, "if you turn and walk out that door, are you saying to me and to God, 'I forever relinquish any right to communicate with God or to ask him for help'? Is that what you want?"

She glared at me with a hatred that was terrifyingly evil. There was some kind of aura around her. I felt I was in the presence of a stick of dynamite a millisecond before the explosion.

She turned on her heel, walked out the door and started down the hall. I went to the door and watched her walk away.

She had taken about fifteen steps when she stopped and looked at me for a long, long moment. Now her eyes were very different. They said, "I'm hurting. Please help me."

I softly called out to her, "Valerie, I really want to help you. Can we talk again?" She nodded yes and walked out of sight.

A New Woman—But . . .
The next time Valerie and I talked, she told me that she had gone back to her apartment and frankly faced the questions I had posed. Did she really, once and for all, want to relinquish any possibility of a relationship with God? Was it really God she was angry at, or people who pretended to have a relationship with God?

Then she said, "I've asked God to forgive me. I've asked him to come into my life and to lead me. I want to have a relationship with him. I want his love and forgiveness. I want his guidance and friendship. But I don't want to be like those other religious people!"

Valerie's life changed drastically. Hostility drained away from her relationships with other people. She started smiling more often. Her face had a new radiance and peace. In the following months she grew rapidly in her spiritual life and soon she was deeply involved with spiritual discipling and training of other people. Our family became sort of a substitute home for her.

The Other Valerie

In spite of all the changes, a heavy cloud hung over Valerie's life. It was only a matter of months before she started to slide into depression and withdrawal. The slide was so severe that she had to be hospitalized because she attempted to take her life.

Months of hospitalization stretched into years. Therapists didn't seem to be able to break through. And when they did, they touched only one of her multiple personalities.

Gradually the story came out. Valerie's father, the evangelist, would take her with him as he went from city to city. Frequently they would be gone two or three weeks at a time.

Valerie felt very special to be chosen as the only child to go with her father. She also felt as if she were a confidante to her father, because he told her about the stresses he felt from being an evangelist. She also felt important because he told her she had a special ability to make him relax and feel good when she lovingly massaged his body.

Valerie's mother was a very austere, cold woman, and Valerie never felt close to her. But she was glad to be with her father. She enjoyed his talking. She enjoyed massaging his body and felt a special closeness to him when he massaged her body as they slept together on their trips.

Valerie was very young when she started traveling with her dad. The closeness was a gradual development. But within a few years he was using her to meet his sexual needs.

A part of her wondered if she should tell her mother or if her father ever talked to her mother. A small voice inside her said, "This doesn't seem right." At the same time, the trips enabled her to be so close to her father. It made her feel good to see that she could do something for him that no other woman could do. Increasingly, she looked forward not only to satisfying her father, but to having him touch and satisfy her.

The incestuous relationship continued into her mid-teen years. However, by that time she wanted out and started avoiding her father as much as she could and finding reasons not to travel with him.

As Valerie began to understand what had happened and how her father had exploited her, she started to develop multiple personalities. One was the bad girl who had an incestuous relationship with her father. Another was the good girl, a virgin, who was saving herself until she was married to the right man. Her first personality was clumsy and ugly. Her second one was an attractive and intelligent girl.

Not Really a Family

As Valerie discovered more about her father's sickness, she began to learn that the whole family was sick. Her cold, harsh mother was, in fact, having an incestuous relationship with Valerie's brother. Valerie further learned that even though her mother knew what was happening to Valerie, she refused to intervene or even acknowledge it.

To this day the parents refuse to admit anything ever happened. "It's all the imagination of the children," they say. However, even though Valerie is now married with children of her own, her father still invites her to go on trips alone with him.

This is a very troubled family, but Valerie is the one who has paid the highest price. She's the one who spent years in the psychiatric wards and thousands of hours in counseling, plus chemical and electro-shock therapy. The parents deny anything happened—but Valerie carries the scars!

Now the question. Should these evil parents be forgiven?

Upon hearing a story like this, something in the human personality says, "I want vengeance! I want to drag those parents through shark-infested waters while the sharks bite off piece after piece of their bodies. No, I want something that will last longer, with more hurt. Maybe I could wire them onto a giant rotisserie and let the fire slowly singe their bodies until they die."

But the question always comes back, Is even *that* enough? What will finally be enough to pay for the evil behavior of that father and mother against Valerie?

Each of us has a list of the ways people have violated us. Part of that list may be conscious—all *too* conscious. We may remember it or react to it every day of our lives. Other parts of that list may be submerged in our unconscious, but they continue to affect us. Unfinished forgiveness from our past injects its deadly poison into every thought and action.

Unforgiveness is like a leak in the big underground storage tank at a gas station. Gasoline seeps into the ground, finds its way into the water supply and contaminates the whole town's drinking water. Yes, only a few drops are released each day. But the leak must be stopped so that the contamination will be stopped.

Look at your list of people who have wronged you, then remember this idea:

I cannot change my past,
but I can forgive my past.

Sometimes forgiveness is viewed as a simple step: Someone wronged you, so you either forgive him or her or you don't. The all-or-nothing view of forgiveness doesn't work for many people; forgiving a damaged childhood is not that simple.

Forgiveness has many levels. Any level you can achieve along the road to forgiveness will help you become more completely healed. Let's look at seven levels of forgiveness.

Level 1: Recognize that you have been violated.

Superficial forgiveness is not real—and it will not drain off the emotion of the silent anger waiting to explode within you.

You cannot give something to someone if you do not own it. Imagine that you and I are standing in front of a jewelry store, and I say to you, "Pick out any watch you want. It's yours." That's a great idea, but the problem is that I don't own the watch. I must buy the watch, own it, before I can give it as a gift to you. Likewise, Level 1 of forgiveness means first owning the fact that you have been violated.

People don't want to recognize the pain of their past for many reasons. Sometimes it's just too disturbing to handle. By the time people become adults they may want simply to block out the event, because if they remember it, they're going to have to do something with it.

But acknowledging your pain is the first level in the process of forgiving your past.

Level 2: Feel your indignation and anger caused by the violation.

Sometimes anger becomes the energy enabling us to look honestly at our painful past as well as to press on with the forgiveness process. Usually we think of anger as a negative factor, but in the early levels of forgiveness, anger becomes a valuable tool.

It's important to realize that at Level 2 we are clearly not saying to the person, "I forgive you. I take you off the hook." We are doing exactly the opposite. We are recognizing the full scope of the problem. We are digging around to make sure that we get at every small dimension of feeling related to this violation.

Not long ago I was refinishing a little table. I sanded out the chipped marks and smoothed the surface so it would be ready to take the new enamel. But when I started to put the paint on, it bubbled up. I asked my painter friend what was wrong. He said it probably had an old coat of lacquer, which is not compatible with enamel. He told me to use paint remover and a wire brush. I had to make sure I got all the old lacquer off or my new paint would continue to bubble up.

Anger helps you to identify all that "old lacquer" so that as you begin to reconstruct your life, you won't have the past bubbling up to ruin your new growth. Anger helps you prepare for your later decision of whether or not to forgive and which parts to forgive.

At the anger level it's also possible to block. Frequently adult children of divorce stop anger from doing its full work because we've been taught by our parents not to be angry, not to express negative feelings—"Don't cry, don't get angry." This long-term conditioning causes us, even as adults, to feel we are wrong if we get angry.

At this stage, anger is your ally in the process of forgiveness.

Level 3: Grieve over what you have lost.

Reading through Chapter 15 about grieving your losses was preparing you to be healed. In addition, those ideas and the feelings you experienced were helping you to move to Level 3 in the forgiveness process. Clearly understand, grieving over losses in your past does not mean that you are forgiving the people who were involved. You have not yet made that decision.

However, if grief, like anger, is not handled first, unresolved grief will cause any forgiveness that is offered to be very superficial. And the person who is offered forgiveness will sense that the forgiveness is not deep enough. In addition, your own life will continue to experience unconscious hurt because you have not fully grieved.

Forgiveness is an act, yes, but it is also a process involving many individual acts. Someday down the road you may be able to say, "I have forgiven that person." But when you do, it will have involved many levels in the forgiveness process.

Imagine a grade-school boy who has a natural ability to play football. In fact, he is exceptionally talented, handling himself and the ball with grace and ease. It would be unfortunate if a coach would say, "My grade-school son is so talented that I'm going to let him play in some of the practice games with my college team."

That would be bizarre. The boy may be very talented for his age, but in order to play with college boys, he needs more physical growth, quickness and mental discipline. Now he will be humiliated. In fact, if someone doesn't rescue him, he'll not only be crushed physically, his self-image will also take a beating and he may believe he should never play football again.

In the same way, grieving is an essential step in the forgiveness process. Even though you may feel ready to forgive, resist that temptation to rush the process. Follow each level so that when you grant forgiveness, it will accomplish all that you hope it will.

Level 4: Consider the implications if you forgive.

At this level of forgiveness you're asking, "If I do forgive, what does this mean?" This is the time to wrestle with dozens of different questions, such as:

- ☐ Who needs to be forgiven?
- ☐ What if they don't ask to be forgiven?
- ☐ Can I ever trust them?
- ☐ What will reconciliation mean?
- ☐ How much involvement is safe?
- ☐ Will I continue to be hurt?

Each person has his or her own list of questions. In a sense, you play the "what if/then what" game with yourself. For example, "*What if* I forgive him and he says, 'Oh, Jim, you've always been too sensitive. You shouldn't let a little thing like that hurt you.' *Then what* will I do?"

Gradually figure out an answer to your own question. For example, tell yourself, "I'll say to him, 'Ralph, we're different people. A remark like that might not hurt you, but it deeply offended me. Even though you hurt me, I'm offering to you unconditional forgiveness.' "

What does forgiveness mean? Let's clear the air on several things. To forgive does not at all suggest:

☐ The other person was not wrong.

☐ It really was only a small matter after all.

☐ They can't be blamed for their weaknesses.

☐ A few words of apology will erase the feelings from a long-standing problem.

☐ They didn't know what they were doing.

☐ I caused them to act or react that way.

As you think about the implications of forgiveness, you also need to decide, "Whom should I forgive?" Suppose you immediately pick out your father. But is he the only one? What role did your mother play? Were your grandparents contributing parties who also need to be forgiven? You may discover a great deal of anger toward other relatives, toward your dad's job, even anger toward God himself.

Think about specific offenses against you. Divide them into two categories: What the offender(s) deliberately did and what the offender(s) unintentionally did.

My parents argued when I was a very young child. It probably never occurred to them that I was being affected by their fighting and by my father's disrespect of my mother. They might have thought I was too young to absorb those feelings. Those were unintentional offenses.

On the other hand, when my mother held my hands in the flames on our kitchen stove to stop me from playing with matches, that act was intentional. Actually, what she did was probably a mixture of the way she was corrected as a child and her deliberate choice of what she thought was the best punishment for me.

If I Forgive, I Do Not Deny

Whenever we consider the implications of forgiveness, we are wrestling with what forgiving will mean to us. In forgiveness you say, "I forgive you for the offense you committed against me. It was real, it hurt, but I'm not going to seek revenge or punishment against you for your act."

Another question you ought to think about is, What is the difference between forgiveness and denial? Frequently I say to Sally after we've had a conflict, "Forget it, just forget it," instead of saying, "I forgive you."

Instead of facing the issue and quickly running through the levels of forgiveness honestly, I get rid of the problem by hiding it. My denial puts Sally in an awkward spot. Is she really forgiven, or am I just blocking it out of my mind?

Those two actions are very different for her and for me. If I forgive her, she is really set free and there's no leftover residue of anger in me. If I just block it out, she is unsure of her status, and I've just submerged the hurt to become part of my giant internal pool of anger, waiting to bubble up at any moment.

You also need to face what you're going to do when you remember the offense again or feel the pain and anger again. Forgiveness is an act that takes place at one moment, but our memory is not wiped out. Thousands of experiences may trigger those feelings all over again. What will you do when you feel that pain and anger again?

If you regress to one of the earlier levels of forgiveness, start again at that level. Briefly feel the pain and anger. Again, touch the grief that you felt. Think about the implications of forgiving or not forgiving. Eventually you will be able to move to the next stage.

Can I Forgive Myself?

As you wrestle with the implications of forgiveness, also ask, "Am I willing to forgive myself as easily as I'm willing to forgive other people?" Frequently in problems between people, both people are somewhat guilty.

In Valerie's case she clearly was violated. Her father introduced Valerie to a sexual experience that was totally immoral. However, as she moved along in years, she began to realize that even though she came to hate her father's advances, she also had enjoyed his closeness and the sexual experience itself.

The reasons Valerie's healing took so long are that (1) she was unable to face and resolve the fact that her father had violated her, and (2) she was unable to forgive herself.

As you think about forgiving yourself, ask the question, "If I saw a little child who was unable to forgive himself or herself, how would I feel toward that little child? What would I say?" Now translate that tenderness and coaching attitude to yourself.

If you offer forgiveness to everyone but yourself, you likely will be caught in a cycle from which you can't escape. You will remember the pain and be forced to forgive other people over and over again for the same issues, but you will not be free. Forgiveness must ultimately release them *and you* from your past pains.

At any level it's possible to block the process. As you consider the implications of forgiveness, you might say to yourself, "It's too much. I'm going to stop thinking about this. I'm going to take myself entirely out of the forgiveness process." Don't quit! Be brave and move onto the next level of forgiveness.

Level 5: Ask,"Why should I forgive this person?"

In a chapter entitled "Forgiveness" in the book *The Courage to Heal,* the authors blatantly tell their readers who are struggling with trying to forgive a person, "Why should you? First they steal everything else from you and then they want forgiveness too? Let them get their own [forgiveness]. You've given enough."[1]

Unfortunately, these authors are suggesting a vindictive approach which allows no opportunity for healing. Life is painful and often very, very unjust. However, the basis for forgiveness is not the intensity of the hurt but your need to release the burden you have been carrying.

As you put yourself into Level 5 of the forgiveness process, you'll be asking the hard question, "Why should I forgive?" No matter whether the pain was great or small, the violation against you was unfair.

Lewis Smedes says, "Forgiving is only for people who are fair to the wretched fact of unfair pain. You will forgive only when you dare look at people eyeball to eyeball and tell them that they are responsible for what they did."[2]

When we wrestle with the question, "Why should I forgive?", we must ask, "What are the alternatives?" There are only two: revenge or denial.

We've already discovered that denial won't work. It just moves the event, pain and anger from your conscious mind to your unconscious. The offense continues to surge within your personality like a volcano, looking for any excuse to erupt and spew the red hot lava of anger and rage over anyone nearby. So if denial won't work, that leaves revenge.

Revenge won't work, either, because it ultimately doesn't satisfy anyone. Successful revenge happens only in the movies. In one of my favorite films, "The Sting," there is a classic line as Paul Newman and Robert Redford are about to get even with a gangster who killed a friend of theirs.

Paul Newman mentions the half-million dollars they're going to trick the gangster out of and says to Redford, referring to Redford's desire for revenge, "Kid, this has got to be enough, because this is all we're going to get." Robert Redford smiles and says, "It's enough."

What Else?

In real life, though, revenge doesn't work that way. Look at your newspaper or TV news as they report gang wars. A gang member crosses into another gang's territory and is killed. The other gang retaliates, so the first gang must retaliate again. There is never any moment when the body count is evened up.

Smedes says, "An eye for an eye becomes a leg for a leg and, eventually, a life for a life. No matter what our weapons are—words, clubs, arrows, guns, bombs, nuclear missiles—revenge locks us in an escalation of violence. Gandhi was right: if we all live by 'an eye for an eye' the whole world will be blind. The only way out is forgiveness."[3]

If denial won't work and if revenge is never-ending—then forgiveness is the only alternative left. Forgiveness unglues us from our past. Forgiveness allows us to turn away and look at the flowers, the blue sky, the smiling faces of people around us in the present.

Forgiveness helps us to heal. Our past will never be healed by revenge or by denial. It can only be healed by forgiveness.

Why should you let that person who has already damaged your life continue to damage you? Think for a moment—whenever you remember that past event you will experience over and over again the pain and anger of that event.

But forgiveness is like taking a gas torch and cutting off the ball and chain that has been attached to you for all these years. Your forgiveness breaks the power that the other person has had over your life.

Make no mistake, forgiveness is not saying:

☐ your parents were right

☐ the abusers were right

☐ the act was right

Neither does forgiveness mean you don't have a right to:

☐ protect yourself

☐ limit contact

☐ refuse information

☐ file legal or criminal charges

Forgiveness does not take the other person off the hook of responsibility—forgiveness takes the hook of pain out of your mouth!

Level 6: Grant a grace forgiveness.

The focus of forgiveness must always be *grace*. Forgiveness is always unmerited. In the last analysis, no one can ever earn forgiveness. It must be granted as a free gift by the person who has been offended. Yes, it helps if the offender says, "I'm sorry," but forgiveness does not automatically follow an apology.

People have used a number of techniques to help them offer forgiveness. In *Making Peace with Your Parents,* Harold Bloomfield suggests making a list of all of the things that caused pain in your childhood. Avoid generalizations, such as "I hate my parents." He suggests, for example, "I resent that you slapped me at school in the first grade in front of my friends. I resent feeling like you never wanted me to be born."[4]

Bloomfield reminds the reader that you are doing this exercise to get rid of anger, not increase anger.

Then he encourages people to visualize their parent and tell them, "I know that you've loved me, but I have some things that I want to talk to you about." Then choose one or two events and explain your feelings to your parents.

Some people have found it helpful to put a picture of their parent in a chair and sit in front of the chair while explaining childhood feelings. Others find it helpful to have a friend listen to the imaginary conversation with the parent. Then the two people talk about the pain that was felt and how the parent might react.

Your parents' divorce has had a powerfully negative effect on you. Now you offer forgiveness to them, not because they deserve it or even asked for it, but because it is the only way for you to be free.

"Grace forgiveness" means:

☐ I understand the full scope of my pain and anger.

☐ I understand that this person has not earned my forgiveness.

☐ I forgive this person freely and permanently.

☐ I give up any thought of revenge or punishment.

☐ I refuse to take advantage of any guilt that my offender may feel.

☐ I will not hold a grudge.

☐ I will not intentionally replay this event.

Grace forgiveness, I've found, is easier when I visualize the problem being handed to God and I hear God say, "Let me take care of this for you."

After we understand grace forgiveness, forgiveness becomes an act of our will. We can either choose to pout, be angry, withdraw, be cold, or we can forgive and relinquish the person, all of the hurt and all of the future results into God's hands.

Catherine Marshall wrote a marvelous book entitled *Something More* in which she talks about the meaning of forgiveness and how she learned to forgive. She quotes a part of the Gospel of Mark, "If you hold anything against anyone, forgive him, so that your Father in heaven may forgive you your sins."[5] Then she says, "The scope and inflexibility of Jesus' teaching on forgiveness staggered me. Obviously I was missing something."[6]

In 1971 David duPlessis visited Catherine Marshall. As they talked about why prayers sometimes weren't answered, David tied together the concept of praying and our granting forgiveness to other people. He said,

By our unforgiveness, we stand between the other person and the Holy Spirit's work in convicting him and then helping him. By stepping out of the way through releasing someone from our judgment, we're not necessarily saying, "he's right and I'm wrong." Forgiveness means, "he can be as wrong as wrong can be, but I'll not be the judge." Forgiveness means that I'm no longer binding a certain person on earth. It means withholding judgment.[7]

Catherine Marshall then explains that she and her husband, Len, would spend about thirty minutes each morning in separate rooms, listing any persons they needed to forgive. "After that we would meet together for verbal prayer release of each person on our list. Then we would tear the lists into small bits, put them into a large manila envelope. Eventually we would burn them."[8]

Catherine and her husband found that this simple process of forgiving anything they held against anybody gave them a deep sense of inner peace. They also discovered that as they released the person to God, dramatic changes took place. They watched tragic alienation between family members and friends miraculously be healed. God was allowed to work in each person without the threat of anger or revenge destroying the process.

But what if the memory of your awful experience comes back? Will you ever get over the pain? Will you ever forget?

Forgiveness doesn't mean that your memory of the event is wiped out. But the pain is gradually taken away, and you will increasingly see the event as an experience God is using to produce a positive quality in your character.

Level 7: Meet with the offender.
A face-to-face meeting with the person who has wronged you should accomplish two major goals:

1. Tell the person specifically how he or she offended you. The information should be given factually, not with the anger and grief of Levels 2 and 3. Avoid general accusations such as "You always made me feel dumb"; instead, give a specific example of a hurtful event. Information should also be given in enough detail so that the person understands you are not just glossing over the violation. Presenting the facts means that you tell the person how his or her choices and actions affected you emotionally and in your life direction.

That person needs to clearly understand that when you offer forgiveness in the next few moments, you are not sweeping the offense under the rug.

A definite violation was committed. You have been affected. Now the violator fully knows the facts.

It would be great, after you have explained the problem to the offender, if he or she would come forward with a clean, honest, believable apology. But that may not happen. If he or she tries to dismiss it with a remark such as, "Oh, that was a long time ago—let's not make a big deal out of it," you can follow up by saying, "I find it offensive that even after you know how I was affected by your actions, you're still trying to brush off the incident."

The person may realize at that point that you're not going to roll over and play dead. He or she may then be willing to acknowledge the wrong and ask your forgiveness. If that person does ask your forgiveness, it makes your next step relatively easy.

However, the offender still may not ask your forgiveness. Your offender may do to you as my father has done to me. Since he feels he has never been wrong in his life, he doesn't say, "I'm sorry." The closest he has ever come, when I have confronted him with what he has done in my life, is to say nothing.

My father's typical response to me is, "You've studied too much psychology." Or, "Don't let little things affect you so much. Quit making a big deal out of everything." In other words, whenever I mention the past problems, he goes on the attack. He starts to bully me. He says it's all my fault. In essence, he says, "If you weren't such a weird person, there wouldn't be any problem."

If your parents or the persons who have violated you do not acknowledge their wrong nor ask for forgiveness, that still should not deter you from your next step.

2. Grant forgiveness—then let go. Remember, in no way can your parents or another person earn your forgiveness. Many of life's damaging experiences can never be repaid. Remind yourself, "It is not because they are worthy. It is not because they have tried to compensate for my loss. Nor is it because they've apologized. It is only because of God's grace."

Whatever the situation, you are granting forgiveness so that both of you can go free. I've learned from experience that I can forgive another only because God has personally forgiven me. A verse that has had a powerful effect on me is, "forgiving each other, just as God in Christ also has forgiven you."[9]

Forgiving a person is really an unnatural thing to do. It flies in the face of our natural human bent to defend our rights and punish evil. We are crusaders by nature. We know right from wrong, and we clearly understand when we have been wronged. Forgiving someone is directly counter to our inherent nature and opposite of all that our culture believes and practices.

But . . .

But forgiveness is the only solution. Smedes reminds us that vengeance will never satisfy us. He says,

Recall the pain of being wronged, the hurt of being stung, cheated, demeaned. Doesn't the memory of it fuel the fire of fury again, reheat the pain again, make it hurt again? Suppose you never forgive, suppose you feel the hurt each time your memory lights on the people who did you wrong. And suppose you have a compulsion to think of them constantly. You have become a prisoner of your own past pain; you are locked into a torture chamber of your own making. Time should have left your pain behind; but you keep it alive to let it flay you over and over.

He goes on to say,

The only way to heal the pain that will not heal itself is to forgive the person who hurt you. Forgiving stops the reruns of pain. Forgiving heals your memory as you change your memory's vision.

When you release the wrongdoer from the wrong, you cut a malignant tumor out of your inner life.

You set a prisoner free, but you discover that the real prisoner was yourself.[10]

When you go to grant forgiveness, look the person in the eye. If that person is no longer alive, look at his or her picture and say, "What you did really affected me. But here and now I forgive you. I will stop replaying the event. I will give up any thought of revenge or punishment. I will refuse to take advantage of you for what has happened. I give you totally into God's care and keeping."

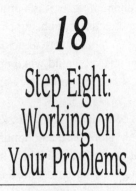

18
Step Eight: Working on Your Problems

V ALERIE, WHOM I DESCRIBED IN THE PRE-
vious chapter, is so different now. She is married, has children and has
completed her doctorate in psychology. She struggled for many years with
multiple personalities and the threat of her husband leaving because it was
so stressful for him to live with her. But now she has worked through the
various steps of healing so that she is a successful wife, mother and therapist whose specialty is working with abused children.

The Coming of Health

I'm also healing. My anger is subsiding, along with the depression.
Thoughts of suicide are not a constant companion as they were before I
made the decision to get better.

My dreams at night have been an indicator of my progress. Before the healing process began—and remember it is a process and not a quick fix— I frequently had terrifying dreams. I was being chased by a giant bear, lion or other wild animal. These animals were ferocious, snarling, and ready to pounce on me. At that moment I would wake up in absolute terror. Sally often told me that shortly before I woke up, I had begun whimpering or started running in bed.

As the healing process continued, I still had the savage animals chasing me, but frequently I would stop, raise my hands and mimic the beast. I would snarl and growl at him so that he would stop in his tracks. Usually my snarling and growling was so loud and ferocious that Sally would awaken me.

As healing progressed, however, the ferocious animals began to disappear. Or if they did appear, I started chasing *them*. The gradual disappearance of these animals has been one of the tangible signs of my recovery.

Dreams Are Friendly Allies

Dreams help us piece together insights about what's going on in our lives. I don't believe that dreams replace either Scripture or prayer, but dreams are another tool God uses for our personal growth and development. My counselor had encouraged me, "If you ever are awakened by a dream, go back to sleep and see if you can pick up the threads of the dream to get further meaning and insight."

A pivotal dream came after I was about ten months into the recovery process. I dreamed that I was in a large park. Two delightful ponds were on this land. Lots of people were on the beach, enjoying the sunshine, the water and each other. Then, tragically, the land was taken over by a developer who put a supermarket on one end of the property and covered the lakes with six inches of asphalt to make a giant parking lot.

I felt very sad that the pleasant lakes were gone, smothered with this awful, thick, black asphalt. Many other people objected to the developer's doing this, too. Finally the developer conceded to building a tunnel from the nearby town to the lakes underneath the asphalt. (In dreams, you know, anything can happen. It doesn't have to make logical sense.)

The lakes were still there, with the asphalt suspended about six inches above the water. People drove through the tunnel in order to swim in the lake, but the area was totally dark under this oppressive six-inch layer of asphalt.

I was swimming in the lake with my snorkeling mask. Each time I came up for air, I found it difficult to get my breath because the asphalt was so close to the water. At one spot I came up for a breath, but there wasn't room for me to get any air. I was suffocating! I woke up in a cold sweat.

Face the Terror

I lay on my bed, shaking with fright. I was suffocating under that thick, black layer of asphalt.

After a bit, I remembered the words of Earl, my counselor. "Go back to sleep and pick up the threads of the dream." As soon as my heart stopped racing, I drifted off to sleep.

Soon I was back in the lake, swimming around. I swam toward the place where the asphalt touched the water—the place where there was no air. This time as I swam to the spot, some kind of force suddenly blew a giant hole in the asphalt. It wasn't a force from above the asphalt but from beneath. The water wasn't exploding; some unseen force simply blasted the asphalt away.

My feelings were joy and elation, because now I could see the sunshine. I could breathe all the air I wanted, even though a lot of the lake was still covered with this terrible asphalt. Now there was a giant hole so that people could use the lake as it was intended to be used.

When I told Earl my dream, he responded by saying, "That's symbolic of your life! Your father, like the contractor, spread a thick, black layer of oppression over your life so that your pleasure has been smothered. It's also interesting," he said, "that the force came from underneath the asphalt, as if God were giving you the breathing room that you needed. You no longer are being smothered by the oppressive control of your father. You *are* getting better!"

Are *You* Getting Better?

My concern at this point is to ask, "How are *you* doing?" Remember, you're on a journey. Think of it as paddling a canoe across a giant lake. You aim your canoe in the right direction and paddle. In the middle of the lake you may feel you're not getting any closer. But be encouraged and keep on paddling in the right direction; you *are* getting there.

Frequently, while you're in the healing process, it will appear that you are having more problems rather than fewer. The truth is, you're not actually having more problems; you simply are more aware now.

You will never forget what has happened in your life, but you will notice a growing sense of peace. Yes, the offenses happened, but now you are able to transform those bad things into positive forces that will help you become a stronger person, better able to help other people.

Seasons of Growth

Your healing process is an on and off situation. It's best to work hard at it for a few months, then take a break. Let yourself rest. Give yourself permission to slow down for a while. Think of life as a series of seasons. Spring and early summer are rapid growing periods for trees, while during late summer, fall and winter, the trees are stabilizing their new growth, setting on buds for the next spring, and resting.

As you work on your problems, remember that the steps of recovery are not always logical, sequential steps. Frequently you'll be bouncing back and forth as you work on different problems. You might find yourself fairly well recovered in the area of anger, but not in your ability to trust people.

Recovery is a process, and you are growing in many, many different areas. You're handling such issues as guilt, shame and fear of abandonment. You're also trying not to control people as you get your emotional needs met in healthy ways. It's important that you not replace one symptom with another, but keep moving (even if slowly) toward health.

Recovery is a feeling that we belong, that other people are to be trusted, that they contribute something to us and we do to them. It's a feeling that the world is basically safe and a relationship with God is not a fearful experience but a friendly one.

As you work on your problem areas remember these facts and take heart:
- Recovery is a process
- Recovery cannot be done alone

☐ Recovery involves facing our painful past
☐ Recovery means learning how to feel
☐ Recovery improves our self-image
☐ Recovery changes how we act
☐ Recovery affects our choices
☐ Recovery reduces all-or-nothing thinking[1]

How Do We Work on Our Problems?

Let's get started in the nitty-gritty process of working on your particular problem areas. My purpose in this next section is to guide you step by step through the process. First we'll review a few areas we've already looked at. Then we'll focus in more depth on some key areas.

1. Decide to be healed.

Many times throughout this book I've talked about motivation. Working on your problems takes time, deliberate thought and energy. Really wanting to be healed is what will keep you going. You have to *choose* to begin.

I've also found that belonging to a group which is asking me at each meeting how I'm doing, seeing a counselor on a regular basis, and reading recovery books has helped to keep my "wanter" working. Let's assume you've got the motivation and you genuinely want to work on your problems.

2. Locate helpers who will deliberately encourage you to work on your problems.

It's great to have people listening to your story. You need that. But, in addition, look for people who are going to push you to actually *work on* your problems and not just *think* about them.

The most helpful people will gently nudge you in directions of healing. At the same time, they will supportively assure you that you are not a strange person, you are worthwhile and you have an important contribution to make in the world.

3. Identify the major dysfunctional areas in your life.

At first my personal list of problems which I wanted to solve had only anger on it. It was the one thing I didn't seem to be able to control. But as I started reaching out for help, deciding to get healed and reading books, I found my personality opening up more, and my list grew.

On one particular afternoon I added unwillingness to trust people, lust and perfectionism. A few weeks later I added competitiveness and a fear of being known. A few months later I added control and depression. A few months after that, I jotted down cynicism.

It's helpful to put your problems or issues down on paper so that you can remind yourself every few days of the areas you want to work on.

One of the latest areas that I have added to my list is truthfulness. It wasn't that I didn't tell the truth. I simply stretched it as far as it could possibly go and still technically be the truth. On some occasions I clearly knew that I was leaving people with a wrong impression. I justified myself by saying, "I am telling the truth, they're just not understanding the truth. That's their problem." Even though truthfulness was a later addition to my list, it's one of the things that I've found easy to monitor and measure. The change helps me to feel good about my recovery.

4. Work for guaranteed change.

You are sure to see improvement and healing if you apply these next four concepts while you work on your dysfunctional areas.

□ *Get in touch with your feelings.* Suppose you have decided to work on your problem of needing excessive control of people and circumstances. Your goal is to reclaim your emotions. You're trying to discover what feelings you associate with the need to control.

In my situation, I discovered a very controlling father who had to have things his way. As a child, I reacted by trying not to make waves. I tried to "fix things"—to keep everything quiet and together, to keep peace and make everyone happy. I continued those tactics into my adult life and marriage by trying to control every event and person in my family.

I also discovered that my desire to control people is connected to my being shamed and made to feel worthless as a child. My parents were not on the sidelines cheering me on. Instead, I felt they were peering over my shoulder, expecting me to do something wrong and ready to pounce on me. Correcting a child is appropriate. Shaming and belittling a child, however, does permanent damage.

Now, I want to control events so that no one will be shamed—neither I nor other people. I have found it necessary to repeatedly caution myself against shaming or belittling my wife, coworkers or other people with whom I feel competitive.

I have had a wonderful, growing freedom as I've recognized where this controlling part of me came from, what it has done in my life and the lives of people around me. I can actually—with God's help—change my behavior. I felt a great sense of release when I said to Sally, "I don't want to shame you or anyone anymore. I want to relinquish control and allow people to be more human and individualistic."

I guarantee healing in your life as you begin to get in touch with your feelings related to your major dysfunctional areas.

□ *Share what you are learning.* You will also get guaranteed life-changing results as you share about your past and your present through writing and through talking to a group, your spouse, a counselor or friend. The very process of telling your story helps you make changes. When I told Sally that I did not want to control her or shame her, my statement changed my actions and produced a stronger commitment between the two of us. Almost every day since then I have apologized to her for some way, often very subtle, in which I have shamed her.[2]

Sharing your story also transforms you to be a person who is now working on the problem, rather than being destroyed by your problem. As you share with a counselor or a group, they will cheer you on. They believe in you. As you hear yourself tell the story, you'll get insights into your past. You'll see how your past has influenced and controlled your present. Wonderfully, those past memories will begin to change, and you'll find some of your dysfunction quietly sliding away.

□ *Reconstruct your past.* You will notice overall improvement in your sense of peace and well-being as you look at how your past has affected your current dysfunction. You can then restructure your past so that old childhood feelings are not affecting you today.

Even though you had a poor start, you can now begin to nurture, honor and heal that wounded boy or girl inside you. Then that great "little kid" in you can play, be joyful and creative, and no longer be controlled by the bad stuff from your parents' dysfunction. Let's look at some practical ways to do this. You can begin to reconstruct your past.

Reparent your inner child. Earlier, I told you about that Saturday morning when my brother and I were beaten. I described how, as an adult, I imagined myself walking into the room and telling the boys the truth, comforting them and giving them an accurate concept of God. I was reparenting those children.

I've also found it helpful to go back into some of my other childhood experiences with the awareness that God has his arm around my shoulder. Together we explore this painful time in my life. God's presence gives me the stability I need so that I don't fall victim to the childhood feelings of loneliness, abandonment and shame.

With God's presence I'm able to view it from an adult perspective. "Yes, that was wrong!" God agrees, but at the same time, he doesn't want me to be bound to the pain of a child. He wants my feelings to be current. I am now loved by God and people. God is transforming those past negative parenting experiences to make me a strong, helping person today.

A very helpful suggestion to me was to locate a picture of myself as a child and become friends with that little kid. I found an old snapshot of my brother and me when I was about ten years old and he was about seven. I had the picture blown up to an eight-by-ten, framed it and hung it where I see it every day as we eat.

I really was a cute kid, even though I was skinny and looked like an abandoned orphan. Often I've said to myself, "Why wouldn't anyone like a kid like that? He looks like a terrific little guy with lots of potential." That kid in the picture and I have now become good friends.

Let old memories heal. The goal is to bring adult truth to your old memories. As a child, you developed thought patterns and behaviors to defend yourself. You don't need those childish defenses anymore. You're an adult, and you can refuse those childhood protections in your current life.

When you first begin to work on your problems, you'll probably feel that most of your past was bad. I found it difficult to remember good stuff, but part of the healing of old memories is to fill in the gaps. You will realize that your home life was bad, but it wasn't all bad. What were the good experiences?

In the early stages you may deliberately block out good experiences because you want people to be sure to understand that you were a victim. Divorce wasn't something just between your parents. You were affected too. You may want to make sure your parents are punished.

But as you begin to reparent the inner child, allowing God to help you heal those old memories, you'll begin to recall that good things also happened. I remember my dad teaching us how to box, swim and paddle a canoe. He taught us many of the skills related to building construction. As I healed, I went from focusing on the negative events to allowing the good memories to come back.

Don't force yourself too early to remember the good stuff. As you reparent your inner child and the painful memories start to heal, the blank spaces will be filled in. This new, more balanced picture of your past will also help you feel more at ease with yourself and your family.

Reconstructing your past is a difficult task. We can compare it to learning a new language. There's lots of repetition, new sounds and new ways of using your tongue and mouth. Slight inflections of words carry special meanings. Reconstructing your past is also a learning process that won't be accomplished by only a few sessions with a counselor or a few experiences of reparenting your inner child. Like a new language, it will take lots of practice!

I have also found it helpful to think of past memories as compact discs. As I hear one bad memory replaying itself over and over in my mind, trying to control me, I hit the eject button. Then mentally I put on a different disc, a here-and-now disc. I choose a disc that shifts my attention to how the past has formed me to be a better person today because of the hard time I went through.

My new adult memories remind me that I have special insights about people because of my dysfunctional family. I am a better people-helper because of the tough stuff I have experienced. Without those negative things, I might not have the opportunities and insights I have today. Yes, much of my past was bad, but it also served me well by making my adult life more effective.

I have also found it helpful to return some of my bad memories to my parents. As a child, I assumed the responsibility of trying to get them together and help them love each other. I tried to cover up the bad situation in my home and the fact of my parents' sexual problems. As an adult, I've now said to myself, "That's their problem. I'm not responsible for it. They can have their problem back."

Compare it to receiving a magazine in the mail that you didn't order. You're not obligated to pay for it. Neither are you obligated to pay the return postage. Just write across the label, "Refused. Return to Sender." I find it helpful to consciously do that as I remember some negative childhood experiences. They are not my fault, and I'm not going to carry that ball-and-chain of responsibility any longer.

☐ *Improve your relationships.* I have guaranteed that you will heal as you get in touch with your feelings, share what you are learning and reconstruct your past. Let me add a final guarantee to the list. You will feel a greater *overall sense of peace* as you improve your relationships.

Make a list of all the people important to you. Then look again at your earlier list of major dysfunctional areas. Now ask yourself, "How can I improve my relationship with these people specifically in the areas of my dysfunction?"

For example, one of my daughters and I have agreed that we will be truthful. When we talked on the telephone on my birthday, she asked, "How old are you today?"

I jokingly said, "I'm thirty-eight."

She responded, "Remember our pact, Dad."

I was embarrassed, but I also appreciated the fact that she held me accountable. I do feel as if I'm thirty-eight, but the truth is, I am fifty-eight. I said, "I'm sorry, I'm trying to be honest, but old habits are hard to break."

Being truthful in small areas has also helped me to be more honest with Sally. When there's a little conflict between us, it's easy for me to see where she is wrong. In the past, I have tried to ignore the truth that I also was wrong. So being truthful with Sally means I recognize that I was at fault as well. When she asks for forgiveness, I now try to say, "Yes, I forgive you," rather than, "Forget it," which was the way the old me did it. Saying "forget it" was an extension of my denial system.

Being truthful touches hundreds of areas of my life. Each time I am careful to be honest, I feel better about myself, and my overall sense of peace increases.

Improving relationships with my parents does not mean that I fall back into being "little Jimmy." I'm now a responsible adult. When they start to treat me like Jimmy, it's important for me to gently but firmly let them know, "I'm not Jimmy; I'm an adult." Improving the relationship does not mean letting myself be absorbed by their marital dysfunction. I'm sorry that they've had marital problems for sixty years, but I am not to blame. Neither should I carry their guilt and shame.

When I visit my parents, typically they take turns getting me in a corner and complaining to me about the other one. Before I started into the healing process I took their marital situation on myself. I became their dumping ground. Now I must say to myself, "I'm sorry you've had these problems, but now I'm trying not to allow your problems to automatically become mine."

"It doesn't mean that I don't want anything to do with my parents. I just don't want to be manipulated by their pain." When I am with them, I continually need to remind myself that I need to be true to myself. I must not get sucked again into the negative things I experienced as a child—control, manipulation, shame and emotional abandonment.

Come Out, Wherever You Are

When I was a kid, we used to play these giant neighborhood "Kick the Can" games. It was a rather sophisticated form of hide-and-seek, or at least I thought so.

One person stood at a large fruit juice can in the center of the street, eyes closed, and counted to twenty-five. Everyone else went to hide. The "it" person who stood at the can was responsible for finding all the other people. As soon as he or she spotted another kid, they both ran back to the can. If "it" got there first, the person who was discovered would have to stand by the can as having been captured.

Gradually, "it" would capture many of us. But occasionally a person in hiding was able to sneak in and kick the can while "it" was out looking. Then everyone who had been found could go hide again. "It" had to put the can in the middle of the street and count to twenty-five again.

The game went on and on, rotating players in a random sort of way as people got bored. Occasionally, however, one or two would be hiding so well and for so long that everyone else would have been captured. The game would be at a stalemate. So "it" would holler, "All-ee, all-ee in free." In other words, "I give up. You can come in free, and we'll start the game all over again."

I want to say to you, you don't have to hide anymore! You don't have to stay hidden all alone, afraid of getting caught. I'm hollering out to you loudly and clearly, "All-ee, all-ee in free."

Come back to home base. Join the rest of us who have been found. Come on in and be part of the gang—the healing group. It's okay to leave your secret place of isolation and shame. All-ee, all-ee in free!

19

Step Nine: Maintaining and Enjoying Your New Life

I WALKED INTO THE HOUSE ONE EVENING AFTER work and gave Sally a passionate lover's hug. In a few minutes I was on the floor, playing with our kids who wanted my attention. Now I was in the role of playmate with our girls. In a few more minutes the roughhousing got too rough, and I had to correct one of the girls in the role of a correcting father.

The telephone rang—someone needed help. The person was struggling with leftover baggage from childhood. In those moments I became a counselor. At the same time, the phone conversation reminded me that I was struggling with similar pain from my own childhood. So briefly I became that inner child again. I wore at least five hats that evening, but I was only one person.

Each of us is very complex. We wear many different hats. If we're going to maintain our newly restored life and enjoy it to its fullest, we must realize that improvement will come about only as we heal the whole person—the one under all the hats.

Take hope! Any area of your life that gets healed will have a positive impact on the rest of your life and will make it easier for the other areas to heal. Even if you don't think of yourself as fully recovered, keep strengthening the restored areas and keep on growing in the areas that still need work.

Alcoholics Anonymous has taught us that a person is always an alcoholic, but he or she can be a recovered alcoholic who has not had a drink for many years. You will always be an adult child of divorce, you will never change that status, but your painful past doesn't need to continue controlling the way you feel and act today.

Just as the recovered alcoholic is always on guard, so the adult child must always be on guard. I don't expect you to live in a cloud of gloom saying, "Oh poor me. I've come from a divorced home." Rather, say to yourself, "Yes, my parents were divorced, but I'm on the road to recovery and I'm doing my very best to maintain the recovery that I've achieved."

In this chapter I want to walk you through some practical suggestions to help you maintain the recovery already accomplished.

1. Remind yourself of your positive insights and traits.

You are more sensitive, you understand people better, you know without being told what other hurting people feel, and you're automatically better able to help. Because of your being raised in a dysfunctional home, you've gained psychological insights that other people spend thousands of dollars to learn in graduate school!

Also remind yourself that you have a better life focus now. You've cleaned out the debris. Your energy can flow with less resistance. It isn't wasted worrying about a lot of junk out of your past. Now your energy can be focused on projects and concerns you never had time for in the past.

Another positive result is your deeper relationship with friends. People actually know you and you know them. You probably are closer to your small group than you ever were to some of your blood relatives. It's a wonderful, secure feeling. But you might never have found that meaningful relationship if it hadn't been that you were such a desperately needy person.

2. Give yourself permission to relax.

If you need help, read Tim Hansel's book *When I Relax I Feel Guilty.*[1] You've decided not to be such a perfectionist and workaholic; now back that up with some real-life relaxations. Take your calendar and start building in some fun times for you. Regularly treat yourself.

Jerry, a hard-driving, high-energy university student, sat in my office, totally dejected and depressed. He wondered what was wrong with him. Life seemed to be a total drag. He didn't want to be around people, and his meditation time with God seemed to be a worthless waste. I asked him to spend the next week keeping a record of what he did every half-hour during his waking hours.

When he returned a week later, his calendar was filled from six in the morning until eleven-thirty at night. I asked him to circle the half-hour sections that were his times of resting—relaxation times that built him up. He looked over the chart and circled a total of three hours in the whole week.

Then I asked him, "Why does the book of Genesis record that God rested on the seventh day? Was the infinite God 'pooped out' from all his work of creation?"

He smiled at me and said, "Of course, God wasn't tired."

"Then why?" I pressed him.

A sheepish grin spread over Jerry's face, "It was a pattern for us."

"Okay," I said, "show me where one-seventh of your waking hours are designated to restoring you."

That was the beginning. I gave Jerry permission to relax. He started to modify his schedule and within six weeks his whole personality began to change. He thought I was some sort of miracle worker. "Not at all," I said. "We just reduced your 121-hour work week to a more manageable 70 to 80 hours and allowed for some relaxation."

3. Remember your physical body.

If you are young, you can probably punish your body and get away with it. But, as you hit each new decade, that becomes less and less true. When you abuse your body, it doesn't bounce back so quickly, and your emotions are going to be affected. Your ability to cope with problems will be reduced. So commit yourself to the following:

☐ Regular physical check-ups.

☐ Daily exercise that gets your heart-rate to 120 beats per minute for at least twenty minutes.

☐ A healthy diet, low in meat and processed foods and high in complex carbohydrates, fresh fruits, vegetables and grains. Follow the current advice of qualified nutritionists.

☐ Regular sleep, eight hours a night, plus a few one-to-five-minute naps throughout the day.

☐ Weight control so that you are within a few pounds of your ideal weight.

I've discovered that when I eat better and stay away from sugar and caffeine, I have more energy. As I exercise, I also have more emotional energy. Exercise changes our body chemistry by increasing the number of endorphins, those positive little critters in our brains that help us to better handle stress and depression. In addition, eating right and exercising helps me to feel better about my body because my weight is under control.

4. Take time to reflect.

A regular, daily quiet time helps to keep life in perspective. It's a time for you to play that library of positive mental CD's you've been collecting, to remind yourself of how far you've come and how you've benefited from your negative childhood experiences.

A daily quiet time also allows God's hope to invade your life. Read a section of the Bible each day, perhaps the Psalms. You will identify with the writer's struggles. Then you'll find hope for your life.

5. Work to enrich and expand your relationships.

Friends and acquaintances of today may move to other parts of the country. Keep expanding your base of friends and deepening your relationships so that as normal changes occur, you will always have an adequate friendship base.

If you have difficulty starting or building deep relationships, you might enjoy reading my book entitled *Friendship*, which teaches you specific skills for starting and deepening friendships.[2]

No relationships will survive without energy to keep them going. It's like the fire in my family room fireplace. I build a fire by first putting some small sticks on the bottom. Next I distribute a layer of medium-sized sticks, and finally I put larger logs on top. Now it's ready to light. As the fire gets going, it's a great sight, with the wonderful light and warmth spreading over the whole room.

The fire continues to grow to a magnificent stage where the logs become large burning embers. You can almost see the fire all the way through the logs. Shortly after this stage, however, the logs start to disintegrate. A lot of hot embers remain, but if I don't put on some additional wood, I may end up with no fire at all.

Relationships don't keep burning by themselves. You need to keep adding fuel, adjusting and adapting, much the same as you do with a fire.

Keep trying to improve all of your relationships: with your friends and friends' children; with your parents, spouse, children, their spouses, grandchildren; with cousins, nieces and nephews, old classmates. None of those relationships can be taken for granted. All of them require continued investment of time, words of kindness, telephone calls, and little notes or gifts for special occasions.

That wonderful small group of yours that seems closer than family also needs tending. Tell them again how grateful you are that they have invested their love and care in you. Maybe it's time to cook up a special event for your group. How about a ski trip or a day at a retreat house? How about rafting down a river, hiking or maybe something as simple as ordering in a ton of pizza to your place and listening to great music or watching a funny video together?

Enjoying and maintaining your new life requires constant investment, but it's worth it. Look at the progress you've already made.

6. Align your activities and your work with your gifts.

Most adult children of divorce have learned to live by doing what other people expect them to do. As you move through the healing process, you've begun to see more clearly who you are as a person. You've been shaking off some of those old "ought to's" that were placed on you by other people. Now, clearly focus your energies and interests in every part of your life to match the abilities God has given you.

A few years ago I was asked to be the dean of a West Coast seminary. It was a tempting offer because it was a wonderful opportunity to influence the direction of an institution and the lives of young men and women training for ministry.

Sally and I spent two days at a mountain retreat with a planning specialist who repeatedly asked us, "What are your gifts and abilities? If you could do *anything*, what would you do? If you accept this position, what will you get and what will you give up?"

After two days we realized that this position would not be a good match for us. It would require surrendering much of our travel, writing and counseling with mid-life people. The offer was flattering, but it didn't match our life vision. We turned it down.

7. Enrich the lives of other people.

You help other people grow as you help them understand their childhood, who they are today and how they can be healed. The people you help will thank you for your contribution. You are an important guide for their lives. At the same time, helping someone else heal will cause you to enjoy and maintain your new life.

Don't be afraid to talk about your past as you help people. Your freedom to speak will be another indication that you are well along the road to recovery and to maintaining your health.

8. Expect to succeed.

Look at all the progress you have made already! You have every reason to believe that you will continue to grow. You are gaining additional valuable insights into yourself and how to correct dysfunction as you relate to others.

At some point you may say, "Wow, I've grown so much. I don't see how I could change any more." Or you might even think, "As I get older I'll probably stop growing."

I remember telling my father when I was sixteen years old that people over thirty ought to be shot. Life was over and they might as well be put out of their misery. When I got into my middle thirties I realized I was still growing and learning, even though psychologists at that time were saying that people over thirty-five probably couldn't learn or change much.

When I turned forty-five and had a severe mid-life crisis, I thought I had nothing more to offer to the world. I felt I was too old to do anything effectively. Yet it was after that time that I began my book writing career and earned two doctoral degrees. After age forty-five Sally and I started our ministry to mid-life families all across the world. After age forty-five I taught at a seminary.

Now here I am, finishing this book at age fifty-eight. Many of my college classmates are talking about retirement, but I'm looking forward to all of the exciting things that are yet going to happen in my life.

I told Sally a few days ago, "It would really be nice if each person could live two or three parallel lives. Then I could be a writer, inventor, sailor, college president, grandfather, musician, explorer and film producer. One of me could be sailing around the world, while another one of me finished this book and another was out camping with my grandkids."

You have achieved a great deal. Healing has taken place in many areas of your life. Don't retreat; let the world be blessed by your healing.

9. Let your special voice be heard.

You have an important contribution to make to the world. Whenever you doubt that, just remember Ludwig van Beethoven. We think of him today as a great composer. Truly he was one of the greatest.

But he also had a very tough life, marked by a great deal of unhappiness and deep depression. He seemed to be a man who never really fit with people around him. He had continual conflicts with his wife, quarreled frequently with his friends and was deeply worried by a nephew he loved very dearly.

Beethoven always wanted to be a singer as well as a great pianist. Unfortunately, when he was still a young man, he began to lose his hearing. It's difficult to be a singer or a pianist if you can't hear.

By the time he was forty-eight, in 1818, he was totally deaf. That's what makes his story truly amazing. Five years after he was unable to hear even the faintest sound, he finished his fantastic Ninth Symphony.

Think about it. He never heard the symphony, he just thought it. He could move his fingers on the keyboard and conduct the whole orchestra perfectly, but the sounds were only in his mind.

But what if—what if he had decided to let his troubles or his handicap keep him from composing? What a loss for all the millions of us who have been emotionally carried along, as if we were on the back of a bird, to new heights of joy and exaltation as we've listened to Beethoven's Ninth Symphony—a symphony of joy and praise to God. Right now you can almost hear those final kettle drums beat out the praise, "Hallelujah, hallelujah!"

Wow! When I get to heaven, that's one of the things I want to do. I want to lead a magnificent orchestra and choir in some of the great masterpieces. Maybe Ludwig will let me have a turn after he's had a chance to conduct and *hear* his Ninth Symphony for the first time.

Part Four
Helping
the Helpers

20
How to Help Adult Children of Divorce

*T*HIS BOOK HAS BEEN ADDRESSED MAINLY *to the person who is from a home where there was an emotional or legal divorce. This chapter, though, is for you if someone you care about—your spouse, a good friend, perhaps your own parent—is a child of divorce.*

The suggested steps that follow may be things you're already doing. Good! Keep it up, and try the other steps as well. You may be the person who can make a life-changing difference in your adult child of divorce!

Day after day we receive calls and letters from people across the United States, as well as overseas, whose marriages are coming apart. Brad and LeAnne are two of those people.

LeAnne met Brad in her first year of college. He was a senior when they fell madly in love. They got married after he graduated. Because he went on to medical school, LeAnne gave up her own college aspirations and went to work. She was a very bright young woman who had planned to be a medical doctor but settled for being the wife of a doctor.

Three years after marriage they had their first child. LeAnne took on the double load of a full-time job and raising the child by herself because Brad was gone all the time. Being mother, father and financial provider for the family was a heavy load. But she thought all of her sacrifice would pay off someday.

After medical school there were the intern years, more children and more bills to pay. LeAnne kept working full-time.

Shortly after Brad completed his internship, he had a great opportunity to buy into a medical practice. But to do that would put a giant financial strain on the family. So, you guessed it, LeAnne kept working, being both mother and father to the kids, trying to help Brad get launched.

Soon Brad was pushing for an expensive house in the "doctors' neighborhood" of their town. LeAnne liked the added prestige, but she didn't like the idea that she was going to have to continue working.

In addition, Brad felt it was necessary for him to drive a Porsche and belong to the local country club. Sometimes it bothered LeAnne that Brad had this addiction—keeping up with the other doctors, continuing his social climbing. In reflective moments she thought, "I haven't progressed at all, but I've made it possible for him to go through medical school and take extra time in his internship for specialization. I've made it possible for him to have a family and his luxuries because I've sacrificed. But what's happening to *me?*"

By the time Brad and LeAnne reached the end of their thirties, LeAnne was exhausted. She was still working full-time, but now she was parenting teen-age kids. Brad was gone most of the time. Their marriage was only a certificate, not a reality.

Brad began to take long trips by himself. At first it was to medical conventions, with a few days added for golf or skiing. Then it was unexplained vacations by himself, nights out of town and afternoons when he was missing from the office.

One Thursday afternoon Brad came home early, took LeAnne into the family room and said, "I don't love you. I've been dating someone else for over a year. I want to marry her. I want you to divorce me, and I want you to let me go in peace. I don't want you to hold anything against me."

LeAnne's first reaction was shock and disbelief. It soon turned to intense anger, followed by rage. She exploded, "How dare you use me all of our married life to advance your own career and get all your toys, and then dump me. On top of that, you really want me not to hold it against you? You're crazy!"

She felt betrayed and exploited. How could she approve of what he was going to do? "Forgive you? Pretend that nothing happened? Not on your life!" she snapped. Each time I think of Brad and LeAnne I get very angry. How could he use her and then throw her away like a banana peel? How could LeAnne have let him get away with it all those years?

After LeAnne and Brad got involved in marriage counseling, they discovered that the pattern of Brad's exploitation of LeAnne could be traced back to his dysfunctional home and his parents' divorce. He had felt very lonely and rejected by the kids in his church youth group. As a teen, he decided he would be rich and successful, no matter what it took. Brad never intended to abuse LeAnne; he just had to have more toys, a more powerful position, more respect—something more that would make him feel good.

All their married life LeAnne avoided talking about her real-life desires and her feelings of being exploited. She had learned not to make waves. Besides, she kept thinking their situation would get better.

Brad was shocked as he began to realize that he had been using LeAnne. He was also startled as he became aware that the other woman was just another one of those "toys" that he craved to help fill the gaps from his childhood.

The good news is that Brad and LeAnne began to work on Brad's past. As a result, their marriage started to improve. He didn't need the girlfriend and, for the first time in their marriage, Brad was genuinely concerned for LeAnne's growth and achievements. They're on the way to recovery.

Even though LeAnne was explosively angry with Brad when he told her about the other woman, over the following months she was the key player for Brad's personal healing and their marriage restoration. In the midst of her anger, we coached her about steps to take to help Brad and save their marriage.

Maybe you're facing uncomfortable feelings as you try to relate to your adult child of divorce. It's tough trying to connect to a person who continually mistrusts, feels insecure, is sometimes perfectionistic and may want to do some things that could destroy your relationship or his or her career.

In the next several pages I want to walk you through some of the suggestions that LeAnne found to be helpful.

1. Understand your adult child of divorce.

This first step is a big assignment! But gradually you will be able to do it. Understanding what children of divorce have experienced will help you piece together the puzzle so you will know why they react the way they do. They have a reason for that anger that erupts, those periods of depression, or their desire to avoid seeing or talking to their parents. There's a cause for why they mistrust, try to control, want to make everything perfect. There's a reason why sometimes they're deceptive, cynical or even suicidal.

Understanding what your adult child of divorce has experienced will also help you to realize that you—his or her mate, son, daughter or friend—are at risk. Adult children of divorce tend to form family units that duplicate some of the same patterns of their own parental family and its dysfunction.

In fact, you may discover that you are a codependent as LeAnne was; that is, unintentionally you may have been drawn into an unhealthy pattern of relating. In fact, if the adult child of divorce is your mate, your marriage likely has been threatened and may indeed be in as serious trouble as was LeAnne and Brad's marriage. You may also feel cheated, exploited or abandoned by your mate—the adult child of divorce who is duplicating his or her parents' dysfunction.

You may also discover that *you* have come from a dysfunctional family. You may realize you have been keeping the family secrets, trying to forget the pain that you experienced in your parental family. Often victims marry victims. We tend to attract each other. Or sometimes a person with a need to rescue other people marries a victim, and neither realizes he or she is simply enabling the other to remain dysfunctional.

Learn all you can in order to be the most positive help to your adult child of divorce. You need to develop a healthy emotional base, in order not to perpetuate dysfunction.

2. Commit yourself to long-term support.

It took adult children of divorce many years to develop those negative patterns that are a deep part of their lives now. Healing from these dysfunctional patterns is not going to happen by two visits to a counselor, reading a book or attending a weekend retreat. Realistically, you're probably looking at a few *years* of fairly regular and intensive work.

But no two people are exactly alike. Typically, the first year is a time when people discover how large the problem really is and how many areas of their life have been affected. That's a painful process. The second year generally includes lots of anger and grief as they remember their past and face their losses.

As they move through that second year, they are likely to start shaking off their victim mentality and come to terms with facing and forgiving the past. In other words, this second year will be a year of pain as they work on their problems.

During the third year in the process, adult children of divorce will continue to work on problems, but they're going to experience a lot more bright, sunny days. They'll frequently talk about feeling much better. You'll notice the difference.

However, the process is not completed even then. It will continue for many years because adult children of divorce are like alcoholics. Some of those poor patterns of thinking and behavior will pop up from time to time. It will be necessary for them to keep living a lifestyle of recovery, rather than assuming after a few years that everything's completely better.

3. Accept your adult child of divorce nonjudgmentally.

It's helpful to remind yourself that whatever your friend or spouse says is what he or she feels. It may not be what you feel about a situation, but you must accept his or her perception without criticism and without trying to straighten him or her out.

Consciously be that person's friend and feel that person's pain. Try to put yourself into that one's experiences and feelings. How would you have reacted? How would you have felt? What would you have said then or now?

Think of yourself as being inside that person's head and looking out at life through his or her eyes, re-living the past. Suddenly you will become compassionate, and your focus will change from correcting to caring.

4. Provide safety.

These people have been deeply hurt. They need your protection. They need to know that you believe them and you're not going to put them down. If you further shame them because they are not getting better faster, they are likely to pull away from you.

You'll have to assure them that you are their ally and that you will absolutely keep in confidence the things they share with you. Being confidential means that you commit yourself *never* to share their problems with another person. In addition, providing safety assumes that you will not use what you learn about them in a power play to take advantage of their vulnerability.

At times you will have to be the strong shield that protects them from their parents and the past. You'll be the one making the excuses and handling a sudden change in plans. Yes, you'll have to diffuse the guilt trips and manipulation from the parents who caused so much dysfunction and still reinforce it.

5. Listen carefully.

You may become the dumping ground for the adult child of divorce. Therefore, you need to learn to listen. Listening is a very special skill; we're not talking about conversation, where you share back and forth. Listening is one-sided. You encourage the person to speak freely about any area he or she wants to share.

Listening also implies that you draw the person out. As he or she begins to share, you must make it easy to keep on sharing.

Listening means you accept at face value what is said. Listening is not debating, nor is it the time to correct their erroneous perceptions. Those times of giving balanced information will come later. Right now you can best help them by practicing the skill of listening.

If these skills I'm talking about are difficult or new to you, you might find it helpful to read through the book I mentioned earlier entitled *Friendship*.[1]

Using your listening skill with your adult child of divorce will help him or her grow more rapidly. You also will feel better about your relationship because you are making a positive contribution to the person's healing and recovery.

6. Encourage your child of divorce to keep working on healing.

The authors of *The Courage to Heal*, in a section entitled "How to Help," point out that adult children of divorce are very fragile, vulnerable and not really sure how to handle what's happening in their lives. The authors suggest that helpers do the following:

☐ Believe the survivor.

☐ Join with the survivor in validating the damage.

☐ Be clear that abuse is never the child's fault.

☐ Educate yourself about the healing process.

☐ Don't sympathize with the abuser.

☐ Validate the survivor's feelings.

☐ Express your compassion.

☐ Respect the time and space it takes to heal.

☐ Encourage the survivor to get support.

☐ Get help if the survivor is suicidal.

☐ Accept that your relationship will be rocky as the survivor heals.

☐ Resist seeing the survivor as a victim.[2]

7. Be prepared to change and be flexible.

There'll be days when they feel very close to you. At other times they will treat you as if you are an alien. They may need your help on the spur of the moment. Some of your own plans may go out the window. The emphasis is on two words: *be there*. Be there when they need you. Being there may also mean being sensitive enough to get out of the way when they need to do some growing on their own.

8. Give them permission to do what is healthy for them.

Adult children of divorce frequently are perfectionistic. They're workaholics, driven by guilt and obsessed by control. Give them permission to relax. Make it possible for them by helping with some of their work load or suggest things you can do together for relaxation.

Give them permission to seek help. Talk to them about the benefits of counseling and of joining a recovery group. Give them permission to spend the time and money so healing can take place.

9. Reinforce the changes you see.

Adult children of divorce feel inadequate. They think they are inferior. They feel alone and abandoned. Your words of encouragement will help them to keep going in the hard, painful times when they feel like giving up.

Be their cheerleader. Look them in the eye and tell them when you see any change, when you are aware of any new insight, or when you see them forgiving their past. You can also cheer them on as you see their anger. What I just said was not a "typo." Anger sometimes gives people the power to explore their past, and it opens the door for the grieving process. Walk with them in their anger as they face their childhood.

Congratulate them at every point along the recovery road. Sally has been my greatest booster. When I haven't wanted to spend the money for counseling, she has assured me that I'm worth it. She says, "If you get recovered, we both will enjoy life more." She has encouraged me to get into a small group, and has cheered every bit of change that she has seen.

This morning as I was spending quiet time, reflecting on where I once was and where I am now, I again said to myself, "If there is one person to get praise for my recovery, Sally's the one. She has been my glue, my stability and my cheerleader."

God Works with You

A wonderful account in the Bible records the incident of Lazarus being raised from the dead.[3] He had been dead three days. Jesus deliberately stayed away so there would be no question that Lazarus was dead.

When Jesus did arrive on the scene, he told the people to believe God. God could do anything. Then he told them to roll the stone from the opening to the tomb. After they did, Jesus called down into this deep cave, commanding Lazarus to come out.

Lazarus did come out, but he was bound from head to toe in grave clothes. Jesus instructed the people to unwrap him and let him go free.

The point I want you to see in this magnificent account is this: God has all power. He is able to raise a dead person. But then why didn't he also roll away the stone and unwrap Lazarus?

To me, it's a picture of the cooperation between God and man. He asks us to do what we can do, and he does for us what we are unable to do.

The healing of your adult child of divorce is not something you can pull off by yourself. But neither are you left out of the process. God wants you to do what you can do to help. And he promises to be working in the very depths of this wounded person where you cannot touch.

You are not alone. God wants your special person to recover even more than you do. In addition, millions of other helpers who have experienced healing are part of a large army reaching out to help heal your adult child of divorce.

As I finish writing this book, I'm listening to a stirring symphonic piece. All the musical talents are needed—composer, director, each player, plus the sound technicians and even the manufacturer of my CD—every person is vital to the end product. You also are a vital component in the symphony of wholeness for your adult child of divorce.

Appendix A

How to Start a Support Group

I want to walk you through this exhilarating process of sharing what you are learning with a small group. Let's divide our discussion into some convenient chunks, such as how to get started, covenants or agreements, structures that will take away the guesswork, possible problems and, finally, the future.

1. How to get started.

Think of two or three people with the following qualifications:

a. You have some degree of relationship with them.

b. They come from divorced or dysfunctional homes.

c. They would benefit from learning healing skills and attitudes.

After you have identified these people, plan to use the next two to four weeks to enlist one of these friends to become a partner with you in sharing these healing skills and attitudes with a group of four to eight other friends. Ask God to help you identify that special person.

Share with your potential partner the information that appears in the next few pages. You will want your friend to be able to make a decision on the basis of complete facts.

You might give them a copy of this book and say something like this: "I have been reading this book, and it has been a big help to me. I was wondering if you would be willing to look it over and perhaps the two of us could start a small group to discuss the ideas in it.

Maybe we could meet with a group of four to eight other people on Thursday mornings at 6:30 for about an hour before we go to work. It looks as if it would take us about fifteen to twenty weeks to get through the book. In the process of sharing, we would get to know each other better and also begin to heal from some of our childhood hurts."

It's important that your friend understand fully what is involved in starting the group so that he or she can make an intelligent decision. If the first friend does not feel comfortable after looking over the book, go to the next person on your list. When you get your first person committed as your partner, you are on your way.

The two of you should then make a list of people who might become a group in this learning experience. Follow the same approach you did with your first friend. Give each person a few days to consider the decision to join you in this adventure. For this group to be effective, it must be kept to a relatively small number—four to eight people. Because not everyone will be able to join your group, you will have to ask more people than the number you want. But soon you will have your group rounded up.

2. Covenants.

Carefully think through what you are going to do as a group so that everyone knows exactly what to expect and can agree to the process. It's helpful to actually write out covenants, or agreements, in order for everything to be up-front about what is expected. A preliminary covenant should be drawn up by you and your first friend. Then as you recruit people, you can intelligently tell them what's going to happen. At your very first meeting of the total group, go over the covenant agreements in detail so that everyone has opportunity for input. Each person should fully own the covenant.

A covenant should cover most of the following areas:

- ☐ Where to meet
- ☐ Time
- ☐ Day of the week
- ☐ Length of each get-together
- ☐ Content to be covered
- ☐ Goals to achieve
- ☐ Format of each session
- ☐ Who will be the leaders or facilitators
- ☐ Outside homework
- ☐ Refreshments (if any)
- ☐ Visitors to the group
- ☐ Social events
- ☐ Confidentiality
- ☐ Other items important to your special group

Try to be as specific as possible as you think about what you want to do. Encourage the other members to share in the covenant process, so that your group won't fall apart in three or four weeks because some of them thought you were going to do something very different from what you're doing. The purpose of the covenant is to eliminate hidden agendas and to help each person fully own the group as his or her own.

Let me coach you a bit more about the previous list. A once-a-week meeting is probably adequate. Meet for an hour to an hour and a half. Probably fifteen to twenty weeks is going to be long enough. Find the best time of day and the best day of the week for everybody.

A simple way to handle the content is to cover one chapter of the book each time, except the first and last meetings.

At your first meeting, focus on getting to know each other. Do some initial sharing, such as the generalities of job, your family's divorce or dysfunction, religious experience, reasons for wanting to join the group and what each person hopes to get out of the group. Talk about the covenants and make sure that they are fully owned. It might also be helpful to assign tasks to different people for the next meeting.

For the following weeks, you could use a chapter a week as the content for your meeting. The last week should be a wind-down session including evaluation and planning for the future.

3. Structures.

Regarding format, I would suggest the following general structure:

15 minutes—Share what happened to you during the past week

30 minutes—Discuss a chapter of the book

15 minutes—Commit yourselves to each other for personal change

10 minutes—Pray for each other

5 minutes—Assign tasks for next week

a. *Sharing* should be included each week. Group members can share something about what has happened in their lives during the past week related to their changing attitudes or commitments they made last week. Sharing will intensify the learning process and will help to sustain the week-by-week growth.

b. *Discussion* is the second segment of your time together. You should assume that each person has read the particular chapter or section under discussion. One person should be assigned each week to develop questions for the discussion. Good questions will not have yes, no, or simple answers.

Good questions push people to wrestle with concepts, ideas and problems which might not ordinarily be tackled. Good questions are tied to the healing process and attitudes. Discussion time should flow logically into the commitment time.

c. *Commitment* is an important part of your time together. Someone should be assigned to oversee this segment as group members share how they plan to think or act differently during the following week. The group should affirm these important yet often difficult commitments.

d. *Pray* before the group separates each week. Pray specifically for each other's work, family, other friends, church and community. It's okay to pray for the world, but be careful not to get too far off target. Your prayer time should target on helping each of you grow in the healing process.

e. *Assignments* or homework should be expected because each person ought to be:

☐ reading in preparation for the next meeting,

☐ practicing his or her commitments,

☐ preparing to lead the sharing, discussion, commitment, prayer or assignments for the next meeting.

Ideally, the group should share leadership by rotating responsibilities so that every person in the group has an opportunity to lead each part of the meeting.

4. Potential Problems.

a. *Inadequate covenants.* If you invite your friends into a group by saying, "Hey, I'm getting a bunch of people together on Thursday night for awhile, would you guys like to come over?", each person will come with his own agenda. One guy is coming to use your VCR and big screen TV. Another guy wants to shoot pool. One of the other guys hopes to spend some time working on your antique car. Unless the covenants are spelled out very completely, you can almost count on problems.

b. *The third or fourth meeting.* At this point, group members begin to feel they know each other fairly well and are committed to the group direction, or else they want out because they misunderstood the original covenant. During this meeting, it might be helpful to bring up the covenant issues to make sure everyone feels comfortable. Modify small areas to help everyone feel at ease. If there are major misunderstandings, perhaps it would be good to form two groups to meet different expectations.

c. *Social events and visitors.* Extra meetings held outside your normal weekly structure are a good time for social events or visitors. If you try to turn the regularly scheduled weekly meeting into a pool party or trip to Disneyland, you may not accomplish either the social or the recovery purposes. Visitors to regular meetings always cause a group to regress. When a new person is present, everyone becomes more hesitant to share.

It is great, though, to have social events outside your regular meetings. Social events can whet visitors' appetites for the friendships and healing that you are experiencing in your group. Who knows, maybe when your group finishes this course, you could split up and start four new groups. Each of you from the original group could be the facilitator of a new group. What an impact if each of you committed yourself to reproduce what you are experiencing! Gigantic changes would take place in families, businesses, communities and churches, as well as in each individual's life.

d. *Winding down.* Stopping is hard. It's better to plan when to stop and how to stop, rather than letting the group go on indefinitely until members lose interest. You all deserve a party to celebrate your growth as you end the group. So plan something special to commemorate your time together.

e. **What of the future?** Winding down is much less sad if you plan for the future. Would you like to stay together as a group and study another book, or take on a new direction such as fixing up a widow's house or starting new groups?

You may not want to leave each other. Why not form several new groups but all meet together weekly? Spend the early part of your time sharing as a large group, then split off into two to four small groups at the same location. That way you can keep the groups small and still continue to enjoy each other. Everyone can share your joy and growth.

Planning the future will help each person feel successful about concluding the group and will help them move beyond the loneliness and aimlessness people feel when a group breaks up. Another opportunity for growth and healing is ahead!

Appendix B

How to Find a Support Group

Many support groups and counselors are willing to help you. However, not many groups are specifically identified as helping only adult children of divorce. The following resource groups will be able to help you find support groups or counselors in your area. (Since some addresses or phone numbers may change after this book is published, consult your local church, Christian radio station, telephone directory assistance or reference person at your local library.)

For Counselors
Focus on the Family
Counselor Referral Dept.
Pomona, CA 91799
(No box number needed)

Christian Support Groups
Overcomers Outreach
2290 W. Whittier Blvd., Suite D
La Habra, CA 90631
213/697-3994
(National and international network)

New Hope
2801 N. Brea Blvd.
Fullerton, CA 92635-2799
714-529-5544

Recovery Partnerships
P.O. Box 11095
Whittier, CA 90603

Alcoholics for Christ
1316 N. Campbell Road
Royal Oak, MI 48067

For Secular Support Groups
Al-Anon/Alateen Family
Group Headquarters
1372 Broadway
New York, NY 10018
800/356-9996

National Association for Children of Alcoholics
31582 Coast Highway, Suite B
South Laguna, CA 92677
714/499-3889

Appendix C

Suggestions for Choosing a Counselor

1. Talk to trusted friends or leaders in your community to get their suggestions for counselors. If you feel uncomfortable asking a friend, call a pastor of a large church, a Christian medical doctor, or an administrator of a Christian school or college for their recommendation of a counselor who specializes in dysfunctional families.

2. Make sure that your counselor has a degree that qualifies him or her to be a professional counselor. One helpful degree is an M.A. in marriage, family and child counseling. Other degrees are Ph.D. or M.D. with a specialization in psychology. All counselors should be appropriately licensed by your state. (Some states, though, do not license at the master's degree level.)

3. Remember that more education does not necessarily mean better help. Experience is the key, specificially in the area of dysfunctional family counseling. A person with a doctorate who has just finished school may not have had enough experience for your needs.

4. Be sure to ask about fees before you go to see the counselor. Some medical insurance covers the cost of psychological counseling, and many counselors have a sliding fee, depending on your income. Also, inquire about the number of times per week or per month the counselor will want to see you and the overall projected number of sessions.

5. Another consideration would be whether the counselor fits with you personally. Do you feel comfortable with this particular person? Can you trust this person? Do you like the counselor's style and personality? If not, it is important to seek out another counselor with whom you do feel comfortable. Don't be afraid to switch counselors.

6. Commit yourself to three or four sessions as a trial period with the counselor. Often the first session is not a good representation of future sessions. More than one meeting will be necessary for you to make an accurate decision about a particular counselor.

7. If you are married, encourage your mate to go to the counselor for a few sessions to understand how your dysfunction has affected your marriage.

(Note: The counseling process is speeded up if you are also involved in a small support group and reading widely in your particular area of dysfunction.)

Appendix D

Survey for Adults Whose Parents Have Divorced

First, we would like to ask some general information about you and/or your parents.

1. Your age when your parents divorced _____

2. Reason for their divorce, as you perceive it _____
_____

3. How many years has it been since your parents' divorce? _____

4. How many times have *you* been married? _____

5. Your occupation _____

6. Your birthdate _____

7. Your education level _____

8. Your zip code number _____
_____

Now we would like to ask you a series of general questions indicating how you were affected by your parents' divorce.
   (Important note: As you consider the following questions, ask, "Did my parents' divorce *cause these traits* or feelings in me?")

1. Did you feel cheated out of part of your life because of your parents' conflict and divorce? (circle one number)

Very Much					Somewhat				Not at all	
10	9	8	7	6	5	4	3	2	1	0

2. Were you physically abused because of your parents' conflict and divorce? (circle one number)

Very Much					Somewhat				Not at all	
10	9	8	7	6	5	4	3	2	1	0

3. Were you sexually abused because of your parents' conflict and divorce? (circle one number)

Very Much					Somewhat				Not at all	
10	9	8	7	6	5	4	3	2	1	0

4. Were you emotionally abused because of your parents' conflict and divorce? (circle one number)

Very Much					Somewhat				Not at all	
10	9	8	7	6	5	4	3	2	1	0

5. Did you suffer financial hardship because of your parents' conflict and divorce?

Very Much					Somewhat				Not at all	
10	9	8	7	6	5	4	3	2	1	0

6. Did you reject or withdraw from your family because of your parents' conflict and divorce?

Very Much					Somewhat				Not at all	
10	9	8	7	6	5	4	3	2	1	0

7. Were you afraid to date or marry because of your parents' conflict and divorce?

Very Much					Somewhat				Not at all	
10	9	8	7	6	5	4	3	2	1	0

8. Did you feel torn in your allegiance between your mother and father because of their conflict and divorce?

Very Much					Somewhat				Not at all	
10	9	8	7	6	5	4	3	2	1	0

9. Did you feel disoriented or dysfunctional at school or work because of your parents' conflict and divorce?

Very Much					Somewhat				Not at all	
10	9	8	7	6	5	4	3	2	1	0

10. Did you feel extra responsibilities were forced on you because of your parents' conflict and divorce?

Very Much					Somewhat				Not at all	
10	9	8	7	6	5	4	3	2	1	0

11. Did you become a parent or counselor to your mother and/or father because of your parents' conflict and divorce?

Very Much					Somewhat				Not at all	
10	9	8	7	6	5	4	3	2	1	0

12. Did you become a parent or counselor to your siblings because of your parents' conflict and divorce?

Very Much					Somewhat				Not at all	
10	9	8	7	6	5	4	3	2	1	0

13. Did you feel that you caused your parents' conflict and divorce?

Very Much					Somewhat				Not at all	
10	9	8	7	6	5	4	3	2	1	0

14. At the time of your parents' conflict and divorce, did you feel . . .

a. angry

Very Much					Somewhat				Not at all	
10	9	8	7	6	5	4	3	2	1	0

b. anxious/afraid

10	9	8	7	6	5	4	3	2	1	0

c. personally rejected

10	9	8	7	6	5	4	3	2	1	0

d. powerless

10	9	8	7	6	5	4	3	2	1	0

e. unhappy

10	9	8	7	6	5	4	3	2	1	0

f. lonely

10	9	8	7	6	5	4	3	2	1	0

g. abandoned

10	9	8	7	6	5	4	3	2	1	0

h. worthless

10	9	8	7	6	5	4	3	2	1	0

i. hostile

10	9	8	7	6	5	4	3	2	1	0

Now we would like to ask a series of questions indicating how you are currently affected by your parents' divorce.

1. Do you still have to guess at what a "normal family" is because of your parents' conflict and divorce?

| Very Much | | | | | Somewhat | | | | Not at all | |
| 10 | 9 | 8 | 7 | 6 | 5 | 4 | 3 | 2 | 1 | 0 |

2. Do you feel stunted in your personal development because of your parents' conflict and divorce?

| Very Much | | | | | Somewhat | | | | Not at all | |
| 10 | 9 | 8 | 7 | 6 | 5 | 4 | 3 | 2 | 1 | 0 |

3. Have you blocked out part of your past because of your parents' conflict and divorce?

| Very Much | | | | | Somewhat | | | | Not at all | |
| 10 | 9 | 8 | 7 | 6 | 5 | 4 | 3 | 2 | 1 | 0 |

4. Have you had trouble establishing or maintaining good personal relationships because of your parents' conflict and divorce?

| Very Much | | | | | Somewhat | | | | Not at all | |
| 10 | 9 | 8 | 7 | 6 | 5 | 4 | 3 | 2 | 1 | 0 |

5. Is it difficult for you to follow through on projects because of your parents' conflict and divorce?

| Very Much | | | | | Somewhat | | | | Not at all | |
| 10 | 9 | 8 | 7 | 6 | 5 | 4 | 3 | 2 | 1 | 0 |

6. Has lying become a common pattern of your life because of you parents' conflict and divorce?

| Very Much | | | | | Somewhat | | | | Not at all | |
| 10 | 9 | 8 | 7 | 6 | 5 | 4 | 3 | 2 | 1 | 0 |

7. Do you tend to judge yourself too strictly because of your parents' conflict and divorce?

| Very Much | | | | | Somewhat | | | | Not at all | |
| 10 | 9 | 8 | 7 | 6 | 5 | 4 | 3 | 2 | 1 | 0 |

8. Is it difficult for you to have fun and relax because of your parents' conflict and divorce?

| Very Much | | | | | Somewhat | | | | Not at all | |
| 10 | 9 | 8 | 7 | 6 | 5 | 4 | 3 | 2 | 1 | 0 |

9. Do you take yourself too seriously because of your parents' conflict and divorce?

| Very Much | | | | | Somewhat | | | | Not at all | |
| 10 | 9 | 8 | 7 | 6 | 5 | 4 | 3 | 2 | 1 | 0 |

10. Do you overreact to situations over which you have no control because of your parents' conflict and divorce?

| Very Much | | | | | Somewhat | | | | Not at all | |
| 10 | 9 | 8 | 7 | 6 | 5 | 4 | 3 | 2 | 1 | 0 |

11. Do you constantly seek approval and affirmation because of your parents' conflict and divorce?

| Very Much | | | | | Somewhat | | | | Not at all | |
| 10 | 9 | 8 | 7 | 6 | 5 | 4 | 3 | 2 | 1 | 0 |

12. Do you feel that you are different from other people because of your parents' conflict and divorce?

| Very Much | | | | | Somewhat | | | | Not at all | |
| 10 | 9 | 8 | 7 | 6 | 5 | 4 | 3 | 2 | 1 | 0 |

13. What age were you when you decided you needed to take care of yourself? _____

Now we would like you to write a *brief comment* for each of the following questions. Please briefly include any of your feelings, actions, and your way of relating.

1. How did you feel toward your parents
During the conflict? _____

After the divorce? _____

Now? _____

2. How did/do you handle your parents' divorce when it comes up in conversations?

3. List the *three biggest problems* you have faced because of your parents' conflict and divorce.

a. _____

b. _____

c. _____

4. Please discuss in more detail *how the worst problem* listed above has affected your life such as work, school, friends, God, self-image, dating/marriage, sex life, use of drugs or alcohol, and your personality. If you need more space, use a separate page.

5. What most helped you to survive *at the time* of your parents' conflict and divorce?

6. What would *most help you now* to handle the stress you are currently facing because of your parents' conflict and divorce?

7. What problems do you *anticipate facing in the future* because of your parents' conflict and divorce?

_____

Is there anything else you would like to tell us about the affect on you of your parents' divorce? Please write your comments here or on a separate page.

The process of filling out this survey will accelerate your healing and growth.

Notes

Chapter 1/Who Are These Adult Children from Legal or Emotionally Divorced Families?

[1]Jim Conway, *Friendship* (Grand Rapids, Mich.: Zondervan, 1989).

[2]John Bradshaw, *Healing the Shame That Binds You* (Deerfield Beach, Fla.: Health Communications, 1988), p. 45.

[3]Neil Kalter, "Long-Term Effects of Divorce on Children: A Developmental Vulnerability Model," *American Journal of Orthopsychiatry* 57 (1987):587-600.

[4]Archibald Hart, *Children and Divorce* (Waco, Tex.: Word, 1982), p. 18.

Chapter 2/A Growing National Awareness

[1]David Van Biema, "Learning to Live with a Past That Failed," *People*, May 29, 1989, p. 79.

[2]Ann Goetting, "Divorce Outcome Research: Issues and Perspectives," *Journal of Family Issues* 2 (1981):350-78; Mavis Hetherington, *Children and Divorce in Parent-Child Interaction: Theory, Research, and Prospects*, ed. R. W. Henderson (New York: Academic Press, 1981); Cynthia Longfellow, *Divorce in Context: Its Impact on Children in Divorce and Separation*, ed. George Levinger and O. C. Moles (New York: Basic Books, 1979).

[3]Mavis E. Hetherington, Martha Cox and Roger Cox, *Effects of Divorce on Parents and Children in Non-traditional Families: Parenting and Child Development*, ed. Michael Lamb (Hinsdale, N.J.: Lawrence Earlbaum, 1985); Steven L. Nock, "Enduring Effects of Marital Disruption and Subsequent Living Arrangements," *Journal of Family Issues* 3 (1982):25-40; Richard A. Kulka and Helen Weingarten, "The Long-Term Effects of Parental Divorce in Childhood on Adult Adjustment," *Journal of Social Issues* 35 (1979):50-78.

[4]"Divorce and Students," *InterVarsity Magazine*, Fall 1988, p. 11.

[5]Paul Amato, "Long-Term Implications of Parental Divorce for Adult Self-Concept," *The Journal of Family Issues* 9 (1988):201-13.

[6]Judith S. Wallerstein and Joan Berlin Kelley, *Surviving the Breakup: How Children and Parents Cope with Divorce* (New York: Basic Books, 1980), p. 211.

[7]Judith S. Wallerstein and Sandra Blakeslee, *Second Chances: Men, Women and Children a Decade after Divorce* (New York: Ticknor and Fields, 1989).

[8]Anastasia Toufexis, "The Lasting Wounds of Divorce," *Time*, February 6, 1989.

[9]Herbert L. Gravitz and Julie D. Bowden, *Recovery: A Guide for Adult Children of Alcoholics* (New York: Simon & Schuster, 1987), preface.

[10]Ibid.

[11]John Bradshaw, *Healing the Shame That Binds You* (Deerfield Beach, Fla.: Health Communications, 1988), p. 58.

[12]Personal letter, August 12, 1988.

Chapter 3/What Has the Adult Child Lost?

[1]Thomas Farragher and Dale Rodebaugh, *Orange County Register*, February 2, 1989, A3.

[2]Kent McGuire, "Adult Children of Divorce: Curative Factors of Support Group Therapy" (a doctoral research paper presented to the faculty of the Rosemead School of Psychology, Biola University, May 1987).

[3]Claudia Black, *It Will Never Happen to Me* (Denver, Colo.: Medical Administration Company, 1981).

[4]Mavis Hetherington, Martha Cox, and Roger Cox, "The Aftermath of Divorce," in *Mother-Child Relations*, ed. J. H. Stevens, Jr., and M. Matthews (Washington, D.C.: National Association for the Education of Young Children, 1978), p. 175.

[5]Rebecca L. Drill, "Young Adult Children of Divorce," in *The Divorce Process: A Handbook for Clinicians,* ed. Craig A. Everett (Binghamton, N.Y.: Haworth Press, 1987), pp. 183-84.

Chapter 4/Cheated out of Life

[1]Alexandra Smith, "Cambodian Women Believed Blinded by Horror of Slayings They Witnessed," *Orange County Register,* September 10, 1988, A-3.

A Harvard Medical School report on boys on death row suggests a similar denial response: "Eight of the fourteen had injuries severe enough to require hospitalization; nine had serious neurological deficiencies. Twelve had been brutally abused, and five had been sodomized by relatives. Their parents had a high rate of alcoholism, drug abuse, and psychiatric hospitalization. The boys had tried to conceal all this during their trials. They preferred to be seen as bad rather than admit that they were psychiatrically impaired, intellectually inadequate, or victims of sexual abuse." These young men facing death had such strong denial systems that they were unable to admit the problems in their parental home. However, their dysfunctional environment probably was the major factor in the destructive outcome of the boys' lives ("Boys On Death Row: More Mad Than Bad?" *Harvard Medical School Mental Health Letter* 3 [1988]:6).

Gravitz and Bowden state that almost three out of four of their clients report "significant memory losses that extend over years of childhood" (Herbert L. Gravitz and Julie D. Bowden, *Recovery: A Guide for Adult Children of Alcoholics* [New York: Simon & Schuster, 1987], p. 39.)

Chapter 5/Damaged Self-Image and Blurred Boundaries

[1]Pia Mellody, *Facing Codependence* (San Francisco: Harper & Row, 1989), pp. 11-13.
[2]Merle A. Fossum and Marilyn J. Mason, *Facing Shame: Families in Recovery* (New York: Norton, 1986), p. 71.

Chapter 6/Dysfunction Breeds Dysfunction

[1]John and Linda Friel, *Adult Children: The Secrets of Dysfunctional Families* (Deerfield Beach, Fla.: Health Communications, 1988), pp. 71-72.
[2]Ibid., pp. 74-90.
[3]Stephanie Covington and Liana Beckett, *Leaving the Enchanted Forest* (San Francisco: Harper & Row, 1988), pp. 40-41.
[4]Archibald Hart, *Healing Life's Hidden Addictions* (Ann Arbor, Mich.: Servant, 1990).
[5]Covington and Beckett, *Leaving the Enchanted Forest,* p. 27.
[6]Andrew Merton, "Father Hunger," as quoted in *Leaving the Enchanted Forest,* p. 27.
[7]Covington and Beckett, *Leaving the Enchanted Forest,* p. 27.
[8]Samuel Osherson, *Finding Our Fathers: The Unfinished Business of Manhood* (New York: The Free Press, 1986), pp. 1-2.
[9]Arthur Miller, *Death of a Salesman* (New York: Viking, 1949), p. 82.
[10]Richard Shelton, excerpt from "Letter to a Dead Father" from *You Can't Have Everything* (Pittsburgh, Penn.: University of Pittsburgh Press, 1975).

Chapter 7/Missing: Normal Life Development

[1]J. Piaget, *The Child's Conception of the World* (London: Routledge & Kegan Paul, 1929); J. Piaget and B. Inhelder, *The Psychology of the Child* (New York: Basic Books, 1969); E. H. Erikson, *Childhood and Society,* 2d ed. (New York: Norton, 1963); E. H. Erikson, *Adulthood* (New York: Norton, 1978); Lawrence Kohlberg, *The Psychology of Moral Development,* vol. 2 (New York: Harper & Row, 1984); James W. Fowler, *Stages of Faith* (San Francisco: Harper & Row, 1981).

Chapter 8/Distrust and Role-Playing

[1] R. Bandler, J. Grinder and V. Satir, *Changing with Families* (Palo Alto, Calif.: Science and Behavior Books, 1976); C. Black, *It Will Never Happen to Me* (Denver, Colo.: Medical Administration Co., 1981); Sharon Wegscheider-Cruse, *Another Chance: Hope and Health for the Alcoholic Family* (Palo Alto, Calif.: Science and Behavior Books, 1981).

[2] David Van Biema, "Learning to Live with a Past That Failed," *People*, May 29, 1989, p. 80.

In our survey we found several indicators that children were taking on more responsibility, or even adult roles, within the families: 63% reported that extra responsibilities were forced upon them; 51% reported they had to counsel or encourage their parents; 36% reported that they began to withdraw or reject their family; 35% reported they had to counsel or encourage their brothers or sisters.

[3] Claudia Black, "Innocent Bystanders at Risk: The Children of Alcoholics," *Alcoholism* 1, no. 3 (1981):22-26; see also Sharon Wegscheider-Cruse, *Another Chance: Hope and Health for the Alcoholic Family* (Palo Alto, Calif.: Science and Behavior Books, 1981).

[4] Herbert L. Gravitz and Julie D. Bowden, *Recovery: A Guide for Adult Children of Alcoholics* (New York: Simon & Schuster, 1987), p. 23;

[5] Gravitz and Bowden, *Recovery*, p. 24.

[6] Ibid.

[7] Ibid.

[8] Ibid., p. 25.

[9] Ibid.; see also Wegscheider-Cruse, *Another Chance*.

Chapter 9/Unsuccessful Marriages and Fear of Parenting

[1] Neil Kalter, "Long-Term Effects of Divorce on Children: A Developmental Vulnerability Model," *American Journal of Orthopsychiatry* 57 (1987):588-89; see also R. Kulka and H. Weingarten, "The Long-Term Effects of Parental Divorce in Childhood on Adult Adjustment," *Journal of Social Issues* 35 (1979):50-78.

[2] Sara McLanahan and Larry Bumpass, "Inter-Generational Consequences of Family Disruption," *American Journal of Sociology* 94, no. 1 (1988):147.

[3] Norval D. Glenn and Kathryn B. Kramer, "The Marriages and Divorces of the Children of Divorce," *Journal of Marriage and the Family* 49 (1987):824.

[4] Norval D. Glenn and Beth Ann Shelton, "Pre-Adult Background Variables and Divorce: A Note of Caution about Over-reliance on Explained Variance," *Journal of Marriage and the Family* 45 (1983):408; see also Bernard Siskin and Jerome Staller with David Rorvik, *What Are the Chances? Risks, Odds & Likelihood in Everyday Life* (New York: Crown, 1989).

[5] Norval D. Glenn and Kathryn B. Kramer, "The Psychological Well-Being of Adult Children of Divorce," *The Journal of Marriage and the Family* 47 (1985):910.

[6] David Van Biema, "Learning to Live with a Past That Failed," *People*, May 29, 1989, p. 82.

Chapter 10/The Outside World

[1] For a discussion of men and women in mid-life crisis, see Jim Conway, *Men in Mid-Life Crisis* (Elgin, Ill.: David C. Cook, 1978); Sally Conway, *Your Husband's Mid-Life Crisis* (Elgin, Ill.: David C. Cook, 1980); Jim and Sally Conway, *Your Marriage Can Survive Mid-Life Crisis* (Nashville: Thomas Nelson Publishers, 1987); Jim and Sally Conway, *Women in Mid-Life Crisis* (Wheaton, Ill.: Tyndale House Publishers, 1983).

[2] Judith Wallerstein, *Second Chances: Men, Women and Children a Decade after Divorce* (New York: Ticknor and Fields, 1989), pp. 299-300.

[3] David Greenberg and Douglas Woll, "The Economic Consequences of Experiencing Parental Marital

Disruptions," *Children and Youth Services Review* 4 (1982):141.

4Paul Amato, "Long-Term Implications of Parental Divorce for Adult Self-Concept," *Journal of Family Issues* 9 (1988):210.

5John and Linda Friel, *Adult Children: The Secrets of Dysfunctional Families* (Deerfield Beach, Fla.: Health Communications, 1988), pp. 58-59.

Chapter 11/Step One: Deciding to Be Healed

1John Bradshaw, *Healing the Shame That Binds You* (Deerfield Beach, Fla.: Health Communications, 1988). .

2John 12:24, New International Version.

3Bradshaw, *Healing the Shame That Binds You,* p. 121.

Chapter 12/Step Two: The Spiritual Link

1Herbert L. Gravitz and Julie D. Bowden, *Recovery: A Guide for Children of Alcoholics* (New York: Simon & Schuster, 1987), p. 103.

2Charles L. Whitfield, M.D., *Healing the Child Within* (Deerfield Beach, Fla.: Health Communications, 1987), p. 127.

3Archibald D. Hart, Ph.D., *Children and Divorce* (Waco, Tex.: Word, 1982), pp. 19-20.

4Matthew 5:45, New International Version.

5John 8:32, The Living Bible.

Chapter 13/Step Three: Joining a Recovery Group

1For an account of our family's struggle with this experience, see Becki Conway Sanders and Jim and Sally Conway, *What God Gives When Life Takes* (Downers Grove, Ill.: InterVarsity Press, 1989).

Chapter 14/Step Four: Remembering Your Past

1Pia Mellody, *Facing Codependence* (San Francisco: Harper & Row, 1989), p. 24.

2John 8:32, New International Version.

Chapter 15/Step Five: Grieving Your Losses

1Charles L. Whitfield, *Healing the Child Within* (Deerfield Beach, Fla.: Health Communications, 1987), p. 86.

2B. G. Simos, *A Time to Grieve: Loss as a Universal Human Experience* (New York: Family Services Association of America, 1979).

3J. Bolby, *Loss* (New York: Basic Books, 1980); Simos, *A Time to Grieve.*

4Sandra D. Wilson, Ph.D., *Counseling Adult Children of Alcoholics,* Resources for Christian Counseling, vol. 21 (Waco, Tex.: Word, 1989), pp. 111-12.

5Daniel Goldman, "Those Who Repress Emotions Tend to Get Sick More Often" *Cincinnati Inquirer,* March 17, 1988, C6.

6Exodus 20:12, King James Version.

7Luke 2: 48-49, New International Version.

8Adapted from Whitfield, *Healing the Child Within,* pp. 102-4.

9Jane Middleton-Moz and Lorie Dwinell, *After the Tears* (Deerfield Beach, Fla.: Health Communications, 1986), p. 120.

10"Adult Children of Alcoholics: Healing the Child Within," seminar in Cincinnati, Ohio, December 1988.

11John Bradshaw, *Healing the Shame That Binds You* (Deerfield Beach, Fla.: Health Communications, 1988), pp. 138-39.

Chapter 16/Step Six: Shaking Off the Victim Mentality

[1]"Break the Chain," Words by Morgan Cryar, music by Ty Tabor. Copyright 1986 by Ariose Music. All rights reserved. Used by permission.

[2]Adapted from *23-Alpha* 1, no.2, April 1989, published by Alpha Counseling, Laguna Hills, Calif.

[3]Ellen Bass and Laura Davis, *The Courage to Heal* (New York: Harper & Row, 1988), p. 167.

[4]Proverbs 23:7, New International Version.

[5]Romans 12:2, New International Version.

[6]Romans 12:19, King James Version.

[7]Charles Sell, *Unfinished Business: Helping Adult Children Resolve Their Past* (Portland, Ore.: Multnomah, 1989), p. 233.

Chapter 17/Step Seven: Forgiving the Past

[1]Ellen Bass and Laura Davis, *The Courage to Heal* (New York: Harper & Row, 1988), pp. 150-54.

[2]Lewis B. Smedes, *Forgive and Forget* (San Francisco: Harper & Row, 1984), p. 130.

[3]Ibid., p. 131.

[4]Harold Bloomfield, *Making Peace with Your Parents* (New York: Ballantine Books, 1983), pp. 30-34; see also Charles Sell, *Unfinished Business: Helping Adult Children Resolve Their Past* (Portland, Ore.: Multnomah, 1989), pp. 149-74.

[5]Mark 11:25, New International Version.

[6]Catherine Marshall, *Something More* (New York: Guideposts edition published by arrangement with McGraw-Hill, 1974), p. 36.

[7]Ibid., p. 38.

[8]Ibid., p. 39.

[9]Ephesians 4:32, New American Standard Bible.

[10]Smedes, *Forgive and Forget*, pp. 132-33.

Chapter 18/Step Eight: Working on Your Problems

[1]John Friel and Linda Friel, *Adult Children: The Secrets of Dysfunctional Families* (Deerfield Beach, Fla.: Health Communications, 1988), pp. 178-81.

[2]A little booklet entitled *I Deserve Respect. Finding and Healing Shame in Personal Relationships* has been a significant help to Sally and me. Since reading it, we have consciously tried not to shame each other or other people. This booklet is an excerpt from a larger book by Ronald Potter-Efron and Patricia Potter-Efron, *Letting Go of Shame: Understanding How Shame Affects Your Life* (Charter City, Minn.: Hazelden, 1989).

Chapter 19/Step Nine: Maintaining and Enjoying Your New Life

[1]Tim Hansel, *When I Relax I Feel Guilty* (Elgin, Ill.: David C. Cook, 1979).

[2]Jim Conway, *Friendship* (Grand Rapids, Mich.: Zondervan, 1989).

Chapter 20/How to Help Adult Children of Divorce

[1]Jim Conway, *Friendship* (Grand Rapids, Mich.: Zondervan, 1989).

[2]Ellen Bass and Laura Davis, *The Courage to Heal* (New York: Harper & Row, 1988), pp. 316-17.

[3]John 11.

Jim Conway, Ph.D.

Jim Conway is president of **Mid-Life Dimensions,** a California-based organization, which offers help to people struggling with mid-life issues, especially mid-life crisis as it affects marriage.

Jim and his wife, Sally, have spoken together at colleges, seminaries, churches and retreat centers on five continents. They were cospeakers on their national daily radio program, **Mid-Life Dimensions,** on more than two hundred stations.

Jim Conway served as a pastor for almost thirty years. He then directed ɪne doctor of ministry program at Talbot Theological Seminary for five years. He holds two earned master's degrees in psychology and theology, and two earned doctorates, a D.Min. in ministry and a Ph.D. in adult development and learning.

He is author of:

Men in Mid-Life Crisis
Friendship

He is co-author of:

What God Gives When Life Takes
Your Marriage Can Survive Mid-Life Crisis
Women in Mid-Life Crisis
Maximize Your Mid-Life

He is a contributor to such books as:

Your Husband's Mid-Life Crisis
Dictionary of Pastoral Care and Counseling
Parents and Teenagers
Encyclopedia of Today's Christian Women
Your Family
Husbands and Wives
How to Raise Christian Kids in a Non-Christian World
Real People

In addition, he has authored over 150 articles in magazines such as **Leadership, Moody Monthly, Impact, Flight Time** and **Review of Religious Research.**

To receive more information about **Mid-Life Dimensions,** or to contact Jim and/or Sally about speaking at a conference, write to:

Jim Conway
InterVarsity Press
P.O. Box 1400
Downers Grove, Il 60515